THE BEDFORD SERIES IN HISTORY AND CULTURE

D0033464

American Social Classes in the 1950s

Selections from Vance Packard's *The Status Seekers*

Edited with an Introduction by

Daniel Horowitz

Smith College

BEDFORD/ST. MARTIN'S   Boston ♦ New York

For Bedford/St. Martin's
President and Publisher: Charles H. Christensen
General Manager and Associate Publisher: Joan E. Feinberg
History Editor: Niels Aaboe
Developmental Editor: Louise Townsend
Editorial Assistant: Richard Keaveny
Managing Editor: Elizabeth M. Schaaf
Production Editor: Heidi Hood
Copyeditor: Barbara Flanagan
Indexer: Steve Csipke
Text Design: Claire Seng-Niemoeller
Cover Design: Richard Emery Design, Inc.
Cover Art: Detail of a scene from the Twentieth Century-Fox production "The Man in the Gray Flannel Suit" (1956). Courtesy of Culver Pictures, Inc.

Library of Congress Catalog Card Number: 94 – 66169
Copyright © 1995 by Bedford Books *of* St. Martin's Press

Manufactured in the United States of America.

1 1
j i h

For information, write: Bedford / St. Martin's, 75 Arlington Street, Boston, MA 02116
(617-399-4000)

ISBN-10: 0–312–11180–0 (paperback)
          0–312–12247–0 (hardcover)
ISBN-13: 978–0–312–11180–9

Acknowledgments

The introduction draws heavily on *Vance Packard and American Social Criticism*, by Daniel Horowitz. Copyright © 1994 by Daniel Horowitz.

The abridged version of *The Status Seekers* by Vance Packard reprinted courtesy of Vance Packard. *The Status Seekers* © Vance Packard.

Page 28: Courtesy of Whitney Darrow, Jr.

Page 191: Cartoon by Ned Hilton from *Look*, August 1959. Cartoons by William F. Brown from *The Girl in the Freudian Slip*, © William F. Brown, courtesy of William F. Brown.

Page 192: Cartoon by James Stevenson of commuters from *The New Yorker*, August 22, 1959. © 1959, 1987 The New Yorker Magazine, Inc., used by permission. Cartoon by James Stevenson of cocktail party from *The New Yorker*, August 8, 1959. © 1959, 1987 The New Yorker Magazine, Inc., used by permission.

Page 193: "Grin and Bear It" by George Lichty, reprinted with special permission of North America Syndicate. Cartoon by Frank Owen from "Today's Laugh," *Chicago Tribune*, August 30, 1961, courtesy of Chicago Tribune. Cartoon by Gardner Rea from *The New Yorker*, September 15, 1962. © 1962, 1990 The New Yorker Magazine, Inc., used by permission.

Page 194: From *The New Yorker*, November 10, 1962.

Page 195: Cartoon by Ed Dahlin. "Moon Probe" by Eric from *Atlanta Journal*, February 3, 1964, courtesy of the Atlanta Journal-Constitution.

Foreword

The Bedford Series in History and Culture is designed so that readers can study the past as historians do.

The historian's first task is finding the evidence. Documents, letters, memoirs, interviews, pictures, movies, novels, or poems can provide facts and clues. Then the historian questions and compares the sources. There is more to do than in a courtroom, for hearsay evidence is welcome, and the historian is usually looking for answers beyond act and motive. Different views of an event may be as important as a single verdict. How a story is told may yield as much information as what it says.

Along the way the historian seeks help from other historians and perhaps from specialists in other disciplines. Finally, it is time to write, to decide on an interpretation and how to arrange the evidence for readers.

Each book in this series contains an important historical document or group of documents, each document a witness from the past and open to interpretation in different ways. The documents are combined with some element of historical narrative—an introduction or a biographical essay, for example—that provides students with an analysis of the primary source material and important background information about the world in which it was produced.

Each book in the series focuses on a specific topic within a specific historical period. Each provides a basis for lively thought and discussion about several aspects of the topic and the historian's role. Each is short enough (and inexpensive enough) to be a reasonable one-week assignment in a college course. Whether as classroom or personal reading, each book in the series provides firsthand experience of the challenge—and fun—of discovering, recreating, and interpreting the past.

Lynn Hunt
David W. Blight
Bonnie G. Smith
Natalie Zemon Davis
Ernest R. May

Preface

Nostalgia and the mass media have shaped our consciousness of life in the United States in the years after the end of World War II. "American High," one historian called the decade and a half after 1945, presumably a time when citizens were optimistic and problems were either few or imaginary.[1] In fact, of course, these years were more complicated. For if it was a prosperous time, it was also one when poverty persisted. If Americans appeared to be becoming more alike, strong differences—of race, class, gender, region, and ethnicity—remained. If some people experienced these as confident years, for others fear persisted—fear of the atomic bomb, of subversion at home, and of Communist expansion abroad.

It is not too much to say that a one-dimensional picture of the 1950s gains its power in good measure from its ability to exclude. The dominant picture of the late 1940s and 1950s, then and to some extent now, relies on the perspective of white, suburban men who worked in large bureaucratic organizations and who wielded a disproportionate amount of cultural power. Vance Packard fits this demographic description. Yet his *Status Seekers* presents a picture of American society in the late 1950s that hardly condoned complacency.

Given the growing interest in obtaining a more accurate and complex understanding of the 1950s, the reissuing of *The Status Seekers* is timely. This book, so widely read in the years immediately following its original publication in 1959, enables us to gain some insight into 1950s suburban America as well as to watch over the shoulder of an author who was disturbed by what he saw. This abridged edition, which remains faithful to the original, is ideal for classroom use. The introduction provides historical context, an assessment of the book's impact, and a discussion of its critical reception. The cartoons in the back of the book also offer vivid evidence of the book's impact. The chronology of surrounding events should help

[1]William L. O'Neill, *American High: The Years of Confidence, 1945–1960* (New York: Free Press, 1986).

students place *The Status Seekers* within its contexts. In addition, the study questions and bibliography, along with the text of the original book, can lead students to a deeper understanding of the postwar period.

ACKNOWLEDGMENTS

The generous assistance of several people helped shape this book in critical ways. Besides having written the original *Status Seekers* in 1959, Vance Packard offered suggestions on what material to include in this republication while allowing me to make the final editorial judgments. Moreover, I wrote the introduction without any interference or advice from him. I believe that this edition of *The Status Seekers* remains true to Packard's original.

At Bedford Books, publisher Chuck Christensen and former history editor Sabra Scribner saw the project's potential at the outset, and current history editor Niels Aaboe reaffirmed its importance at a later moment. With great precision and insight, development editor Louise Townsend and production associate Heidi Hood shepherded the manuscript from draft to publication. Richard Keaveny offered concise and useful editorial guidance, while managing editor Elizabeth Schaaf ably oversaw all aspects of production. Barbara Flanagan's copyediting measurably improved the prose in my introduction and the flow of the edited version of *The Status Seekers*.

Ernest R. May, who wrote a review of *The Status Seekers* when it was originally published, welcomed its reappearance and offered useful suggestions about the introduction. The critical and encouraging comments of Lynn Dumenil, Roland Marchand, Elaine Tyler May, Char Miller, Richard Pells, and Judith E. Smith helped me strengthen the introduction. Gina Rourke provided able research assistance and probing suggestions. As usual, Helen Lefkowitz Horowitz encouraged my efforts from start to finish. I dedicate this book to the memory of my father, William Horowitz, who lived in and challenged the society that Packard described in 1959 but did not live to see this reissue brought to completion.

Daniel Horowitz

Contents

Contents

PART ONE

Introduction:
Social Criticism
in an Age of
Conformity and Anxiety

More than two years before the appearance of *The Status Seekers* in 1959, Vance Packard told his publisher that he was hoping to write a book in which he would be taking a "belt at some aspect of contemporary society." He was looking for a subject that would touch the "'national nerve'" by focusing on "how to achieve a creative life in these conforming times." Many Americans, he wrote his publisher, "resent the growing conformity and sterility of their life where they are left only with the roles of being consumers or spectators."[1]

Because Packard understood so well the tensions other Americans felt between conformity and individualism, classlessness and social divisions, this abridged version of his book *The Status Seekers* provides us with an important window into the 1950s. Packard was a journalist-turned-author who made accessible to a broad audience information that sociologists and others had gathered. More than a third of a century after its publication,

[1] Vance Packard to Kennett Rawson, January 25, 1957, Vance Packard Papers, Rare Books and Special Collections, Pennsylvania State University Library (hereinafter referred to as PPPS).

1

The Status Seekers remains fascinating in its attention to class hierarchies within the suburban middle class that were muted rather than trumpeted in most other mainstream writing of the 1950s.[2] The book appeared at a critical time in American life—after the most chilling effects of the cold war and McCarthyism began to diminish, but before the new political agendas of the 1960s coalesced. It was published when Americans had much to cheer about and much to worry over. On the one hand, relatively widespread affluence and America's dominant position in the world provided encouragement about the nation's present and future. On the other hand, McCarthyism and the atomic bomb engendered a fearfulness among millions of Americans. There were other causes of anxiety. The spread of mass culture, promoting as it did considerable pressures to conform, seemed to threaten individualism. From colonial times to the 1950s, fears of degeneration often accompanied periods of self-congratulation, and the 1950s were no exception. Americans also worried about the relationship between affluence and social class, concerned that economic growth might intensify social divisions or obliterate distinctive ways of life.

When *The Status Seekers* appeared in 1959, the nation was in the midst of a period of economic growth which, though marred by recessions, was nontheless sustained. In the years after the end of World War II in 1945, a number of factors underwrote prosperity. The demographic uniformity of marriage and childbearing patterns increased demand for automobiles as well as for suburban houses and schools. The defense budget, spurred by fear of Soviet aggression, provided investments in new technologies and employment for millions of Americans. Government subsidies for mortgages and for the interstate highway system facilitated the growth of suburbs. It is not hard to understand why contemporaries missed the irony that Harvard economist John Kenneth Galbraith intended when he labeled America in the 1950s "the affluent society" in his 1958 book with that title. In the fifteen years following World War II, the GNP increased, in constant dollars, by a respectable 37 percent. By the middle of the 1950s, for the first time in the nation's history, more employees wore white collars than blue ones. Moreover, many blue-collar workers tasted a middle-class way of life as strong unions and gains in productivity strengthened their economic position. Millions of Americans, many of them the sons and daughters of immigrants and most of them white, moved to suburbs where mass-produced houses, baby boom children, automobiles, televisions, and shopping centers dominated their daily routines. It was an age when social

---

[2] This introduction draws heavily on Daniel Horowitz, *Vance Packard and American Social Criticism* (Chapel Hill: University of North Carolina Press, 1994), which the interested reader should consult for fuller documentation.

observers, including several who were critical of the new conformity, saw white middle-class men as the representative Americans, something reflected in book titles that became part of the language — "the organization man" and "the man in the gray flannel suit."

Although the number of working women increased throughout the 1950s, especially married working women, the message conveyed to all women, whether or not they worked outside the home, was that they should value domesticity over autonomy or liberation. Television, movies, and magazines emphasized the cooperativeness of parents who headed child-centered families. Obviously, the lives of American women were more complex and less compliant than the picture offered by the advertisements, stories, and advice columns of popular magazines such as *The Saturday Evening Post* and *Look*. Yet the media had cultural power. In 1954 the editor of *McCall's* magazine wrote the classic statement on "togetherness," which pictured husbands, wives, and children "creating this new and warmer way of life not as women *alone* or men *alone*, isolated from one another, but as a *family* sharing a common experience." During the postwar period, if the foreign policy of the United States consciously aimed to contain the spread of communism, then it seems in retrospect that American ideology in the late 1940s and 1950s tried — perhaps less self-consciously — to contain American women within the household circle of family responsibilities.[3] As Vice President Richard Nixon told Soviet Premier Nikita Khrushchev when they stood in a model of a suburban American kitchen at an exhibition in Moscow in 1959, the suburban house was the focal point of freedom and abundance. But in a few years, this domestic ideal came under attack. In 1963 Betty Friedan, a writer and later a founder of the National Organization for Women, wrote the immensely influential *The Feminine Mystique*, which described women who had succumbed to pressures to conform when they embraced homemaking, remained sexually passive, and subordinated themselves to men.[4]

To a considerable extent, national politics evoked the contentment, confidence, and anxiety that accompanied affluence. Democrats and Republicans embraced the cold war doctrine of the necessity to contain communism. The Soviets tightened their grip on central Europe, and

---

[3] The best book on family life in the 1950s, on which this summary draws, is Elaine T. May, *Homeward Bound: American Families in the Cold War Era* (New York: Basic Books, 1988), especially pp. 9–14, 20–33, and 162–81.

[4] Otis L. Wiese, "Live the Life of *McCall's*," *McCall's* 81 (May 1954): 27; Betty Friedan, *The Feminine Mystique* (New York: W. W. Norton, 1963). Joanne Meyerowitz, "Beyond the Feminine Mystique: A Reassessment of Postwar Mass Culture, 1946–1958," *Journal of American History* 79 (March 1993): 1455–82, provides a useful corrective to Friedan's picture.

Americans reasserted their historic anticommunism. In 1946, Winston Churchill declared that "an iron curtain has descended across" Europe. A year later, the American president, announcing the Truman Doctrine, committed the nation for the first time in its history to the peacetime use of military aid to allies to stem the advances of a foe. Dwight D. Eisenhower, elected to the first of two terms as president in 1952, served as a symbol of peace, prosperity, and security. A bipartisan coalition accepted the consolidation of many New Deal social programs such as Social Security and federal aid to farmers.

Millions of Americans agreed with molders of public opinion who had articulated a consensus ideology, one that minimized conflict, celebrated what they saw as fundamental values shared by all Americans, and contrasted America's achievement of liberty with the Soviet experience of totalitarianism. McCarthyism, the fear of Communist domination, and the specter of nuclear war undergirded the commitment millions of Americans made to conformity and cold war consensus. This widely shared ideology stood in an uneasy relationship with the anxieties and realities of American life. Without protecting the constitutional rights of those they accused, Democrats and Republicans alike worked to cleanse government, unions, universities, and Hollywood of people they saw as un-American. Anticommunism, which was widespread before the rise of Senator Joseph R. McCarthy in 1950 and persisted after his fall in 1954, suffused American life. The threat of nuclear war, which began with the attack on Hiroshima in 1945 and intensified when the USSR exploded an atomic bomb in 1949, haunted Americans and impelled them to seek security where they thought they could find it. And the "American Century" of world leadership that Henry Luce, the founder of Time Inc., had announced in a famous editorial in *Life* in 1941 no longer seemed as certain as it once had, especially after the Communists took over China in 1949, the Soviets detonated their first atomic bomb the same year, and war broke out in Korea a year later.

There were more social and ideological fissures in the 1950s than most celebrants wished to acknowledge. For neither husbands, wives, nor children did the traditional home usually measure up to expectations. A silent generation, a label critics used to describe apathetic college students of the 1950s, may have reigned on American campuses, but millions of young Americans identified with the apolitical rebelliousness portrayed in the 1955 movie *Rebel without a Cause* or with the antic humor of *Mad Magazine*. In the mid-1950s the Beats, a handful of writers who articulated what many others only sensed, questioned the nation's materialism and commitment to bureaucratic routine. Most important, in the mid-1950s the civil rights struggle intensified, revealing to many white Americans the presence in the nation of African Americans who pressed their demands against a segregated society and called for attention to how discrimination and prejudice contradicted a complacent consensus.

Additional evidence of unresolved problems was not hard to find. Conflicts and tensions remained—across the lines that separated parents and children, men and women, homosexuals and heterosexuals, African Americans and whites, rich and poor. Women faced hostility as they tried to hold on to their wartime jobs. Though many in their ranks grew more affluent, the working class hardly disappeared. Clear fissures persisted between skilled and unskilled workers and, in the middle class, between managers and clerks. Contradicting the picture offered by proponents of prosperity, suburban development was generally affordable for only the upper 40 percent of the population, especially families headed by managers and professionals. To be sure, there were mass-produced working-class suburbs such as Levittown; but even these proved the general rule that exclusively white neighborhoods defined suburban life. Given the combination of prosperity and uncertainty, people grew increasingly preoccupied with symbols of status. In suburbs and office buildings, minor distinctions in style resulted in exaggerated differences in status. By 1960, the distribution of income was not substantially different from what it had been in 1945. In 1960 the top 5 percent of the population controlled more than half of the nation's wealth, while the bottom 20 percent held only one-twentieth. As many as one in four Americans lived in poverty—African Americans and Latinos in inner cities; whites in Appalachia; African Americans, whites, Indians, and Chicanos in rural areas; the elderly and single mothers across the nation.

Despite all of this evidence of diversity and inequality, politicians, business leaders, journalists, and some intellectuals articulated a consensus ideology as they celebrated the benefits of the "American Way of Life" in the 1950s. With varying degrees of exaggeration, they pictured a nation where democratic capitalism had produced ever-expanding prosperity, which in turn had brought about a harmonious and increasingly egalitarian society. Although many of the social commentators worried about the adverse effects of affluence, by and large they remained confident that the United States was the best place on earth. As workers earned income once reserved for the middle class, as expert managers replaced greedy capitalists, as the pot full of immigrants melted, and as poverty disappeared, these opinion makers confidently asserted, social divisions between classes and ethnic groups had diminished. Unlike what had happened in the Soviet Union, in America mediating institutions such as family, church, and voluntary association stood between the individual and the state. Many observers remained convinced that the limited welfare state, administered by experts, was beginning to solve many of the problems Americans faced at home. Looking beyond the nation's borders, publicists of American exceptionalism boasted of America's uniqueness, sure that with God on their side the American dream would triumph over the Communist nightmare.[5]

As a journalist and writer, Vance Packard was responding principally to the image fostered in the late 1940s and 1950s by the business community and the mass media. Yet it is also important to understand him in relation to American intellectuals who varied in their stance toward the ideological consensus that shaped much of the nation's public discussion. Some, like novelist Norman Mailer, philosopher Herbert Marcuse, sociologist C. Wright Mills, and critic Irving Howe, vigorously dissented from consensus ideology and visions of a near perfect America. However, many influential American intellectuals—sociologists David Riesman and Daniel Bell, political scientist Seymour Martin Lipset, cultural critics Dwight Macdonald and Mary McCarthy, theologian Reinhold Niebuhr, literary critic Lionel Trilling, and to a considerable extent Packard himself—approached American society with what one historian has characterized as a combination of "contentment and uneasiness."[6] Yet although they adopted many elements of consensus ideology and found much to admire in America, these liberal anti-Communists offered a sophisticated critique of the impact of affluence on middle-class life. They paid relatively little attention to politics not only because they believed that the New Deal's legacy had more or less permanently solved the problems the Depression had revealed but also because they concluded that the difficulties America faced were not easily amenable to institutional solutions.

Accepting as givens the elimination of poverty and fundamental class divisions by a largely successful capitalism, these critics worried about the psychological and cultural strains that mass culture, especially TV and Hollywood movies, imposed on Americans, suburban men in particular. They focused not on injustice and economic exploitation, the issues of the 1930s, but on the impersonality, uniformity, and manipulation that mass culture seemed to enforce. What bothered them was not poverty and discrimination but the moral issues raised by advertising, standardization, alienation, affluence, monotonous work, and bureaucratic boredom. They

---

[5] This summary draws on Godfrey Hodgson, *America in Our Time* (New York: Random House, 1976), pp. 69–83.

[6] Richard Pells, *The Liberal Mind in a Conservative Age* (New York: Harper and Row, 1985), p. 121.

argued that white middle-class men felt tremendous pressure to belong, to work together cooperatively, to curb their ambition and individualism, and to be sensitive to the opinions of others. Instead, liberal intellectuals urged white middle-class men to take risks and to seek autonomy and identity. Their goal was not collective action but private fulfillment, an approach that reinforced the domestic ideal. In the 1950s the ideas of liberal intellectuals formed part of a broad consensus that avoided a direct attack on the social order. In the 1960s a new generation would use this critique of modern culture to more radical ends.[7]

Along with *The Status Seekers,* two other best-selling books captured the mood dominant in much of America in the 1950s. In *The Organization Man* (1956) William H. Whyte, Jr., explored the lives of white middle-class men who worked in large bureaucracies. In *The Lonely Crowd* (1950) David Riesman examined the world of upper-middle-class men who lived in major metropolitan areas. Like Packard, Whyte and Riesman emphasized the costs of affluence, the dangers of conformity, and the problems of personal autonomy. All three writers rejected both nineteenth-century individualism and 1930s communitarianism, focusing instead on how to achieve self-determined individualism within the existing social order. They recommended strategies that would enable readers to demystify society's codes in order to achieve greater personal freedom. They tended to believe that social problems could be solved by the psychological healing of the individual and therefore failed to embrace programs for fundamental transformation of the social order. None of them really grappled with political solutions to the problems their analyses revealed.

THE MAKING OF A SOCIAL CRITIC

Vance Packard's life prepared him to be an author of a popular book that explored status striving, social changes, and opportunity in suburban America during the 1950s. Born on May 22, 1914, in Granville Summit, Pennsylvania, he spent his early years as what he later called a "backwater farm boy" on his parents' farm in the north central part of the state.[8] The experiences and memories of the world in which Packard spent his youth provided a set of values that shaped his career. His early years on a farm undergirded his vision of an America based on family, community, hard work, and individualism. Growing up in a Methodist household provided

[7] The preceding summary relies heavily on Pells, *Liberal Mind,* especially pp. 185–88.

[8] Vance Packard, "Behavioral Changes in Americans since 1950," unpublished essay, March 1993, p. 1, author's possession.

him with a moral basis for judging a postwar America that was dominated, he believed, by suburban sprawl, urban blight, conspicuous consumption, rampant commercialism, invasion of privacy, and fragmentation of the family. As a writer he romanticized the conditions that existed during his childhood and much of Packard's later critique of midcentury society came from his own heartfelt assessment of the virtues of the life he had left behind.

In farm communities like Granville Summit, Packard believed, the lines between men and women were clear yet intersecting. With family, kin, and community integrated, there was little room for unbounded individualism. Because people relied on hard work more than on superficial symbols of social class, a rough egalitarianism held the community together. People bought and sold goods and services but they did not systematically use market yardsticks to judge people's worth. Day in and day out, they understood the human and concrete dimensions of work. They relied on products they themselves made or purchased, items which they rarely imbued with qualities they did not inherently have. Husbands and wives, parents and children, farm owners and neighbors worked together as partners, without relying excessively on the exchange of money or experiencing sharp social divisions. Middlemen, speculators, immigrants, and African Americans, though present in the local communities in small numbers, lay outside the boundaries of the stories farm people commonly told about their own lives.

In 1924, around the time of Packard's tenth birthday, his family moved from Granville Summit to the town of State College, Pennsylvania, where his father took a job at Penn State. Packard's father quickly worked his way up from farm hand to foreman and then to supervisor on the university's farms. The move to State College was traumatic for Packard. In 1936 he recalled that the "sudden" shift "worked violently on me." The change from rural community to university town made him keenly aware that he was "a farmer's son dropped in the midst of well-manicured sons and daughters of professors."[9]

In the fall of 1932, Packard made another shift, this one from town to gown when he enrolled at Penn State. Events on campus, across the nation, and around the world awakened his interest in politics. He flirted with left-wing politics: very appreciative of Joseph Stalin's Soviet Union, he nonetheless kept his distance from American radicalism and remained favorably impressed by many of Franklin D. Roosevelt's most far-reaching

---

[9] Vance Packard, application to Columbia University Graduate School of Journalism, 1936, [p. 11], Columbia School of Journalism Archives (hereinafter referred to as CSJA).

New Deal reforms. These years pointed him toward a career that would combine journalism with the social and behavioral sciences. In his work on undergraduate publications, he satirized collegiate customs, sharpened his sense of himself as an ironic observer, and wrote about events at home and abroad. Willard Waller (1899–1945), a sociologist with a personal, demystifying, realistic, and often impressionistic approach, influenced Packard and taught him what it meant to develop an engaged yet ironic intelligence.

In 1936, when Vance Packard graduated from college and moved to Manhattan, he set off on a course that would take him far from rural and small-town Pennsylvania. In the fall he entered the recently established Graduate School of Journalism at Columbia University, earning his master's degree the following June. He then moved to Boston for a job on a tabloid newspaper, where he quickly produced a scoop on a local love story and in turn gained his own daily column. Nonetheless, work on the Boston newspaper did not fully satisfy him and a downturn in the economy and competition with radio for advertising revenues caused the newspaper to terminate his job. In 1938 he moved back to New York to begin a four-year stint with the Associated Press Feature Service, writing human interest stories and weekly reviews of the news. He married Virginia Mathews in 1938 and the first of their three children was born in 1942. In the late 1930s and early 1940s, a series of events at home and abroad — especially the 1939 Nazi-Soviet Pact — prompted him, as it did many of his peers, to rethink his favorable attitudes toward the Soviet Union and to make him more appreciative of the United States.

In 1942, at age twenty-eight, Packard reached a major turning point in his career when he took a job with *American Magazine,* a monthly that appealed to the broad middle of American society and was owned by the conglomerate Crowell-Collier. Like other mass-circulation periodicals of the period, after 1945 *American Magazine* participated in the cold war celebration of American life as it trumpeted an anti-Communist foreign policy, offered a middle-of-the-road take on domestic politics, painted a favorable view of life in American suburbs, and introduced Americans to new items in consumer culture. A typical issue contained expert advice on personal relationships, romantic short stories, how-to articles that featured new products, profiles of famous personalities, and human interest stories that communicated the drama of everyday life.

While working for *American Magazine* from 1942 to 1956, Packard shared many experiences with other white middle-class men of his generation. He bought his first home in the suburbs and then traded up to another, fathered three children, and worked for a large national corporation. In important ways, however, Packard was different. His family resided not in a new, cookie-cutter suburban house but, from 1948 on, in a commodious and distinctive home in New Canaan, Connecticut, an old, wealthy town an hour from Manhattan. In 1953, the Packards also purchased a summer home on Chappaquiddick, an island off Martha's Vineyard, Massachusetts. The Packard household itself was unconventional for its time and place. Packard was a Democrat in a largely Republican community. He did not go into Manhattan to the office on a regular basis, preferring instead to do his research in libraries and write at home. Unlike many of the wives in the community, Virginia worked for money as a schoolteacher and strove to fulfill her dream of becoming a professional artist. With Vance and Virginia encouraging their children to test the limits of conventional behavior, life among the Packards was characterized by creativity, expressiveness, and nonconformity. Yet if the Packard household differed from those of the readers of *American Magazine,* it resembled them in some important ways. Like many suburban dwellers, in social terms the Packards were relatively insulated. The only poor, working-class, or African American people the children met were those who helped in and around the house.

Hell's Bells (1983), a novel by Packard's daughter Cindy, offered an embellished but generally accurate account of the Packard household in the 1950s. She wrote that her youth "was anything but the safe, sane childhood one would infer" from the wealthy community in which the family lived. Her parents were not "employed like normal folks." The fictional mother, under the cover of being a writer, could appear in public like "a typical suburban Mom" and involve herself "in an unending social whirl." Success enabled the father to become even more of an " 'absent-minded professor,' " a phrase that "covered his multitude of sins quite nicely." Thus he was "incredibly stupid about matters which did not interest him," such as how to operate a dishwasher or make a bed. Instead, when he was not writing or roaming the house "at all hours," he was dabbling in politics, playing golf or the stock market, remodeling the family's homes, and giving lectures "on the evils of a technological society."[10] Watching "Ozzie and Harriet" on television provided the children in the novel with no guidance as to what life was really like. "I was aware my parents fought," Cindy Packard noted, "but in that combative household, who didn't?" The parents taught their offspring "to think of life as A Great Challenge," expecting them to succeed and be creative but not particularly caring what they "excelled at." The children, raised by a "trial-and-error" approach, were "a diverse menagerie." Antic inter-

[10] Cindy Packard, *Hell's Bells* (New York: Atheneum, 1983), pp. 17, 18, and 20.

actions in the public realm plus "absolute privacy in one's own domain" dominated the household.[11] During the 1950s and 1960s, Vance Packard appeared to many of those who met him as an unassuming, fundamentally decent, and ambitious person. Driven but not egotistical, Packard was unpretentious as a person. He spoke in direct, colloquial language and seemed less cosmopolitan than he was. He portrayed himself as a country boy among sophisticates, not someone who had the social skills or background to belong in the world of New Canaan and Ivy League graduates. He had boundless energy and curiosity, always trying to figure out what made people tick and things work. In public situations he usually stayed in the background, following rather than leading. He was often in his own world, acting very much like an absent-minded professor.

In his writing for *American Magazine*, Packard articulated a vision that mediated between his own commitment to postwar liberalism and pressures from the editors who were, in turn, hostages to advertisers. His articles celebrated the spread of affluence throughout America in a way that minimized the existence of poverty, highlighted the position of independent entrepreneurs, exaggerated the extent to which America had become a middle-class society, and emphasized the gains of some blue-collar workers. Even though he evoked a world dominated by heterosexuality and the nuclear family, he offered a mild challenge to domesticity by writing about husbands struggling to be more egalitarian and wives moving beyond the confines of the home while happily fulfilling their domestic duties. In the articles he authored when he was free from an editor's intervention, his embrace of consensus ideology paled in comparison with the celebratory expressions dominant in the worlds he knew best — where business publicists, advertising executives, and more conservative magazine writers held forth. In the best of his pieces, Packard offered an implicit critique of American society, putting some distance between himself and the fairyland picture of American life that dominated public discussions during these years. Yet compared with the liberal anti-Communists' critique of America as a mass society, Packard's reservations, like his demeanor, seemed understated.

In the mid-1950s, when mass-circulation magazines faced intensified competition from television, Packard's autonomy decreased further and he rarely had much freedom to write what he wanted to. His success at formulaic articles, while it advanced his career, made him restive with the restraints he faced and intensified his ambivalence about the success he had achieved. The pressure to satisfy editors and advertisers, present

[11] Packard, *Hell's Bells*, pp. 5, 7, 8, and 9.

from the beginning, became especially intense as the situation at *American Magazine* became dire. By 1953, as television and special-interest publications were taking more advertising revenue away from *American Magazine* and similar periodicals, red ink covered the balance sheet of the publishing conglomerate. Those in control struggled for survival, pressuring writers to turn out articles that would enhance the sales of consumer goods advertised in their pages. "So the magazines began prostituting themselves to attract ads," Packard recalled. Every issue, he later remarked, "had to have a food article, a do-it-yourself article, a travel article, and a kiss-ass-with-big-business article because the advertising department told us we needed them."[12]

Packard was in a perfect position to see the intersection of money, power, and writing, a situation that taught him how rarely corporations worried about the welfare of their customers and employees. Working for owners who collected their dividends but demonstrated little concern for the magazine's long-term health left Packard with a sense of the danger posed by wealth unconnected with productivity or responsibility. However ambivalent he may have been about writing stories of suburban life and new consumer goods in a way that aided advertising, his assignments placed him close to the center of American middle-class life. The years at *American Magazine* gave him an intuitive sense of what worked with the largely suburban, white, middle-class audience of his generation. Working for a popular magazine sharpened his ability to research and write with extraordinary speed feature stories that were easily accessible to a broad range of middle-class readers. These years also made him a keen observer with an eye for telling details. Moreover, working in New York on *American Magazine* amply exposed him to the pressures of the advertising world. That world—with its hype, its emphasis on self-promotion, its sensitivity to the market, and its focus on style—was something Packard both absorbed and disliked.

Forces beyond his control were numbering his days as an employee of Crowell-Collier. The corporate survival strategies did not work and with the August 1956 issue *American Magazine* ceased publication. Because of the effectiveness of his contribution to *American Magazine*, Packard was the only person from the editorial section transferred to one of the company's other popular publications, *Collier's*.[13] But the day before Christmas 1956, it too folded. Now Packard faced a critical situation. Long-term unemployment seemed in the offing. Competing with televi-

---

[12] Vance Packard, quoted in Michael Nelson, "What's Wrong with Sociology," *Washington Monthly* 10 (June 1978): 44.
[13] Vance Packard, interview with author, New Canaan, Conn., April 23, 1987.

sion's situation comedies, variety shows, live dramas, and action adventures, the mass-circulation magazines were not able to maintain sufficient advertising revenue. Packard crossed his fingers and hoped that he could become a book author. In early 1957, he collected unemployment checks as he tried to sustain himself as a freelance writer.

The Hidden Persuaders (1957), followed by The Status Seekers in 1959 and The Waste Makers in 1960, became the trilogy that ensured Packard's position as an author and social critic, enabling him to achieve what no other American nonfiction author has done before or since—have three different books in the number one position on the nonfiction bestseller list in four years. With these books, he was able to capitalize on his experience with the world of Madison Avenue, parlaying his knowledge into commercially successful critiques of society. Published in April 1957 by David McKay Company, The Hidden Persuaders, an exposé of advertising, was an immensely successful and influential book. It remained at the top of the list of nonfiction bestsellers for a year; in the next decades, it sold over three million copies in the United States and abroad. The phrase hidden persuaders entered the American language. With considerable justification, advertising executives worried about the impact of a book that awakened the nation to the dangers of deceptive and invasive appeals to consumers.

Even though The Hidden Persuaders made him a famous writer, in the spring of 1957 Packard worried about his future. In May he wondered if he was coming across "as a perceptive and incisive observer of the contemporary scene, or . . . as a radical, arm-waving sensationalist."[14] Yet he was soon at work on what would emerge as The Status Seekers. By the summer of 1957 Packard had settled on an examination of status consciousness and social divisions in America. He later termed The Status Seekers the "lightest" of any of the books he authored. Yet at the time, he wrote that he hoped it would be "a contribution to scholarship," albeit "in compelling terms that will assure it a wide readership."[15] Though this second bestseller drew on material from its predecessor, more immediately his editor at McKay brought to his attention a marketing study that sparked his interest in the larger issues of social class and patterns of consumption.[16]

[14] Vance Packard to Kennett Rawson, May 11, 1957, PPPS.

[15] Vance Packard, interview with author, New Canaan, Conn., December 20, 1990; Vance Packard to Kennett Rawson, Friday night (probably early 1959), PPPS.

[16] Packard, interview, December 20, 1990; Packard to K. Rawson, Friday night; Eleanor Rawson to Vance Packard, July 18, 1991, Vance Packard Papers, Packard residence, New Canaan, Conn. (hereinafter referred to as PPNC); Eleanor Rawson, interview with author, New York, January 16, 1991; Vance Packard to author, April 23–24, 1987, author's possession.

To the task of producing the book, Packard brought the skills of an investigative reporter and an ability to decide early on a structure and then set up a filing system. He stuffed folders with clippings from newspapers, popular magazines, government studies, academic journals, trade publications, and notes he had taken while reading and thinking. For *The Status Seekers* he did fieldwork, carrying out eight "informal" but "intensive" investigations.[17] In addition, he went to Rochester, New York, for several weeks to examine patterns of leadership and discrimination.[18] With his appearance as an "earnest, four-square American," Packard was able to get unsuspecting people to talk with him.[19] He also spoke with academics who were experts on aspects of his study and to professionals (usually in the employ of corporations) trying to reshape the world. Though there was no one with whom he discussed the content of his books in a sustained way, he tried out his ideas and solicited readings of his manuscripts from a number of friends, relatives, and colleagues. As a researcher he was more interested in absorbing, assimilating, and synthesizing than in generating new concepts and formulations. Once he had accumulated enough information, he went through the folders. As he noted concerning a later project, he would spend a considerable amount of time reading what he had collected, "first looking for interrelationships and things that seemed of particular interest for making some point or other. Then I went back and did it all over again to shape the surviving material into chapters," developing a "flow" for each section.[20]

Once he completed the research in the spring of 1958 and began writing, Packard and his family traveled for several months in Europe, placing the material for the book in a trunk on the top of his car. "While his seventeen-year-old son drove across the Alps last summer," a reporter noted, "author Vance Packard sat in the back seat peering over the preliminary notes" for the book. "As his family strolled leisurely through sunny Italian streets," the story continued, "Mr. Packard stayed in his hotel room correlating piles of sociological material. While they shopped and saw the sights, he delved deep into a stack of research data dealing with America's class structure."[21] Upon returning home, Packard completed the writing, sending the manuscript to his publisher by November 1958.[22]

[17] Vance Packard, *The Status Seekers* (New York: David McKay, 1959), p. 10.

[18] Vance Packard, interview with author, New Canaan, Conn., April 9, 1986.

[19] William Hart, telephone conversation with author, May 15, 1992.

[20] "Packard, Vance (Oakley)," *Contemporary Authors*, New Revision Series (Detroit: Gale Research, 1982), p. 375.

[21] "Back Seat of Car Doubles as Office for Vance Packard," clipping from New York University newspaper, June 1959, CSJA.

[22] Vance Packard to author, June 16, 1993, author's possession.

SOCIAL CLASS AND
AMERICAN SUBURBAN LIFE
IN THE LATE 1950s

In writing *The Status Seekers,* Packard was reacting to claims of those who
embraced American exceptionalism—the belief in, not necessarily the
reality of, American uniqueness and openness—and asserted that affluence was increasing social mobility in America and decreasing class and
ethnic divisions. He questioned the conclusion, common among market
researchers and even among those intellectuals who celebrated the results
of prosperity, that sustained economic growth was turning the nation into
a classless society. Rather, he asserted, "under its gloss of prosperity"
the nation was becoming more socially divided as people scrambled "to
find new ways to draw lines that will separate the elect from the non-
elect."[23] The immediate context for Packard's assertions was an editorial
in *Life* that, he later remarked, "exulted that the United States had finally
achieved the 'most truly classless society in history.' "[24] Similarly, in 1955
the editors of *Fortune* hailed "the rise of the great mass into the new
moneyed middle class," a change that was "erasing old class lines" and
elevating "proletarians" into "America's booming new middle-income
class." The lines between income groups were becoming "remarkably
penetrable," "inconspicuous consumption" was making spending patterns
more uniform, and people were trying "to keep *down* with the Joneses."[25]
Claims such as these prompted one observer to comment that "there is
subconscious agreement among the vast majority of Americans that the
United States is not evolving *toward* socialism but *past* socialism."[26] The
question of whether postwar Americans had greater opportunities for
social mobility than their ancestors or than contemporary Europeans
evoked quite varied answers. While some social scientists argued that
opportunity was diminishing, others emphasized the continuing uniqueness and openness of American society. A distinguished anthropologist
wrote that "perhaps one should avoid the word 'class' with its misleading
European connotations and speak of 'status groups.' "[27] Against this
background, Packard argued that the nation's "fantastic" extent of afflu-

[23] Packard, *Status Seekers,* p. 8.
[24] Vance Packard, "A Commentary," *Trans-Action* 2 (January–February 1965): 17–19.
[25] Editors of *Fortune, The Changing American Market* (Garden City, N.Y.: Hanover
House, 1955), pp. 14, 21, 57, 67, 79, 80, and 250.
[26] Frederick Allen, *The Big Change: America Transforms Itself, 1900–1950* (New York:
Harper and Brothers, 1952), p. 291.
[27] Clyde Kluckhohn, "Mid-Century Manners and Morals," in *Twentieth Century Unlimited: From the Vantage Point of the First Fifty Years,* edited by Bruce Bliven (Philadelphia: J.
B. Lippincott, 1950), p. 304.

ence, by strengthening the "barriers and humiliating distinctions of social class," was intensifying status striving.[28] Where liberal intellectuals traced the origins of the problems of mass society to mindless consumers, Packard blamed consumer culture developed by capitalists.

A series of factors, he argued, had transformed American society. With work in large national corporations increasingly fragmented and impersonal, employees derived less social prestige, job satisfaction, and self-esteem from their labor. With opportunity blocked and status striving exaggerated, Packard argued, millions of Americans were suffering emotionally. Frightened "by the anxieties, inferiority feelings, and straining generated by this unending process of rating and status striving," Americans were constantly trying "to surround themselves with visible evidence of the superior ranking they are claiming."[29] Shut off from social advancement and bored with their jobs, blue-collar and white-collar workers could feel they were getting somewhere by increasing material consumption. Consequently, people consumed "flamboyantly, much as the restless Roman masses found diversion in circuses thoughtfully provided by the emperors." Advertisers and market researchers were foremost among the villains who persuaded people to seek satisfaction through consumer goods, not jobs. Advertisers intensified consumers' feelings about status by encouraging the achievement of success and status through self-indulgence. At the same time that they promoted the vision of a classless society, Packard noted, advertisers exaggerated the importance of specific ways of identifying status.[30]

Packard worried that a decline in social mobility might undermine what he saw as the American dream of abundant opportunity, a vision that at moments rested on a nostalgic view of America's past. Although he divided people into five social classes, he saw the real chasm between the "Diploma Elite" and the "Supporting Classes." It was becoming increasingly difficult for a person to rise in larger businesses without an education beyond high school. He cautioned against exaggerating the extent to which members of the working class had entered the middle class, noting that "many of the new white-collar jobs are essentially manual or require little skill." Yet he remained worried that blue-collar workers, especially union members, had made gains in income or social position significant enough to threaten the middle-class status of some white-collar workers. "The better-paid blue-collar working people such as craftsmen and foremen," he argued, "are coming to dominate the middle-class

[28] Packard, *Status Seekers*, p. 3.
[29] Packard, *Status Seekers*, p. 7.
[30] Packard, *Status Seekers*, pp. 9–10 and 307–8.

positions in our society." He reserved some of his ire, usually muted, for organization men "who have successfully shed their rough edges of individualism" and especially for those who "manage to become rebels at night," turning into "wicked wits and flaming liberals in the safety of their patios and favorite bars."[31]

One of his principal solutions to the problems of a status-conscious society was to enhance the understanding of one group by another. By comprehending the entire society and not just their particular place in it, Americans might "lead more effective lives, and quite probably more serene ones." Packard's second solution was opening up opportunity. He criticized college-educated and economically comfortable Protestant men, who he believed should have had the least cause for concern about social position, for erecting barriers against Jews in corporations, clubs, and neighborhoods. Packard's solution to the problems of blocked mobility was to make class distinctions less burdensome by ensuring that the society discovered people of real talent and then helped them fulfill their potential. He advocated open access to higher education, especially for "all of high native ability" and those discouraged by the high cost or by "an environment of resignation, ostracism, and hedonism."[32]

The book-buying public rushed to read what Packard had written in The Status Seekers. It remained number one on the bestseller list for more than four months and on the list for a year. It helped develop Packard's career as a celebrity, and he appeared on major television shows. As would happen with the language of women's liberation twenty years later, ads used Packard's catchword to hawk goods. Cartoonists had a field day with The Status Seekers (see pp. 191–95). The title of the book also earned a place on the list of phrases—like 1984, Future Shock, and Feminine Mystique—that entered the language at home and abroad. Translated into more than a dozen foreign languages, Packard's book would reach millions of people around the world. More than three decades after publication of the second book in the trilogy, the notion of status seeking still served as a reference point for discussions of social striving in America.[33] In 1991, an African American journalist told Packard that thirty years earlier her mother, who had a "keen interest in class," read The Status Seekers "most likely for pointers."[34]

The letters ordinary people sent Packard soon after the publication of

[31] Packard, Status Seekers, pp. 8–10, 26, 35, 98, 102, 116, 124–25, and 276.
[32] Packard, Status Seekers, pp. 340, 346–47, and 351–52.
[33] See, for example, "The New Status Seekers," Los Angeles Times Magazine, December 27, 1987/January 3, 1988, front page.
[34] V.B.M. to Vance Packard, July 29, 1991, PPNC. To preserve anonymity, I have used initials to identify Packard's correspondents.

The Status Seekers reveal some dimensions of the book's impact. They provide real evidence of how people made sense of Packard's book in the context of their own lives and prove that people read books from the perspective of their own experiences.[35] Many people wrote to brag about, decipher, or puzzle over their own position in American society. For example, a woman from a distinguished southern family commented that she "subscribed to the *American Heritage* and owned the eleventh edition of the *Encyclopedia Britannica* and was once invited to Newport but couldn't go. Will that do?" she asked Packard.[36] With an even greater sense of urgency and of the problematic nature of status came a letter from a woman in a midwestern industrial city. Married to an owner of a barber shop, with a son in a private boarding school in New York, and a public school teacher herself, she found her family in the anomalous position of having more income than status. People, she observed, responded in two distinctive ways: some pigeonholed them as " 'rich,' " " 'four-flushers,' and 'fakers,' " while others snubbed them because "we 'ain't got nothin',' but act like 'big shots.' " Turning to Packard for help and denying that they were " 'climbers,' " she asked how she and her husband might meet "a couple or two with whom we feel congenial, with whom we can exchange visits occasionally without this underlying feeling of animosity, or rivalry."[37]

The success of *The Status Seekers* also underscored the vacuum created by developments in academic sociology. In 1960, a high school teacher from a small city in the Midwest thanked Packard for writing books that, compared with the "dense volumes" by Harvard sociologist Talcott Parsons, were readable and personal. "Those in the sociological field," he remarked, "may not think too highly of you for putting your personal self in the book." Sociologists, he concluded, "seem to think that sociological research and communication must be as impersonal as a washing machine." A friend of this teacher who taught high school sociology had told him that Packard was a "popularizer" who lacked depth and had "the nasty habit of dashing in where even fools would fear to tread" and that he was "really not in sociology," by which he meant that he was "not a full professor at a big, high status university." Five years later, the teacher wrote Packard again. After remarking that he appreciated Packard's books because they told "truths that most 'good' people would just as soon ignore," he noted that "the 'experts' in sociology apparently have little use

[35] For an exploration of reader response theory, see Janice A. Radway, *Reading the Romance: Women, Patriarchy, and Popular Literature* (Chapel Hill: University of North Carolina Press, 1984).
[36] E.D.S. to Vance Packard, December 2, 1958, PPPS.
[37] A.E. to Vance Packard, June 11, 1960, PPPS.

for you or your wares." In a class he took during the summer, a sociologist at a university told him that Packard's work was "not a 'safe' or 'reliable' or 'scholarly' source." His guess, which reflected the ironic role of status in the situation, was that "these boys are jealous of you—of your fame or notoriety and of the great amount of money you make" out of what academics felt was " 'phony' " scholarship and " 'glib' " judgments.[38]

The most dramatic evidence of the impact of the book on some readers came from a nurse. "There are two or three situations," she remarked in 1960, "resulting in a release of joy normally attributable to orgasm—a new idea, a phrase that writes itself, or a *real* feeling of accomplishment. It is with this feeling I finished your book."[39] More typical were the testimonials to the book's impact that came from people who prided themselves on their avoidance of status seeking. A person from Chicago reported staying awake until five o'clock in the morning to finish *The Status Seekers*. "I feel that my life has been immeasurably enriched by reading and understanding your book." Long fearful of articulating the ideas Packard now expressed, this person was grateful that "there are men such as you to bring these truths to the attention of the world."[40] An African American woman from a city in the Midwest talked of how "intensely" the study held her interest, attacked people for spending and not saving, and hoped that what Packard wrote "will awaken and enlighten the masses about some of the true values of life which seem lost."[41] Probably with unintended irony, an antique dealer from Pennsylvania asserted that America was "doomed" because the entire economy, based "on trying to get others to covet things which they do not even need," violated one of the Ten Commandments.[42]

Moreover, there is considerable evidence that the book had special appeal to people concerned about prejudice and limited opportunity. Several Jews wrote Packard to discuss discrimination.[43] He also heard from people who were downwardly mobile, without college degrees, aspiring but fearful, or worried about the implications of blocked social mobility. An especially poignant example was a woman from the state of Washington who wrote because she believed Packard was sympathetic to the plight of people America might push aside. The wife of a farm laborer who was "white of Latin heritage," she proudly described how she and her family lived frugally. They did not drink alcohol and they drove a nine-year-

---

[38] H.K. to Vance Packard, August 1960 and September 29, 1965, PPPS.
[39] G.R. to Vance Packard, February 2, 1960, PPPS.
[40] M.G. to Vance Packard, January 26, 1960, PPPS.
[41] V.H. to Vance Packard, August 22, 1959, PPPS.
[42] J.K. to Vance Packard, October 16, 1960, PPPS.
[43] For example, see L.A.F. to Vance Packard, August 29, 1961, PPNC.

old automobile, "for transportation, not show." Every day she read to her two young daughters, choosing authors such as Charles Darwin, Thomas Mann, and Carl Jung. How many people of higher social status, she asked Packard rhetorically, read books by writers such as these? How many members of the Junior League, Episcopal church, and Rotary Club "want their children to become understanding, educated ladies and gentlemen?" In a remark laden with implications about ethnicity, gender, and class, she remarked that she hoped her daughters would "attend a good college," become "ladies, not women," and "marry educated non-conforming gentlemen, not college men." Ending the letter, she said "I remain a friend," as if to tell Packard how important it was to have the ear of a sympathetic and authoritative person who wanted to strengthen America's commitment to equal opportunity.[44]

GROUNDBREAKING STUDY OR "*KITSCH* SOCIOLOGY"? THE RESPONSE OF CRITICS TO *THE STATUS SEEKERS*

Favorable reviews of the book captured the contribution and impact of *The Status Seekers*. Book trade and library journals offered especially positive appraisals, with one claiming that it contained information "brought together intelligently, interpreted with imagination, and effectively presented" and another seeing it as "a penetrating book that provides a thorough and disturbing portrait of the more unlovely aspects of the American social landscape."[45] A professor from North Carolina credited it with making "a substantial contribution to fuller and more accurate understanding of the dizzy vortex that is contemporary America."[46] *Newsweek* hailed the book as "a fascinating view of contemporary pride and prejudice."[47] A writer in a Christian publication called the book "a masterful piece of conscience-pricking" because "it so truthfully exposes raw nerves by laying bare the ambiguity of many of our motives."[48] The reviewer in a Philadelphia newspaper said that the book "should be read by every American who wishes to understand the society of which he is a

---

[44] J.L.D. to Vance Packard, no date, PPPS.

[45] Harold Lancour, *Library Journal* (April 15, 1959): 1275; *Booklist* (May 1, 1959): 470. Because many of the reviews are most conveniently found in clippings in PPPS, they often lack the basis for a complete citation.

[46] Joseph S. Himes, *Journal of Human Relations*, p. 304.

[47] *Newsweek*, May 4, 1959, p. 106.

[48] William H. Hudnut III, *Christian Century*.

part. If the reading dismays him, his dismay could prove salutary."[49] *The
Status Seekers,* commented one newspaper reviewer, "packs a wallop that
will be felt from coast to coast." It belonged, he continued, "in the library
of every American who is concerned with the future of his country."[50] A
college professor wrote that the book belonged "in the great tradition of
American protest literature," filled as it was with "horrified fascination,"
"righteous moralism," and "outraged" optimism."[51]

Despite the success and influence of *The Status Seekers,* it was hardly
immune from criticisms. Sociologists, New York intellectuals (the name
historians use to describe the group of writers who dominated American
intellectual life in the 1950s), reviewers in cosmopolitan publications, and
people from a variety of political perspectives raised important questions
about the book. Some found Packard too critical of America. For example,
one observer asserted that he was wrong when he argued that American
society was becoming more rigid and social mobility more difficult to
achieve.[52] Likewise, political scientist Seymour Martin Lipset asserted in
1959 that the basic problem with the book was its misuse of "scientific
evidence to construct a prejudiced and partisan case" that wrongly argued
that the United States was becoming less egalitarian. Lipset cited studies
demonstrating that Americans were satisfied with their work, that rates of
social mobility and opportunity were steady if not improving, and that
access to higher education was enhancing opportunity.[53] A number of
people criticized Packard for being nostalgic. Informed by neither "a
scholar's concern [n]or a reformer's zeal," wrote sociologist Lewis Coser,
The Status Seekers was "anchored in nothing more substantial than a guilty
nostalgia for a supposedly less status-conscious and hence less anxiety-
ridden past."[54]

Critics took Packard to task for emphasizing small-town values,
celebrating American ideals, and oversentimentalizing the past. The most
sustained argument along these lines came in 1961 from the historian
Loren Baritz. Writing in *The Nation,* he compared Packard with other
backward-looking reformers. Baritz cited the references in Packard's
books to suburban houses as homesteads, to self-sufficiency, to individualism, and to New England villages, all of which conjured up a "notion of the
nineteenth-century pastoral as the measure of our degeneration." Baritz

---

[49] Ben Ray Redman, *Philadelphia Bulletin,* May 3, 1959.
[50] Barney Ballard, review in unidentified newspaper, May 1, 1959.
[51] John Lydenberg, *New Leader,* September 21, 1959.
[52] Robert J. Havighurst, *Personnel and Guidance Journal* (February 1960): 512.
[53] Seymour M. Lipset, "Vance Packard Discovers America," *Reporter* 21 (July 9, 1959):
31–33.
[54] Lewis Coser, "Kitsch Sociology," *Partisan Review* (Summer 1959): 480–83.

saw Packard as "still a spiritual citizen" of the nineteenth-century small town, whose "self-appointed task is to convince those Americans most committed to the twentieth century to become villagers too." Consequently, Baritz incisively noted, although Packard criticized "industrialism and—even—capitalism," he nonetheless accepted "the situation which gave rise to the things he now finds unpleasant." Baritz asserted that Packard shied away from the realization that waste, economic growth, rising profits, and a cornucopia of consumer goods were essential to the American economy. Packard, he stated, was a proponent of a "nostalgic" or "anachronistic liberalism" whose solutions of "pious wishing and wet hankies" relied on the ignorance of "considerations of power."[55]

The Status Seekers also came in for attack because some believed that under the guise of social criticism it was an advice book that offered Americans lessons on how to seek status. Those who corresponded with Packard made clear how important the book was in helping them to evaluate their social position. As sociologist William Petersen noted, its appeal lay "in the social climber's ambivalent stance toward social climbing." Packard, he asserted, provided a formula "that had been perfected long since in moral tracts against pornography." First came "up-to-date Emily Post," a detailed description of the tricks by which one could achieve new status. There followed the denunciation of "status-seekers as an unworthy lot." Petersen concluded that "such careful catering to a widespread need suggests that the author is a good businessman."[56]

Another line of attack emphasized that Packard was merely a popularizer who offered a superficial analysis of American society. Thus Coser saw the book as an example of "kitsch sociology," a "spurious reproduction" that reshaped scholarship in a way that eliminated all nuances. Packard, he wrote, frightened "the jaded reader," then aroused his "guilt and anxiety," and finally reassured him with homilies about the possibilities of individual happiness.[57] In his classic 1960 essay warning of the threat that "masscult" and "midcult" posed to high culture, the cultural critic Dwight Macdonald wrote of Packard as "an enterprising journalist" who had "manufactured" best-selling books "by summarizing the more sensational findings of the academic sociologists, garnering the results with solemn moralizings, and serving it up under catchy titles." Middlebrow culture, a category Macdonald pejoratively used to attack culture that pretended to creativity without achieving it and in which he included the

[55] Loren Baritz, "Of Time and the Ostrich," The Nation (January 1961): 82–83.
[56] William Petersen, "Reply to Mr. Packard," American Sociological Review 25 (June 1960): 408–9.
[57] Coser, "Kitsch Sociology," pp. 480–81

widely read novelist John Hersey, the Book-of-the-Month Club, the musical *South Pacific*, and Packard, was "a peculiar hybrid" that resulted from the "unnatural intercourse" of "High Culture" with "Masscult." In the process, Macdonald asserted, mass culture pretended "to respect the standards of High Culture while in fact it water[ed] them down and vulgarize[d] them."[58] Similarly, Mary McCarthy, a prominent New York intellectual, remarked that books on "mass culture for the mass audience," such as *The Status Seekers* and *The Organization Man*, "had become the latest form of pornography—'the mirror on the ceiling of the whorehouse.'"[59]

Critics also found Packard's politics ambivalent or shallow. Although Lipset believed that Packard probably thought of himself as a rebel who embraced some liberal or even radical position, in fact, he wrote, Packard was a conformist who managed to hide his nonconformity in a book that combined "a critique of commercialism with an espousal of the verities advocated by Herbert Hoover." This was, the political scientist argued, a "foolproof combination that sells books."[60] In the end the criticism Packard offered was harmless, the sociologist Coser wrote, because it set out "to afford its audience the pleasure of deploring a state of affairs which it secretly craves." Flattering the reader, the book made it possible for "him to compensate for his guilt in condoning a meretricious reality by the fake catharsis of verbal condemnation," something "designed to reconcile him to his role as a part of that reality."[61]

Critics who looked at the relationship between Packard's writings and his life probed for contradictions of a personal nature. In typically caustic fashion, *Time* ended its story on *The Status Seekers* by pointing out that the author lived "in New Canaan, Conn., in a twelve-room house (white frame), and has a Weimaraner, just about the highest-status dog available." Writing in *The Wall Street Journal* John Chamberlain, a radical anti-Stalinist turned conservative, remarked ironically that "if Mr. Packard really wants to prove his sincerity about his thesis he will have to sell that home in New Canaan and go back to living in a cave."[62]

Critics such as these captured some of the problems with Packard's works. Not very rigorous in its handling of tough theoretical issues, *The Status Seekers* tended to fudge critical distinctions between class, status, and ethnicity. Critics correctly pointed out the costs of Packard's haste.

---

[58] Dwight Macdonald, "Masscult and Midcult," in *Against the American Grain* (1960; New York: Random House, 1962), pp. 37, 39, and 53–54.

[59] Mary McCarthy, letter to the editor, *Time* 76 (August 8, 1960): 2.

[60] Seymour M. Lipset, "The Conservatism of Vance Packard," *Commentary*, pp. 80–83.

[61] Coser, "Kitsch Sociology," p. 483.

[62] *Time* (June 8, 1959): 102; John Chamberlain, *Wall Street Journal*, April 29, 1959.

He composed more accessible prose than academics, wrote books more quickly than they could produce articles, and had an ability to absorb what more cautious writers would struggle to resolve or qualify. *The Status Seekers* was better at synthesizing the work of others than it was at striking out on an original path. Virtually everything Packard wrote had already been said by contemporary authors. The originality came when he supported his arguments against the benefits of classlessness and affluence with information on how advertisers were trying to increase status identification and thereby class division. What he gained in impact, productivity, and accessibility, he lost in originality and subtlety. What distinguished him from academic sociologists was his ability to bring his critique of classlessness, something others had developed, to a broad audience and make that perspective part of the public debate.

Those who felt Packard produced "masscult" or "midcult" correctly saw his work as patterned and derivative rather than idiosyncratic or original, soothing as much as adversarial. The view of Packard as someone who wrote *kitsch*, a German term for any work—be it writing, artwork, or home design—that is hastily assembled and pretentious, relied on a clearly defined cultural hierarchy in which articles in *American Magazine* and best-selling books ranked relatively low. There was at least one irony in the situation: intellectuals were demeaning Packard's work as kitsch, or debased mass culture, even as he himself protested the spread of mass culture throughout American society, albeit in a manner that his critics felt resembled kitsch. Packard and his adversaries, both ambivalent about what they saw in post–World War II America, combined criticism of and accommodation to the central values and institutions of American society.

THE PLACE OF
THE STATUS SEEKERS
IN ITS TIME

Like many 1950s liberals, Packard assumed that the problems America faced stemmed from affluence, not poverty. He focused principally on the middle class, especially the moral dilemmas raised by success and mass consumption. As was true in much of the social analysis of the 1950s, problems faced by women, African Americans, and the poor were not among Packard's principal concerns. Despite his challenges to the placid consensus of the time, he kept his central focus on the plight of the white middle-class male who lived in a suburb and worked in a large organization. Packard tended to exaggerate the degree to which working-class and lower-middle-class Americans could participate in the affluent society. He seemed most fearful of the impact of social and economic changes on members of the middle class who had no powerful institutions to protect them. Worried about blocked opportunity, he did not focus on prejudice against African Americans. Rather, he reserved his sharpest words for the anti-Semitism of white upper-class men who excluded Jews from major institutions. This focus underscored his tendency to worry more about social problems of the affluent than the problems of those in poverty, a reflection of his location in a wealthy suburb which influenced his own sense of urgency. Nor did he think that it was possible to solve the problems America faced by a fundamental restructuring of institutions or by collective political action; rather, he called for individual resistance to the pressures of affluence and conformity.[63]

There is fragmentary but suggestive evidence that Packard's book was among the forces that shaped political discussions in the United States in the late 1950s and early 1960s, as the nation was shifting from the quiescent politics of one decade to the more active and reform-minded politics of the next. Packard promoted an animus against experts, attacked unquestioned growth, and emphasized the social and psychological costs of status and class. He stressed the quest for meaningful work and for a more democratic workplace, addressed the perils of conformity in corporations and suburbs, questioned discrimination based on ethnicity, and advocated consumer rights. *The Status Seekers* was among the many sources that influenced radicals of the 1960s. In 1962, the Port Huron Statement, the key document of Students for a Democratic Society, the principal organization of the New Left, acknowledged the contribution of Packard in noting that college students paid too much attention to social status when they decided what to wear and whom to befriend and marry; that Americans' "nagging incentive to 'keep up' makes them continually dissatisfied with their possessions"; and that the economy relied too heavily on " 'market research' techniques to deliberately create pseudo-needs in consumers."[64]

Herbert Marcuse, an émigré from Nazi Germany whom radical students considered one of their most influential intellectual forebears, offered a balanced evaluation of Packard's contribution. In 1964, he included Packard's works among the sources that he had found useful for their discussions "of the familiar tendencies of advanced industrial civiliza-

---

[63] In this discussion, I have drawn on Pells, *Liberal Mind*, pp. 130–261 and 346–402.

[64] Port Huron Statement reprinted in James Miller, *"Democracy Is in the Streets": From Port Huron to the Siege of Chicago* (New York: Simon and Schuster, 1987), pp. 334, 338, and 339.

tion." He emphasized "the vital importance of the work of C. Wright Mills, and of studies which are frequently frowned upon because of simplification, overstatement, or journalistic ease," including *The Status Seekers*. "To be sure," he continued, "the lack of theoretical analysis in these works leaves the roots of the described conditions covered and protected, but left to speak for themselves, the conditions speak loudly enough."[65]

However cogent its critics, *The Status Seekers* provides us with a way of understanding American society in the 1950s. Packard's book influenced Americans in a number of ways, not the least of which was in helping to foster the shift from a complacent 1950s to a more questioning 1960s. Packard articulated what many Americans sensed but had been unable to express, as he explained changes in the United States that excited and frightened those who were experiencing them. His moral tone appealed to people who felt something was wrong with affluent America but nonetheless enjoyed comforts their parents had been unable to afford. What some critics saw as weaknesses in his books—their ambivalence, nostalgia, moralism, and slickness—also help account for their sales and impact.

Reflecting the liberal feminism of the late 1950s, Packard discussed the feminization of those on the lower rungs of white-collar occupations, spoke out against job discrimination against women, and bemoaned the way corporations treated the wives of their male executives. He acknowledged the existence of a true lower class, largely African American, that lived in inner cities and lacked steady employment. He recognized the force of segregation in housing and remained hopeful that integration would help the nation achieve racial balance in cities and suburbs. *The Status Seekers* was important because it challenged the celebrations of American exceptionalism so commonly expressed in the 1950s.

Like others, Packard served as a scout or a negotiator in the shift from the 1950s to the 1960s.[66] In the late 1950s, the Beat generation and the civil rights movement questioned the extent of the nation's commitments to justice, equality, and authenticity. Books such as C. Wright Mills's *Power Elite* (1956), John Keats's *Crack in the Picture Window* (1957), John Kenneth Galbraith's *Affluent Society* (1958), and Paul Goodman's *Growing Up Absurd* (1960) prodded the complacent to think about their apathy and the restive to shed their reserve. Packard's book reflected the tone of social criticism of the 1950s at the same time that it heralded

---

[65] Herbert Marcuse, *One-Dimensional Man: Studies in the Ideology of Advanced Industrial Society* (Boston: Beacon Press, 1964), p. xvii.

[66] For the argument that writers of the 1950s served as progenitors of the 1960s, see Pells, *Liberal Mind*, pp. 188 and 401–9.

and influenced the bolder politics of the 1960s. In its earliest stages, during the late 1950s, this renascent sense of social responsibility often lacked specific programmatic content, something that dovetailed well with Packard's approach. His politics appealed to readers dissatisfied with the complacency of the 1950s but unsure of how to create a better society.[67]

[67] After the publication of *The Status Seekers*, Packard sustained himself as a freelance writer and social critic. *The Waste Makers* (1960) was a path-breaking book that explored the impact of planned obsolescence and wastefulness on American life. Though *Pyramid Climbers* (1962) broke little new ground, *Naked Society* (1964) was among the first books, if not the very first, to warn Americans about the full range of new dangers to their privacy. *Sexual Wilderness: The Contemporary Upheaval in Male-Female Relationships* (1968) stood at a crucial turning point in the line of popular books on sexuality. *Nation of Strangers* (1972) examined American experiences with rootlessness. *People Shapers* (1977) took on the task of exploring how scientists were setting out to transform human lives. *Our Endangered Children: Growing Up in a Changing World* (1983) entered the crowded field of treatments of family life. *Ultra Rich: How Much Is Too Much?* (1989) examined the lives of very rich Americans and called for a redistribution of their wealth.

Packard's friend and *New Yorker* cartoonist Whitney Darrow, Jr., created this drawing for a 1986 issue of the Sunday supplement of the *Hartford Courant*. Darrow captures essential elements of Packard's life: book after book emerging from his word processor, one hat placed on another; and his dog Thumper at his feet. Waiting at the ready are reminders of his avocations: bowling paraphernalia; golf equipment with tags from courses on Martha's Vineyard, San Miguel de Allende, Fairfield County, Connecticut; and a sea gull from Chappaquiddick.

The Status Seekers

**An Exploration of Class Behavior in America
and the Hidden Barriers That Affect You,
Your Community, Your Future**

by Vance Packard

Contents

CHAPTER 1

A Classless Society?

What happens to class distinctions among people when most of them are enjoying a long period of material abundance?

Suppose, for example, that most of the people are able to travel about in their own gleaming, sculptured coaches longer than the average living room and powered by the equivalent of several hundred horses. Suppose that they are able to wear a variety of gay-colored apparel made of miraculous fibers. Suppose they can dine on mass-merchandised vichyssoise and watch the wonders of the world through electronic eyes in their own air-conditioned living rooms.

In such a climate, do the barriers and humiliating distinctions of social class evaporate? Do anxieties about status—and strivings for evidences of superior status—ease up notably? And do opportunities for leadership roles become more available to all who have natural talent?

The recent experience of the people of the United States is instructive. In the early 1940's an era of abundance began which by 1959 had reached proportions fantastic by any past standards. Nearly a half-trillion dollars' worth of goods and services—including television, miracle fibers, and vichyssoise—were being produced.

Before this era of fabled plenty began, it was widely assumed that prosperity would eliminate, or greatly reduce, class differences. If everybody could enjoy the good things of life—as defined by mass merchandisers—the meanness of class distinctions would disappear.

Such a view seemed reasonable to most of us in those pinched preplenty days of the thirties because, then, differences in status were all too plainly visible. You could tell who was who—except for a few genteel poor—by the way people dressed, ate, traveled, and—if they were lucky—by the way they worked. The phrase "poor people" then had an intensely vivid meaning. A banker would never be mistaken for one of his clerks even at one hundred feet.

What, actually, has happened to social class in the United States during the recent era of abundance?

A number of influential voices have been advising us that whatever social classes we ever had are now indeed withering away. We are being told that the people of our country have achieved unparalleled equality. Listen to some of the voices.

Some months ago, a national periodical proclaimed the fact that the

31

United States had recently achieved the "most truly classless society in history." A few weeks later, a publisher hailed the disappearance of the class system in America as "the biggest news of our era." Still later, the director of a market-research organization announced his discovery that America was becoming "one vast middle class." Meanwhile, a corporation in paid advertisements was assuring us that "there are more opportunities in this country than ever before." Whatever else we are, we certainly are the world's most self-proclaimed equalitarian people.

The rank-and-file citizens of the nation have generally accepted this view of progress toward equality because it fits with what we would like to believe about ourselves. It coincides with the American Creed and the American Dream, and is deeply imbedded in our folklore.

Such a notion unfortunately rests upon a notable lack of perception of the true situation that is developing. Class lines in several areas of our national life appear to be hardening. And status straining has intensified.

We shall see that the people of the United States have, and are refining, a national class structure with a fascinating variety of status systems within it. These status systems affect a number of intimate areas of our daily lives and have some surprising and preposterous ramifications. At points it will be noted how our class structure now differs from that of other countries. And finally we shall examine several growing areas of cleavage in the American class structure that seem to demand recognition. In particular, I think we should be disturbed by the stratifying tendencies appearing in the places where millions of us work, live, relax, vote, and worship.

Since class boundaries are contrary to the American Dream, Americans generally are uncomfortable when the subject of their existence arises. Sociologist August B. Hollingshead of Yale University found that psychiatrists—supposedly uninhibited, open-minded individuals—"tend to react with embarrassment when the question of social class is raised."[1]

Until recent years, even sociologists had shrunk away from a candid exploration of social class in America. Social classes, they realized, were not supposed to exist. Furthermore, Karl Marx had made class a dirty word. As a result the social scientists, until a few years ago, knew more about the social classes of New Guinea than they did of those in the United States of America.

Editor's Note: I have left the content of Packard's footnotes substantially as he presented them; however, deletion of material from the original body of the book has necessitated some omissions and collapsing of footnotes.

[1] August B. Hollingshead and Frederick C. Redlich, *Social Class and Mental Illness* (New York: John Wiley & Sons, Inc., 1958), p. 162.

Webster defines status as the "position; rank; standing" of a person. (The word can be pronounced either "stay-tus" or "stat-us.") Although present-day Americans in this era of material abundance are not supposed to put differential labels of social status on fellow citizens, many millions of them do it every day. And their search for appropriate evidences of status for themselves appears to be mounting each year. There is some evidence that wives, generally speaking, tend to be more status conscious than their husbands.

The majority of Americans rate acquaintances and are themselves being rated in return. They believe that some people rate somewhere above them, that some others rate somewhere below them, and that still others seem to rate close enough to their own level to permit them to explore the possibility of getting to know them socially without fear of being snubbed or appearing to downgrade themselves.

Many people are badly distressed, and scared, by the anxieties, inferiority feelings, and straining generated by this unending process of rating and status striving. The status seekers, as I use the term, are people who are continually straining to surround themselves with visible evidence of the superior rank they are claiming. The preoccupation of millions of Americans with status is intensifying social stratification in the United States. Those who need to worry least about how they are going to come out in the ratings are those who, in the words of Louis Kronenberger, are "Protestant, well-fixed, college-bred."[2]

Even our children soon become aware of the class labels that are on their families and are aware of the boundaries that circumscribe their own daily movement. If even children know the facts of class, you may inquire, why is it that so many opinion molders have been announcing their conclusion that classes are disappearing?

The discrepancy arises partly as a result of a generalized desire on the part of United States adults—particularly businessmen—to support the American Dream. Also it arises from the widespread assumption that the recent general rise in available spending money in this country is making everybody equal. Class, in fact, has several faces and income is just one of them. With the general diffusion of wealth, there has been a crumbling of visible class lines now that such one-time upper-class symbols as limousines, power boats, and mink coats are available to a variety of people. Coincidentally, there has been a scrambling to find new ways to draw lines that will separate the elect from the non-elect.

A working-class man, however, does not move up into another social

[2] Louis Kronenberger, *Company Manners* (New York: The Bobbs–Merrill Co., Inc., 1951), p. 189.

class just by being able to buy a limousine, either by cash or installment, and he knows it. In terms of his productive role in our society—in contrast to his consuming role—class lines in America are becoming more rigid, rather than withering away.

In truth, America, under its gloss of prosperity, is undergoing a significant hardening of the arteries of its social system at some critical points.

As I perceive it, two quite sharply divided major groupings of social classes are emerging, with the old middle class being split into two distinct classes in the process. At the places where most Americans work, as I will try to show, we are seeing a new emphasis on class lines and a closing-in of the opportunities available to make more than a minor advance. In modern big business, it is becoming more and more difficult to start at the bottom and reach the top. Any leaping aspiration a non-college person has after beginning his career in big business in a modest capacity is becoming less and less realistic.

Furthermore, stratification (formalized inequality of rank) is becoming built-in as our increasingly bureaucratized society moves at almost every hand toward bigness: Big Business, Big Government, Big Labor, Big Education. Bigness is one of the really major factors altering our class system.

In the hierarchy of the big corporation, stratification is being carried to exquisite extremes. Employees are usually expected to comport themselves in conformity with their rank, and generally do so. Industrialists are noting that the military experience millions of our younger generation have had has made them more accepting of rank. (With all this growth of bigness and rank, the best opportunities for the enterprising non-college man today are found not with the large producing company but rather on Main Street, where it is still often possible to start small and grow, or with a small or pioneering producing firm.)

Employees in big offices, as well as big plants, are finding their work roles fragmentized and impersonalized. There has been, perhaps unwittingly, a sealing-off of contact between big and little people on the job. And there has been a startling rise in the number of people who are bored with their work and feel no pride of initiative or creativity. They must find their satisfactions outside their work. Many do it by using their paychecks to consume flamboyantly, much as the restless Roman masses found diversion in circuses thoughtfully provided by the emperors.

Although we still tend to think of equality as being peculiarly American, and of class barriers as being peculiarly foreign, the evidence indicates that several European nations (such as Holland, England, and Denmark) have gone further than America in developing an open-class system, where the poor but talented young can rise on their merits. And they have done this while preserving some of the outer forms of class, such as titled families.

In brief, the American Dream is losing some of its luster for a good many citizens who would like to believe in it. If, and when, the patina of prosperity over our land is ever rubbed off by a prolonged recession, to use the polite word, the new stratifications will become uncomfortably apparent and embarrassing, unless action is taken to broaden the channels for upward mobility.

It is my impression that status lines are more carefully observed in the East and South than in most of the other parts of the country. Californians, with their yeasty social climate, seem the least status-conscious people I've encountered in the nation. This might be explained by the fact that—with their violently expanding economy and their multitude of relatively small new enterprises—they are close to the free-and-easy frontier spirit. In the San Joaquin Valley, some of the most widely and highly esteemed families are of Armenian or Korean background. They have prospered, and their forebears were Early Settlers.

Perhaps I should say a few words about how I came by the material and concepts supporting the views I will develop. First, I have drawn upon eight investigations I have made in the past three years into specific situations bearing on class. These were informal studies, but quite intensive. I have, in addition, discussed aspects of class with knowledgeable local people in eighteen United States states and five European countries; and I have conferred with several dozen sociologists and market-research specialists who have interested themselves in aspects of class behavior.

Most important, in terms of the impact of this book, I have brought together the findings of more than 150 United States sociologists and other students of the social scene who have been investigating phases of our social stratification, and I have tried to assess their findings.

Business groups, I should add, have shown a lively interest in sponsoring studies of class behavior. They have sought to know their customers better. Home developers have been studying the stratification patterns—and status-striving motives—of home buyers. Madison Avenue has been busily trying to understand our tastes and buying behavior by social class. To understand the Chicago market better, the *Chicago Tribune*'s Research Division has spent approximately $100,000 on a comparative study of three homogeneous communities in the Chicago area representing three different class levels.[3] The director, Pierre Martineau, long an

---

[3] Prices in the 1990s are more than five times those of 1959. — ED.

enthusiast of the sociological approach to marketing, has concluded from his many years of studying our class behavior that "the vast majority of people live and die within the boundaries and tastes of their own class."

Finally, Social Research, Inc., of Chicago, has done a number of revealing studies of our class behavior. In a recent one for MacFadden Publications, it analyzed the contrast in emotional make-up of women in the working classes and women in the white-collar classes. The study indicated that, though these women might live in the same neighborhood, there was an "invisible wall" between them in the way they think, live, and even make love. Social Research concluded that social distinctions today are "none the less sharp because they are subtle."

Taken together, all of these studies—requiring several hundred thousand man-hours of research—represent a lode of fascinating and valuable information about how Americans really behave. These investigators often disagree among themselves on the precise nature of the American class structure, and I assume many will disagree with some details of the conception of it that I have arrived at. However, they are virtually unanimous in agreeing that mid-century America very definitely does have a system of social stratification.

My debt to all these investigators is very large. In terms of insights, I owe the greatest debt, perhaps, to E. Digby Baltzell, Bernard Barber, Richard Centers, Milton M. Gordon, Arnold W. Green, August B. Hollingshead, Herbert H. Hyman, Joseph A. Kahl, Russell Lynes, Raymond W. Mack, Bevode C. McCall, Pierre Martineau, C. Wright Mills, Liston Pope, and W. Lloyd Warner.

The chapters that follow will in large part take the form of a roving over the social landscape of America. This exploration may give some readers a better insight into their own behavior and that of their neighbors. Also, it may give them a better understanding of people in their locality who seem uncomfortably different from themselves. For those readers who must, in the performance of their duties (as educators, business managers, public officials, etc.), deal regularly with people of different class levels, this exploration may shed, also, some useful insights on coping with their problems realistically and sympathetically. Finally, I hope that for all readers the exploration will make more apparent some noteworthy points about the current drift of our society.

I. Changes of Status

CHAPTER 2

An Upsetting Era

I suppose I first became interested in social stratification as a farm boy in northern Pennsylvania when my father pointed out to me that one of our cows, I believe her name was Gertrude, always came through the gate first at feeding time. We had about eighteen cows and all the others deferred to her. Later I observed that another, rather runty cow almost always came through the gate last. In fact, each cow seemed to know its appointed place in the lineup. When we bought a new cow who butted and bluffed her way to the top spot within an hour after entering the barnyard, our dethroned Gertrude developed neurotic symptoms and became our meanest kicker at milking time.

To come down—or up—to the human level, every society of any complexity examined by social scientists has revealed a pattern of stratification. There has always been a group that ran things at the top and, at the bottom of the scale, a group assigned to do the dirty work.[1]

Despite the fact that some very ambitious efforts have been made to set up truly classless societies, such societies have never been achieved on any large sustained basis. The most publicized attempt, of course, is that of the Soviet Union. The goal of the class struggle as conceived by Karl Marx was the elimination of the bourgeois class and—after a brief, benign dictatorship of the proletariat—the emergence of a truly classless society. Four decades have passed since the Russian Revolution. The Soviet Union, despite its professions of achieving a society of true equality, is becoming more precisely stratified each year. The need of the expanding industrial machine for a hierarchy of managers and specialists as

---

[1] William Foote Whyte, *Street Corner Society* (Chicago: The University of Chicago Press, 1943), pp. 261–63.

well as workers of varying skills provided, and in fact perhaps demanded, a social structure to match.[2]

A more sincere and genuinely persistent recent effort to establish a classless society is that attempted by the farm collectives in Israel. They were begun nearly a half-century ago and number in the hundreds. Today, the original ideals—complete democracy and complete equality in the sharing of material goods—are still carried out. But social strata have emerged.[3]

The experience of early American efforts to create communistic societies was much the same, with an elite consisting of the most talented or capable ultimately emerging.

America as a whole, since the Revolutionary War, has struggled to preserve ideals of equality in the face of persistent tendencies for elites to develop and consolidate their power, prestige, and wealth. Long after the Revolution, a few families continued to dominate the affairs of many New England towns. Some observers have suggested America came closest to a genuine system of equality of opportunity (as contrasted to the more utopian equality of status) around 1870. The industrial era was just getting started and vast areas of frontier were being opened for settlement and development.

Still, lest we forget it, America by the beginning of the present era (around 1940) had opportunities for upward mobility and social contact that are much less present today. For example:

— Most Americans still lived in communities representing all walks of life.

— Many men of little education still had reasonable grounds for hoping they could rise to the heights.

— Most companies were still small enough so that most employees knew top officials of the companies at least on a nodding basis, and often on a first-name basis.

— There were many lodges and social clubs where men from many social and income levels could and did meet.

— People in most neighborhoods still knew one another well enough personally so that people could be judged for their personal worth rather than by the trappings of status they exhibited.

Beginning with World War II, and still continuing today, an upheaval in the American way of life occurred that has profoundly affected the

---

[2] Alex Inkeles, "Social Stratification and Mobility in the Soviet Union, 1940–50," *American Sociological Review*, Vol. 15 (August 1950), pp. 465–79.
[3] Eva Rosenfeld, "Social Stratification in a 'Classless' Society," *American Sociological Review*, Vol. 16, No. 6 (December 1951).

class structure of America, and caused many to conclude (I say over-optimistically) that we are on the verge of a truly classless society.

For just a moment, let us look at ten changes in our national economy that have affected the class structure (and status striving) in the United States. Taken together they represent a transformation in a nation's way of life.

1. Perhaps most obvious is the truly spectacular increase in individual wealth since 1940, and particularly during the past decade. Even allowing for inflation, our individual buying power has increased by more than half. Some groups have prospered much more than others, but most families have seen paychecks doubling or tripling. As they say along the New England coast, "The rising tide lifts all the boats." The number of families earning more than $4,000 a year after taxes more than doubled from 1950 to 1956. Americans consequently have been living higher off the hog than ever before in their lives. A mass merchandiser of packaged foods is now offering such items as crepes suzette and hearts of palm. And in 1957 more than 50,000 Americans installed swimming pools in their back yards. The greatest rises in income, on a percentage basis, have been among those who had below-average incomes. A higher standard of living for working-class people, however, doesn't necessarily change their class status. The rich, meanwhile, have not been suffering. In one recent year, the number of Americans with annual incomes of more than $100,000 increased by a fifth.

2. This brings us to the second big economic change affecting class: the graduated federal income tax. Some have described it as the great leveler. The federal-government income taxes began rising in the thirties to fight the Depression, and soared even more steeply in the forties to finance World War II. They still remain near the wartime levels.

Despite the laments about high taxes, the number of American families with a net worth of a half-million dollars has doubled since 1945. Most of the very rich manage, one way or another, to hold on to the bulk of their new incomes each year. Meanwhile, corporate lawyers have applied their ingenuity to find non-taxable benefits for key executives.

3. The lessening contrast in the material way of life of rich and poor. The ostentatious turn-of-the-century behavior of millionaires who staged $100,000 parties and smoked cigars wrapped in $100 bills is being soft-pedaled. One probable reason is that the Depression threw a scare into the really rich, and they have learned to be discreet, almost reticent, in exhibiting their wealth. They have learned that in modern America you can exert power only by denying you have it. Another reason for the lessening contrast is the mass selling of standardized goods and services once available only to the better-off. Most American women, regardless of

class, for example, now wear nylons, have permanent waves, buy frozen steaks, and wear clothes that are copies (or copies of copies) of Paris designs.

The increasing difficulty in obtaining servants, because of the availability of higher-prestige jobs, has also diminished the contrast. In fact, the word "servant" is disappearing from the language. A disgruntled reader of the *Wall Street Journal* complained that in order to keep a cook he had to call her a housekeeper, and address her as "Mrs." Even cleaning women are hard to hold. A sociologist in Pennsylvania told me that his cleaning woman not only drives a better car than he does, but has remarked on the fact. She says she just doesn't care for cars more than two or three years old. "She expects my wife to prepare her lunch," he added.

4. The massive shift in vocational skills needed by our economy. We have been seeing demand for skills changing with lightning rapidity. Some occupations are becoming largely or entirely outmoded, and hundreds of new occupations are emerging. The man at the United States Labor Department in charge of the Dictionary of Occupational Titles advised me he had to add 375 brand-new occupations in 1956. (Examples: video recording engineer, automation "programmer," radiation detector, and "port steward" for overseas airliners.)

Looking at the changes in demand in terms of the larger trends, the following two seem most significant in their effect on class structure. One is the really spectacular rise in industries that furnish services (in contrast with those such as mining, manufacturing, and farming that produce goods). As our mechanized farms, mines, and factories have become able to produce ever-increasing amounts of goods with fewer people, the service-field industries (the selling and servicing of goods, and providing insurance, banking, amusement, education, medicine, travel) have been taking up much of the slack.

The other long-range trend of note, and it is really a by-product of the first, is the recent great gain of white-collared workers over blue-collared ones. The service fields are primarily staffed by white-collared people. In 1940, only a third of our employed people were in white-collared occupations. Today nearly half are.

Some observers have enthusiastically seen this growth of white-collars as evidence of a great upthrust of "working"-class people into the "middle" class. There has unquestionably been some social upgrading, but two cautions should be noted. First, a large percentage of the people recruited into white-collared ranks are women who previously didn't work. Second, many of the new white-collar jobs are essentially manual or require little skill, and so represent no real advance in prestige. One happy consequence to the economy of these trends to white-collar, service jobs, however, is that more people now work on a salaried basis rather than an hourly-wage basis and so are less likely to be discharged quickly in case of an economic downturn. This represents a gain for stability.

5. The great increase in moving about of the population. Some people still live in the houses they lived in twenty years ago, but they are rarities. The average American picks up roots about every five years. The result of this geographical mobility is that social status is established less and less by family background and more and more by such currently visible factors as job, consumption standards, behavior, school, club membership, and so on. Furthermore, as we shall see in Chapter 21, all this moving about produces an upsurge in status striving.

6. The great growth in leisure time that has accompanied increased productivity. In the days of Thorstein Veblen,[4] a display of oneself enjoying leisure was one of the better ways to prove one's superior class rating. Then the average man had to work fifty to sixty hours a week. Today the average man works about thirty-eight hours a week, and it is the harassed business executive who is likely to put in the fifty to sixty hours. As a result, leisure has lost most of its potency as a status symbol.

7. The trend toward large, bureaucratic organizations. Everywhere —in both government and private industry—the trend is to bigness. Every spring sees a new burst of corporate mergers. The number of civil servants in the federal government has multiplied ten times in five decades. In industry today, 2 percent of the companies employ a majority of all workers.[5]

8. The shrinkage in the number of small entrepreneurs and self-employed people. Such independent entrepreneurs originally constituted a true middle class in the United States. They found economic security by commanding their own destinies, however small. In Jefferson's day, nearly four-fifths of all Americans were self-employed enterprisers. By 1940 only about one-fifth remained.[6] And today the number has shrunk to approximately 13 percent. The other 87 percent—or the overwhelming majority of our working populace—are now employed by others. We have become an employee society.

This lack of entrepreneurial experience is most vivid in the ranks of our industrial executives. More than three-fifths are the sons of men who, at

---

[4] Thorstein Veblen (1857–1929), an iconoclastic economist and social critic, wrote *Theory of the Leisure Class* (1899). — ED.

[5] Peter M. Blau, *Bureaucracy in Modern Society* (New York: Random House, 1956), p. 2.

[6] C. Wright Mills, *White Collar* (New York: Oxford University Press, 1956), p. 63.

one time, ran their own businesses. Yet, according to one survey,[7] only one executive in six today has ever had such experience.

9. The trend to breaking jobs down into narrow, and if possible, simple specialties. The growth of bureaucratic thinking—with its passion for job definition—is partly responsible for this. More responsible, however, is the emergence of efficiency engineers who know that money can be saved for a company by reducing a job to a simple repetitive level so that any alert twelve-year-old with a capacity for withstanding boredom could handle it. This practice, while saving money for management, reduces the social prestige attached to the job and reduces the employee's job satisfaction and self-esteem.

10. The mass production of homes, with the attendant growth of homogeneous suburban communities. In earlier days, an American community was usually a scale model of all society, with a fair share of butchers, bakers, candlestick makers, creamery owners, manufacturers, laborers. Such towns are relentlessly being replaced by one-layer towns, which encourage birds-of-a-feather flocking.

[7] Mabel Newcomber, *The Big Business Executive* (New York: Columbia University Press, 1955), p. 61.

CHAPTER 3

Emerging: A Diploma Elite

Against the background of economic upheaval just described, what in broad outline is the class system that seems to be unfolding in America?

Several hundred United States sociologists have been applying themselves to this puzzle. Their task is complicated by the fact that class boundaries not only are invisible but often are not acknowledged. According to our creed, they are not supposed to be there. While the investigators still disagree on some points there is, as August B. Hollingshead puts it, "general agreement" that mid-century American society is stratified. Any investigation of status striving should properly begin with an understanding of the current class structure—and its barriers—within which the striving typically takes place.

As I see it, the boundaries of class are best perceived not as fixed lines or ceilings but rather as sieves or bottlenecks. Few investigators now believe that everyone falls neatly into one of four or six or fourteen classes. We are probably closer to the truth when we view the American populace as being arranged along a continuum with an infinite number of possible divisions.

While there is a continuum, it is also true that people will tend to cluster so that a continuum is actually a series of bulges and contractions. The major bulges might be called the major class groupings.[1]

There have been exceptions, but most sociologists have tended to see the primary break in the class structure as between the blue-collar, or working-class, world and the white-collar world. This was seen as the barrier most difficult to pass.[2] Here I would disagree. In the past decade, the most fundamental split in our social structure has moved upward a notch. It is now between the so-called lower middle class and the upper middle class.

This new, more formidable boundary results from the growing insistence on college diplomas as a minimum entry requirement for most of the higher-prestige occupations.

Meanwhile, we have been seeing a revolutionary blurring of the boundary line between white- and blue-collared people. The recent upheaval of our economic system has brought about this blurring. Let us pause for a moment to note what has been happening.

In the past, many investigators have arbitrarily assigned all white-collar workers to a class above *any* blue-collar worker. Thus store clerks and stenographers have been rated above skilled craftsmen. The reasoning apparently was that the white-collared person worked in a world carrying more prestige. The white-collar working world was clean rather than dirty, and it seemed more dignified, more brainy. There was close proximity to management, and people in white collars sought to live in the style of their superiors. The pay not only was better than blue-collar pay typically but usually came in the form of a weekly salary rather than the less dignified hourly-wage form.

Just about every basis on which white-collared clerical people have claimed superior status to blue-collared workers, however, has been undermined in recent years. This applies not only in America but in other advanced industrial nations.

The change may have started during World War II when many people quit office jobs for the more glorified jobs of riveters in shipyards. The

[1] Richard Centers, *The Psychology of Social Classes* (Princeton, N.J.: Princeton University Press, 1949), p. 74.

[2] August B. Hollingshead, *Elmtown's Youth* (New York: John Wiley & Sons, Inc., 1949), pp. 11–48; Joseph A. Kahl, *The American Class Structure* (New York: Rinehart & Company, Inc.), p. 186.

spectacular growth in the number of people finishing high school likewise had an undermining effect. In the past, the high-school diploma was a ticket of admission to a white-collar job. Now, many millions of American youngsters have the ticket, so there is less prestige attached to putting on a white collar. Actually, the color of the collar is losing much of its significance as a label. Many steelworkers don't wear blue collars any more on the job, they wear sports shirts. And so do supposedly white-collared missile engineers.

Furthermore, in hundreds of companies, there has been a sharp downgrading in the amount of skill and dignity associated with the average clerical job. Scientific management procedures and the introduction of office machinery have been creating working conditions very similar to those out in the plant, which simultaneously has been cleaned up and made to look more like an office. Many white-collared office workers—billing clerks, key-punch operators—are actually machine attendants, manual workers in any honest nomenclature. The work of some clerical people is so routinized, dull, and easily learned that people are often chosen for their special capacity to endure boredom.[3]

Finally, in many of the larger plants, the white-collared functionary is isolated from his or her bosses so that even the psychological satisfaction of closeness to management is being denied.[4]

From the male's standpoint, another factor bringing a decline in prestige to clerical work is the fact that many of the jobs in this growing field are being filled by women, who typically command somewhat less money for the same job than men. In the occupations of bank teller, bookkeeper, and cashier, long dominated by men, women are taking over.

The change in status of white-collar jobs is most sharply reflected, however, in the comparative financial rewards of white- and blue-collar employees. At the turn of the century, a white-collar job commanded twice as much money as a factory job. Today, the unionized blue-collar worker has overtaken and moved ahead of the white-collar worker. Sales workers earn less than craftsmen and foremen who typically have three years less schooling.

Perhaps the most spectacular falling off in money and prestige has occurred with retail salesclerks. Still, I found women, as in Greenville, South Carolina, working as low-paid salesclerks rather than taking higher-paying factory jobs because of pride of class. Some felt their family's status in the community could not survive the assumed come-down.

The unions have sought, with only modest success, to exploit the

---

[3] Arnold Green, *Sociology* (New York: McGraw-Hill Book Co., 1956), p. 276.
[4] C. Wright Mills, *White Collar*, p. 204.

growing frustration of clerical and other white-collar workers with such sneering slogans as "You Can't Eat Air Conditioning." Unions feel an urgent need for white-collar recruits because the supply of blue-collar workers, who constitute the great bulk of union membership, is shrinking. John L. Lewis's mine workers' union is one-third the size it was in his pre–World War II days of glory and power. Most white-collar people still aspire to rise, and this makes them poor prospects for the unions. Many are caught up in a panic about their status and strain to demonstrate that they are different from the working class. Meanwhile, many lead lives of quiet conformity trying to live like—and to please—their superiors.

While the boundary between white and blue collar is blurring, the boundary between lower and upper white-collar groups is becoming sharp and formidable. (By upper white collar I mean the managers, professional people, etc.) It has become the great dividing line in our society. And it is becoming more formidable every year.

The boundary is formidable because the ticket of admission is steep: a college diploma of some sort. About one in eight youths today has the ticket. More and more, opportunity at the higher levels begins and ends with the choice of education. After one is educated the mold is usually set. Only rarely will a person who begins in a lower white-collar job without a college degree be able to move across the line into the upper group.

The system of horizontal social strata which I perceive emerging in America is in two great divisions. Within each division there are classes or major bulges. Here appears to be the most graphic way to suggest by generalization the situation that is developing:

THE DIPLOMA ELITE

I. The Real Upper Class
II. The Semi-Upper Class

THE SUPPORTING CLASSES

III. The Limited-Success Class
IV. The Working Class
V. The Real Lower Class

The diploma elite consists of the big, active, successful people who pretty much run things. The supporting classes contain the passive non-big people who wear both white and blue collars: the small shopkeepers, workers, functionaries, technical aides. Here briefly is a description of the five classes, as I see them, that comprise these two main divisions.

I. *The Real Upper Class.* These are the people who are likely to be on the board of directors of local industries, banks, universities, and community chests; who send their daughters to finishing schools and their sons, probably, to a boarding school and, certainly, to a "good" college. They have heavy investments in local land, industry, banks—they probably inherited much of it—and they can swing a great deal of weight around town when they wish. These also include the high-prestige professionals such as the more fashionable doctors, lawyers, and architects who come from well-connected families or have an upper-class clientele. The Episcopal minister also would normally be included here.

These people of the real upper class would have you believe that wealth has little bearing on their social pre-eminence. Rather, it is the gracious, leisurely way of life they have achieved as a result of their innate good taste and high breeding. In smaller communities, "old" family background is especially important.

The real-upper-class people tend to view the new rich as uncouth and will accept them only when the self-made newcomers become so powerful that they must be consulted on the important decisions involving the community and only if they have the right kind of money. (Wealthy undertakers are not typically accepted.)

It is true that only the rarest of the new rich can take on the genteel, austere airs of the old rich without a good deal of practice and observation. But although manners are important, money is more so.[5]

In Northeast City,[6] where I spent several weeks exploring the elite structure of a representative middle-sized metropolis, an old-family social matron talked nostalgically of social relations in the old days. Then, she said, "family" really counted. Many of the best families would never have received the people they do today. But, she sighed, "money is money."

Most communities with a population of more than 10,000 have a fairly well-defined upper class. At the higher reaches of the upper class are what might be called the "upper uppers." They live in the most exclusive sections of large metropolitan areas and are still very rich or very powerful even when viewed on a national basis.

II. *The Semi-Upper Class.* This is the class that sociologists still usually call the "upper middle class." My only objection to that phrase is that it implies "upper middle" is part of a larger body called the "middle class" and so is intimately related to what the sociologists call the "lower middle class," also assumed to be a part of the larger "middle class" body. My contention is that they are becoming two quite distinct clusters and

[5] August B. Hollingshead, *Elmtown's Youth*, p. 70.
[6] Northeast City, where Packard carried out original fieldwork for this book, was Rochester, New York. In giving a fictitious name to the locale of his study, Packard was following the practice of sociologists, who called the places they studied by names such as Elmtown and Yankee City. — ED.

shouldn't be confused. However, I concede that it is convenient to refer to whatever is between upper and lower as "middle." When, subsequently, I cite findings of sociologists who use "upper middle" I will accept their terminology.

At any rate, members of the semi-upper class—to revert to my terminology—are mostly confident, energetic, ambitious people who went away to college, then began a career somewhere away from their home town or neighborhood. Most of them are with fairly large organizations where they are decision makers serving as managers, technologists, or persuaders. The remainder are professional men or successful local businessmen.

Members of this semi-upper class are the hyperactive civic boosters who devote themselves actively to their roles in service clubs and country clubs, and their wives power the local charity drives.

Below the two classes cited, which comprise the diploma elite, is a gulf, and beyond the gulf are the supporting classes. Its members are the people who are, in the words of sociologist Joseph A. Kahl, "the anonymous or little people—the vast masses who can be hired interchangeably to do the routine jobs in factory or office."[7] They are outside the area of decision and play essentially supporting roles as workers, functionaries, or aides.

III. *The Limited-Success Class.* This group is the one still characteristically referred to by sociologists as the "lower middle class." Its members place great store in demonstrating that they are respectable, proper, cultured, and socially above the working masses. They are more conforming, more morally proper, and more active in the churches than any other group.

Virtually all its members have high-school diplomas, and many of them have a year or two of post-high-school training in technical schools, two-year colleges, or secretarial schools.

In offices they are the clerks, excepting the routine machine attendants, and secretaries. On Main Street they are clerks in the quality store or the small shopkeepers or the smaller contractors. In industry they are the foremen, technical aides—a spectacularly expanding group—and skilled craftsmen. They also are the smaller farmers.

In short, they include the lower ranks of the genuinely white-collar world and the higher ranks of the blue-collar world, the aristocrats of labor. Both groups are success minded, but in a different way. The blue-collared elite are at the top of their ladder and so don't worry too

---

[7] Joseph A. Kahl, *American Class Structure*, p. 193.

much about trying to upgrade themselves socially by their choice of status symbols. The white-collared people do worry, and do strive. They feel that they haven't arrived, and wonder if they ever will.[8]

Both the blue- and white-collar members, then, are of roughly equal prestige although their ways of life differ. And they both can be called "limited successes," but for different reasons.

IV. *The Working Class.* The heads of families of this class frequently have not finished high school. They work steadily, in good times, at jobs that require little training and can be mastered in a few days or, at most, a few weeks. They constitute the backbone of the industrial unions and numerically are the largest class (nearly 40 percent of the total).

Most are semi-skilled factory operatives. Others wear white shirts and man machines in offices or work as deliverymen. Still others are truck drivers, miners, filling-station attendants, supermarket clerks and attendants.

Their work often bores them, especially if it is a repetitive job, and they live for the pleasures their paychecks can buy. If you ask them what they do for a living they say, "Oh, I work for Standard." It wouldn't occur to them to explain what they do there. It is too boring, and not a source of pride. While they resent the airs put on by white-collared folks, they like to feel they are good citizens.

V. *The Real Lower Class.* These are the people everyone else looks down upon. They live in the decrepit slum areas that just about every American town has. (Slums are much less apparent in Europe's towns and cities.) They usually leave school as soon as legally allowed, if not before. They work erratically at unskilled or semi-skilled tasks, and try to find their pleasures where they can.

Allison Davis, University of Chicago sociologist, found in a study of the motives of the underprivileged that people in this class are so used to living on the edge of hunger and disaster that they have never learned "ambition" or a drive for higher skills or education. These people are not as frightened of losing a job as the rest of us because they fatalistically expect they will lose it anyhow; and unlike the rest of us they know that even when everything is lost friends and relatives will take them in without any loss of respectability. There is little to lose. "The harder the economic noose is drawn, the tighter the protective circle," Davis reports.

Meanwhile, the unmarried male spends his nights in sexual exploration. He lives in a world, according to Davis, "where visceral, genital, and emotional gratification is far more available" than it is to most of us.

---

[8] Ibid., p. 203.

These people know that most of us look down on them and despise them. There are two natural reactions to this contempt: either kick back, which youths do and then are arrested for juvenile delinquency, or retreat into apathy, which is what the older lowers do. What these people need more than charity or prosperity is recognition.

Quite a few people, it should be noted, do not fit neatly into any of these horizontal identifications. They are in between the major bulges of class, or their characteristics make them hard to place. This is particularly true of many intellectuals, who tend to have high-class tastes and educations with incomes that often do not match. Further, they value nonconformity and so develop their own ways of snooting. Perhaps they get a hideaway on Fire Island or Majorca. And inevitably the less imaginative well-to-do begin copying them by going there.

Genuine eggheads are the working intellectuals who create culture (i.e., scholars, artists, editors, philosophers, novelists, composers, etc.) or who disseminate and interpret culture (i.e., academic people, critics, actors, etc.).

These people tend to develop their own quite tight stratification systems outside the main body of the class system. Most would be very ill at ease trying to converse with a genuine proletarian. They share the diploma elite's ideals about higher education and higher income. And often they are quite avid status seekers within the marginal group they wish to impress. If, as is likely, they live in a "contemporary" home, they will, while visiting other "contemporary" homes, carefully note the kind of eating utensils considered most appropriate for such a house.

Union leaders likewise are among those hard to classify. A study of the power structure in the steelmaking city of Lorain, Ohio, revealed that in recent years union leaders have come to exert a dominant influence in political and school affairs. Furthermore, they are persons of great influence in many civic activities. The influence of upper-class business and professional families in these areas has at the same time been greatly curtailed. Socially, however, the position of the union leaders and their families is ambiguous. They were found to be rated less highly in terms of social status than many business and professional men who had far less influence in the community than they did. This, of course, may be a transitional situation.

CHAPTER 4

Obstacle Course for Outsiders

Now we turn to the other half of the story about our social-class structure. Until recently, most sociologists in talking of our class structure have concerned themselves only with the *horizontal* layers (such as we discussed in the last chapter). People are identified with a layer primarily in terms of *prestige*.

It now seems clear, however, that the American populace is also organized into *vertical* strata, on the basis of *differentness*.

Sociologist Raymond W. Mack told me of an interesting exercise he sometimes gives his students in stratification. He asks them to "place" in the class structure a man with these characteristics: "He is a graduate of Indiana University and has a law degree from Ohio State. His father, a small businessman, was a high-school graduate. His mother had two years of college. He drives a 1958 Buick . . . he has his own law office . . . he is a Methodist . . . he has a $12,000 income . . . his two children are university students." At this point Mack asks the students if they now have the man pretty well pegged as to status. Usually they nod that they have. Then he adds: "Oh, yes, and one other thing. He is a Negro." The last bit of information forces them to readjust the whole concept they have been building in their minds. Mack says the students look at him as though he had cheated because he held back the most important fact.

We tend to think of "minorities" as a minor part of our society. Actually, they constitute more than 50,000,000 of the United States population.

Sociologist Milton M. Gordon, now of Wellesley College, was one sociologist who began wondering uneasily, in the early fifties, if a series of horizontal strata told the whole story of the American class system.[1] The position of the millions of Americans who belonged to various ethnic groups bothered him. Their ethnic status seemed to set them apart with invisible boundaries—and limit their area of "intimate social contact in the adult world"—just as thoroughly as the social-class system (horizontal) based on the prestige of occupation, education, etc. In the past, sociologists had tended to consider Negroes as a caste apart but to assign all other people with ethnic backgrounds to whatever horizontal social stratum best fit them in terms of prestige. Gordon disagreed that Negroes

---

[1] Milton M. Gordon, "A System of Social Class Analysis," *The Drew University Bulletin* (Madison, New Jersey), August 1951.

should be considered apart. As he saw it, their situation differed in degree rather than in kind from that of other ethnic groups.

He proposed that American society is "crisscrossed" by two sets of stratification structures (social class and ethnic class) and that while they should be kept conceptually apart they should both be considered a part of the "full outlines of the social class system."

Meanwhile, August B. Hollingshead had shifted his community investigations from the largely Protestant, old-American Elmtown in the Midwest to New Haven, Connecticut, a city with a heavy ethnic population. He found, as in Elmtown, five main horizontal classes. But as far as socializing was concerned, each ethnic group in New Haven appeared to have its own social structure of five classes. He concluded that New Haven had "parallel class structures."[2] His findings indicated that the community's current structure is "differentiated vertically along racial, ethnic, and religious lines, and each of these vertical cleavages in turn is differentiated horizontally by a series of strata or classes that are encompassed within it." The horizontal classes are based on such prestige factors as occupation, schooling, address. The result, he said, was a social structure that is "highly compartmentalized."

Hollingshead offered a vivid example to illustrate the parallel class structures, each having its elite. He found that New Haven had not one but seven different Junior Leagues[3] for its elite white young women. The top-ranking organization, he reported, "is the New Haven Junior League which draws its membership from the 'Old Yankee' Protestant families whose daughters have been educated in private schools. The Catholic Charity League is next in rank and age—its membership is drawn from Irish-American families. In addition to this organization there are Italian and Polish Junior Leagues within the Catholic division of the society. The Swedish and Danish Junior Leagues are for properly connected young women in these ethnic groups, but they are Protestant. Then too the upper class Jewish families have their Junior League.

"This principle of parallel structures for a given class level by religious, ethnic, and racial groups," Hollingshead said, "proliferates throughout the community." The cultural characteristics typical of each horizontal level carry through all the parallel (or vertical) structures. And the cultural pattern or "master mold" for each horizontal class running through the entire structure is set by the "Old Yankee" core group.

---

[2] August B. Hollingshead, "Trends in Social Stratification: A Case Study," *American Sociological Review*, Vol. 17, No. 6 (December 1952).

[3] The Junior League, founded in 1921, is a series of women's clubs that focus on volunteer activity in local communities. — ED.

The vertical structures based on the differentness of groups overlay—to revert to the grid concept—the horizontal classes based on prestige. They vary, of course, from community to community both in composition and in the proportion of their total membership in the higher-prestige classes.

Here, however, are the four criteria most commonly used by Americans in determining that certain fellow citizens are sufficiently *different* from themselves to justify a wall. The people are differentiated:

1. *By recency of arrival in the locality.* Old-timers in almost any community like to feel they have a monopoly on local prestige, and tend to view all newcomers as upstarts.

Interesting collisions have been developing in many United States communities as a result of the growing industrial practice of dispersing plants into smaller cities and towns. Once the plants are built, managerial personnel in large numbers move in and in some cases feel superior to the town's existing upper class. Gregory P. Stone and William H. Form of Michigan State College followed the progress of one of these massive clashes in a Michigan town of 10,000, which they call Vansburg.[4]

These invading newcomers or "cosmopolites" were oriented in their life style to the sophisticated, blasé, and busy life style of the metropolis. Immediately they "joined together and made status claims that called into question the status of the 'old families' of the community. Rather than attempting to achieve social honor by emulating the life style of the entrenched 'upper classes' the members of this group imposed their own symbols upon the social life of Vansburg and established themselves as a separate status group. They appeared publicly in casual sports clothes, exploited images of 'bigness' in their conversations with established local businessmen, retired late, and slept late. With all the aspects of a coup they 'took over' the clubs and associations of the 'old families.' "

Such wholesale invasions have caused the old guards in many communities to react by emphasizing the importance of ancestry.

2. *By national background.* Hollingshead made an analysis of the ethnic origins of the people of New Haven and found a third were of Italian origin. Other groups in descending order of size were Irish; Russian, Polish, Austrian Jews; British-Americans; Germans; Poles; Scandinavians; Negroes.

"Although all of these groups," Hollingshead states, "have been in the community for at least a half century, they are keenly aware that

[4] Gregory P. Stone and William H. Form, "Instabilities in Status: The Problem in Hierarchy in the Community Study of Status Arrangements," *American Sociological Review*, Vol. 18, No. 2 (April 1953).

their ancestors were English, Irish, Italian, Russian, German, Polish, or Negro." Each group when it arrived kept to itself and developed its own occupational specialties.

He noted that as each newly arriving group has entered the occupational system the groups that have arrived earlier moved up a notch. This same phenomenon—where immigration is massive—has been observed in Hawaii, where planters have imported in succession a half-dozen nationality groups as plantation hands. The Chinese were the first to arrive. Today, few Chinese can be found on the plantations. Most of the men are in the cities in professional, proprietary, clerical, or skilled classes of employment.

3. *By religion.* While the large majority of Americans are Protestant, 36,000,000 are Roman Catholic and 5,500,000 are Jewish. The social philosopher Will Herberg has stated that, as the melting pot gradually dissolves other differences of newcomers such as language and dress, America will coalesce into three great sub-cultures—Protestant, Catholic, and Jewish.

For whatever reason—whether Gentile barriers, Jewish cohesiveness, or both—Jews do tend, as we shall see in a later chapter, to lead a segregated social life. And in many communities they maintain a division among themselves. The quiet, conservative German Jews, the first large Jewish group to reach America, often turn their backs on the more flamboyant and lively Polish and Russian Jews who began arriving several decades later. In some cities, the two groups have their separate elite social clubs.

Catholics, too, tend to split up by national origin. The Irish, in some cities, remain aloof from the Italians; and the Italians do not intermingle much with the Poles.

And Protestants, especially at the elite level, frequently try to draw a line that excludes both Catholics and Jews. Some years ago, one listing of several thousand socially select New Englanders contained only about a dozen Catholics and still fewer Jews.[5]

4. *By pigmentation.* For the one American in ten who is a Negro, the boundaries of status are hardly invisible. To a somewhat lesser extent the same applies to Americans of Chinese, Mexican, or Indian origin. Among Negroes, the color of their skin is almost universally recognized as a barrier to full dignity of treatment from their fellow citizens. Consequently, many of them strain to "marry light" and tend to grant high status to fellow Negroes who have the lighter complexions. While perhaps

[5] Cleveland Amory, *The Proper Bostonians* (New York: E. P. Dutton & Co., Inc., 1947), p. 14.

10,000 light-skinned Negroes "pass" the boundary each year and are accepted as white, these constitute but a tiny fraction of their race. Most of the rest must live with the grim fact that, while a white person can sometimes work up from a low social status to a high one, a colored man can never work up to being a white man. Kimball Young and Raymond W. Mack have pointed out: "A Negro may be a college graduate and an experienced pilot in the U.S. Air Force and yet be rejected as a job applicant by a commercial airline needing pilots."[6]

What some can do, however, is seek to separate themselves as far as possible from the general run of lower-class Negroes through achievement and style of life. Across their caste line they have set up a horizontal social structure based on the white model. And many Negroes have been able to move up from the bottom (Class V) to Classes IV, III and in a few cases to Classes II and I. They have been moving into skilled, clerical, managerial, and professional jobs. Some have built fortunes. *Ebony* magazine estimates that several hundred Negroes now have assets of more than $100,000. They have built their fortunes in real estate, the beauty business, owning restaurants, insurance, baseball, boxing, medicine, and so on. Some of these new-rich Negro businessmen with an all-Negro clientele feel something of a vested interest in segregation.

These higher-status Negroes pattern their behavior after what they perceive to be the white model. They speak softly and precisely to show they are not like noisy, low-class Negroes; they shun emotional religions; they have small families; they encourage their children to study Latin as a mark of culture; and they prefer to shop at higher-class white stores.

The strain of this striving for differentness and superiority is beginning to show, according to Negro sociologist E. Franklin Frazier of Howard University. They are more stiff in their behavior and more desperately absorbed in surrounding themselves with status symbols such as limousines and mink coats than their white counterparts. In fact, Frazier accuses the "black bourgeoisie" of being engaged in such a "wild flight from reality" that it is failing to provide responsible leadership for Negroes as a whole.[7]

Meanwhile, there is evidence that Negroes are no longer the lowest-prestige group among the nation's ethnics. Occupationally at least, many of the Puerto Ricans migrating to the United States—especially the darker-skinned ones—are taking over the most menial jobs. Today, in

[6] Kimball Young and Raymond W. Mack, *Sociology and Social Life* (New York: American Book Company, 1959), p. 194.
[7] E. Franklin Frazier, *Black Bourgeoisie* (Glencoe, Illinois: The Free Press, 1957), p. 235.

New York, it is not uncommon to see a Negro bus driver cussing out a Puerto Rican pushing a hand truck in the garment district. A decade ago it might have been an Irish bus driver cussing out a Negro.[8]

We have, then, a two-dimensional class system. The horizontal levels are based on prestige deriving principally from such social-class factors as wealth, job, education, style of life. The vertical divisions are based on the seeming differentness of people caused by their ethnic background, their religion, etc. For most of us, the horizontal rankings have by far the larger impact on our lives, perhaps because they have a hard economic base and because they affect everybody. During the Depression, for example, many working-class people began to realize for the first time that their common social-class interests as workingmen were far more important to them than the religious, racial, and ethnic rivalries that had separated them. When in the remainder of the book I speak of classes I will be referring to the horizontal ones unless I qualify the reference.

If I were to try to sum up the emerging picture with another figure of speech, I would say that the class structure of the United States is more like a jungle gym than a ladder. Or to be more precise, in view of the gulf developing between the diploma elite and the supporting classes, it is like *two* jungle gyms. One jungle gym is on the ground floor of a building. The other, directly above it, is on the second floor. To move from the lower jungle gym to the higher one, you must go outside and climb up the fire escape of higher education.

We are now ready to examine, in some detail, the indicators of status that are most commonly recognized, and most commonly sought. These marks of status establish the prestige rating we receive in the class structure.

We become assigned to a certain prestige classification on the basis of not one factor but rather the combined influence of a number of factors: occupation, education, residence, family background, behavior, beliefs, income, and so on.

Consumption patterns, too, are extremely revealing. After years of studying them, Pierre Martineau, Research Director of the *Chicago Tribune,* states that our consuming and spending habits equal our position in the social-class structure.

Ideally, we should be judged on our individual skill, responsibility, and personal worth. These factors, however, in our age of movement and

[8] Christopher Rand, series on Puerto Ricans in New York, "Reporter at Large," *The New Yorker,* November 16, November 30, December 7, December 14, and December 21, 1957.

complex organizational structures, are often difficult to judge. We may know that the man who lives three houses down the street has something to do with the fertilizer business. What his responsibilities and income are, however, are not within our area of reliable observation, as they were in former days. Thus we tend to "place" people on the basis of what is visible: such as type of home, automobile, clothing, home furnishings. These are all visible.

In the following section we shall examine a number of these factors that, whether we like it or not, have come to be generally accepted as indicators of status. They include one's home and neighborhood, occupational rank, patterns of spending, patterns of behavior, patterns of mating, patterns of socializing, patterns of beliefs and attitudes, and patterns of indoctrinating the young.

II. Marks of Status

CHAPTER 5

Snob Appeal = Today's Home Sweet Home

The home during the late fifties began showing signs of supplanting the automobile as the status symbol most favored by Americans for staking their status claims. There are a number of explanations for this change (see Chapter 21), but the most important one, undoubtedly, is that with the general rise of incomes and installment buying a luxuriously sculptured chariot has become too easily obtainable for the great multitudes of status strivers. A home costs more money, a lot more. Another explanation is the appearance in profusion of mass merchandisers in the home-selling field, who have become skilled—partly by copying mass-selling strategies developed in the automobile field—in surrounding their product with status meanings.

Experts in home selling have recently cited "snob appeal" as one of the great secret weapons. One strategy, he said, is to drop some French phrases in your advertisements. French, he explained, is the language of the snob. Later in the year, we began seeing newspaper advertisements of housing developers drenched in French. One, penned by a developer in Manetto Hills, Long Island, exclaimed: *"C'est Magnifique! Une maison Ranch très originale avec 8 rooms, 2½ baths . . . 2-Cadillac garage . . . $21,990 . . . No cash for veterans."*[1]

American families in the past few years have been giving more and more thought to the problem of establishing a home that adequately reinforces the status image they wish to project of themselves. And home builders have happily helped the trend along by emphasizing status appeals. William Molster, who directs the merchandising activities of the National Association of Home Builders, confirms this new trend in home

---

[1] Federal legislation made purchasing a home easier for veterans. — ED.

selling. He points out that postwar builders who erected minimum-shelter mass communities to answer the war-stimulated demand are being replaced by the builders who are carefully sizing up the desires and needs of their market. Today, he states, the status symbol in home selling has become a key to large-volume business.

One developer outside Chicago, in describing to me the buyers of his $20,000–$30,000 houses, called them "striving, frightened people." He plays upon both those traits, he happily explained, in promoting the sale of his houses. This man, another enthusiast of the motivational approach to home selling, helps the buyers feel that buying a home in his higher-priced development "means they have arrived."[2]

He has noticed that most of his buyers are newly prosperous people — not the kind who inherit wealth—and the husband has struggled so long and arduously at his pajama factory that he has had little time to demonstrate his love to his wife. Thus, the builder shrewdly offers his house to the neglected lady as something she "deserves."

In moving to a higher-income level, we find the same striving, but in a somewhat more discreet form. Researchers for the *Chicago Tribune,* exploring the attitudes of people in the semi-elite suburb they studied, summed up the prevailing attitude toward homes in this way: "You have to *look* successful. A house is a very tangible symbol of success . . . and the residents regard it as a goal and a symbol, as well as something to live in."

In the Northeast, at least, the top executive is likely to have a gem of an estate, beautifully manicured on the outside, highly polished on the inside. The house will be Georgian, Colonial, Federal, old English, or old French, with clipped hedge or rustic fence, and, inside, a central hallway and period furniture. There will be old portraits or family portraits on the walls of the living room, and, if there is wallpaper—there probably won't be—it will be used just to add decorative touches. Most of the walls will be painted a solid color, usually with dark trim. The rugs will be either a solid-color wall-to-wall type or Oriental. The built-in bookcases will contain mostly leather-bound volumes. The gleaming, mahogany dining-room table will be enhanced with silver candlesticks. The walnut-paneled den, with its green- or red-leather chairs, will have old hunting and sailing prints. The decor probably was supervised by an interior decorator specializing in the executive look.

As you move a block or two away to the vice-presidential-level home, you find much the same but on a less sedate and authentic scale. The

---

[2] In the 1950s, many corporations used motivational research, a market research technique that relied on Freudian psychology. — Ed.

vice-presidents' wives, as Russell Lynes has pointed out, seem "a little quicker to point out the really good pieces of furniture, and to tell you something about the artist who painted the picture over the mantel."

In Texas, of course, you find a little more flamboyance, even in executives. The houses are likely to be the rambling-ranch type, but with expensive details. A Dallas builder, specializing in catering to businessmen who feel a need for homes in the $100,000 to $250,000 bracket, has built one section that he calls "President's Row" because so many heads of companies live there. The houses he builds have such distinctive touches as His and Her bathrooms, color television in the bedroom ceiling, push-button drapes, air-conditioned dog houses, authentic soda fountains, and hallway fountains. "Our clients," he says, "like these little touches of plushiness." And he added, "We try to create a desire to keep up with the Rockefellers. Then, you've got to have snob appeal."

A great deal of thought, on the part of builders, has gone into finding symbols of higher status that will provoke gasps of pleasure from prospective buyers. And the higher-status people themselves have obviously given a good deal of thought to symbols that will produce the same results with guests in their homes.

The favored way to do this, in many areas in America, is by the use of symbols indicating the owner has ties that go back into American history. One of the wealthiest suburban areas in America, the Green Bay Road of Lake Forest, Illinois, still uses gas lights. In fact, the residents have resisted proposals for modernization to the extent of setting up a society for the prevention of improvement of their road. A builder in Charlotte, North Carolina, now is putting flickering gas lamps on the outside of his most expensive models.

In San Jose, California, a builder tries to make each prospective buyer feel like a bona fide frontiersman or woman. His promotions are heavily flavored with historical allusions. They exhort: "TRADE IN YOUR LOG CABIN FOR A BEAUTIFUL NEW FIRESIDE HOME." They offer prospects of "warmth" and the "good things in life for which the pioneers came to this fertile valley in the West." Instead of talking about two-Cadillac garages, they advise prospects that they can park "two Conestogas" in their "extra large wagon shed." The talk about financial terms, however, is strictly twentieth century: "$16,950–$18,450. . . . No Down to Vets."

Antiques, in some cases, become so important for their symbolic value that they are cherished even when their functional value is dubious. If you walk along Beacon Street, Boston, you may note that certain windows have defective panes. The glass is purplish. The defectiveness of those panes is highly cherished. The panes were part of a shipment of inferior glass foisted off on Americans by English glassmakers more than three centuries ago.

In Wichita, Kansas, too, you will find many homes with symbolic features of uncertain utilitarian value. In one development of picturesque houses ($35,000), which look like something out of *Grimm's Fairy Tales,* you may see false holes near the gables. Those false holes have symbolic importance. French aristocrats used to have these holes in their homes as roosts for hunting birds. The symbolic importance of the holes is that only aristocrats in early France were permitted to own guns, and so only they had holes in their gables. The holes were, in an earlier era at least, an important status symbol.

The man who alerted me to this false-hole situation was James Mills, researcher and publisher of *Home Facts* (for home builders). He and his staff have spent two years making a nationwide study of the new trends in home selling. Mr. Mills finds that, in merchandising homes to present-day Americans, "you get a very layered situation." Foremen, he explains, don't want to buy in the same development with workmen. They want to buy a house in another development well known to offer homes at a higher price.

Another common device people employ to enhance their class status through their homes is to add casual but obviously costly touches. One touch coming into increasing popularity is the gold-plated bathroom fixture. Gene Dreyfus, vice-president of Cooperative Homebuilders (northwest of Chicago), showed me a gold-plated faucet, and said he has found it has such tremendous appeal that he is starting to introduce it, as an optional accessory, in some of the houses in his higher-priced ($30,000 to $50,000) development. The gold faucet, he has found, is a little $500 extra that provides the buyer with an excellent conversation piece, and adds substantially to the resale value of the house.

The air conditioner is similarly cherished in many areas as an obviously costly, status-enhancing touch. It has two features of special interest, whatever its utilitarian value, from the standpoint of status enhancement. First, it is still uncommon enough in homes in most areas to provoke conversation. And, second, evidence of its presence can be seen by outsiders passing the home. This visibility factor was a potent force in selling television to the three lower classes in TV's early days. Within a city or development, TV aerials did not begin appearing at random. Instead, they began sprouting in clusters. When one pioneering family put up its aerial for all to see, nearby neighbors felt impelled to emulate the pioneer.

Even today, the TV aerial has symbolic significance in some areas of the nation. In the southwest corner of Michigan, for example, the most conspicuous feature of the landscape is the proliferation of tremendously high TV aerials. Some, on tripod towers, are fifty-five feet in height. Many two-room shacks have thirty-foot towers above them, which might, one would imagine, topple the homesteads if a really strong wind struck.

The status strivers also seek out goods for home decoration that can be pointed to as hand wrought. As iconoclastic economist Thorstein Veblen pointed out some decades ago, hand labor is a more wasteful way to produce goods than machine labor; and so the handmade product, with its crudeness and its imperfections which can be pointed to, and its obvious costliness, is cherished as a status symbol for the well-bred and the well-heeled. The display given, in upper-class homes, to man-blown glassware is a case in point.

Finally, visible signs of culture have their value in conveying the impression of high status. James Mills, the home-marketing expert, argues that one reason the home is replacing the automobile as a favored way for demonstrating status is that a home can be a showcase for "culture." In a home you can display antiques, old glassware, leather-bound books, classical records, paintings. These are things a car can't do. And the American home-buying public currently is on what some building experts call a "Kultural kick." In the mass home market, the room that used to be the "game room" became first the "recreation room" and is now the "den" or "study." Soon, Mills predicts, it will be the "library." Whatever the name of the space, Mills acknowledges sadly, people shove a television set into it and sit around it at night in semi-darkness.

In the matter of color preferences, there is also a parting of the ways along class lines. The Color Research Institute of Chicago has found, from sampling the responses of many thousands of people, that people in the higher classes (higher income and higher education) favor muted and delicate colors, whereas the lower classes like their colors in brilliant hues and large doses. They particularly like the warm, bold reds and orange reds. And, I might add, their preference for paintings (reproductions) for their walls run to orange or pink sunsets, which an upper-class person professes to find revolting, or to highly sentimental scenes, which are equally objectionable to the upper-class person. (Greeting cards preferred by the three supporting classes likewise tend to run to flowers and to what the diploma elite considers to be excessive sentimentality.)

You find much the same sort of separation regarding preference for design as you go down the class scale. The upper class favors the primly severe, the lower class the frankly garish. Pierre Martineau relates that his investigators asked people of all classes to choose, from pictures, their favorite homes and home furnishings. They found people completely different in taste as they moved up the scale. The lower class likes more "frills on everything," whereas the upper class wants things to be "more austere, plain." This showed up, for example, in the preference for sofas. The lower-class people preferred a sofa with tassels hanging from the arms and fringe around the bottom. The high-status people preferred a sofa with simple, severe, right-angled lines. People in the working class, I could add, are prone to attaching an imitation-brick wing onto an aluminum trailer and calling it home.

Social Research, Inc., of Chicago, in its study of the tastes of the Wage Town, or workingman's, wife for MacFadden Publications, found: "The Wage-Town wife thinks in terms of 'decoration' rather than 'decor.' She uses bright colors and bold pattern, and side-by-side mixtures of both. Muted tones and severe lines are apt to be too 'cold' for her taste. What might seem garish to the white-collar wife is 'warm' or 'cheerful' to the Wage-Earner wife." In another study, Social Research, Inc., found that the upper classes in most cases prefer solid-color rugs, whereas patterned rugs become more popular as you go down the scale.

One interesting further distinction between the horizontal social classes is the uneasiness that people in the lower classes feel about socializing with neighbors in developments. Craig Smith, Vice-President of Detroit's Sullivan-Smith, feels that the main difference between blue- and white-collar working people who are thrown together in a development is that the blue-collar people are not gregarious. They feel insecure, and are more likely to become lonely. To illustrate, Mr. Smith said, "We find these blue-collar people resist the idea of sharing a driveway with a neighbor. They are afraid of an argument with the neighbors, or an invasion of their privacy. The white-collared people wouldn't mind."

Privacy is tremendously important, James Mills pointed out, to people of working-class background who may have had to sleep three or four to a room sometime in their lives. They want walls around every room, and they want doors to the rooms, not entry ways. The open layout characteristic of "contemporary" houses, with rooms often divided only by furnishings, frightens them. On the other hand, a West Coast builder of "contemporary" houses has become famous in home-selling circles for his success as a mass builder for eggheads. His open houses, severely "contemporary" and terribly *avant-garde,* have been tremendously popular in an area near the Stanford University campus favored by local intelligentsia. Eggheads have enough self-assurance so that they can defy convention, and they often cherish the simplicity of open layout.

As we move from the horizontal social-class groupings to the vertical ethnic-class groupings, we find even more clear-cut differentiations in preference for homes and home furnishing.

Detroiters who trace their ancestry to Great Britain are most likely to favor what some builders jovially call "Early American gestunk." They want a white fence and the white clapboard house. Mr. Smith pointed out that they like the "snob appeal" (there's that phrase again) of a rustic-looking lantern. They typically want their house to be made of wood. Any brick used should be the reclaimed, ancient-looking kind.

Americans of Italian background insist, more than any other group, on having a dining room even if it means sacrificing a bedroom or chopping up the living room. They have a strong family spirit, and like to sit around the table after a good meal, chatting. They also like what builder Gene Dreyfus calls "lots of goop" in their houses—shadow boxes, splashes of marble, stucco, and rococo furnishings.

As for the Polish-Americans, they like their homes to be "very garish, with loud, screaming colors," according to one builder. (Among Polish-Americans of Buffalo, pink and turquoise are preferred in decorative touches.) Polish-Americans want their houses to be of brick, and they want it to be hard "face" brick. They also demand a large kitchen. Mr. Smith pointed out that they will not accept the supposedly chic, open-beams, or studio-type, construction. It reminds them of the barns they knew back in Poland. Furthermore, they resist the idea of the rear-view living room, so popular with many builders. They want their living room to look out on the street, Mr. Smith explained, and they want a big picture window in that living room, and in that window they want to be able to place an enormous lamp. I thought perhaps Mr. Smith was generalizing, but some months ago I passed through a large Polish section of Chicago and I noticed that fully 80 percent of the homes did indeed have picture windows facing out on the street with huge, often old-fashioned, lamps in the middle of them.

Jewish people (who sometimes are categorized, loosely, as an ethnic group) are, perhaps, most interesting of all in their preference for homes and home furnishings. As Gene Dreyfus put it, Jewish people "don't care about having a back yard." While a prosperous Gentile will want his grounds to be as large as possible (and with a winding driveway), the Jew is a little horrified at the thought of owning a place with large grounds. First of all, he and his wife like to be close enough to neighbors so that they can talk back and forth. Furthermore, frequently the Jewish man has neither the temperament nor the know-how to putter around trimming hedges or repairing screen doors, or other delights of the do-it-yourself. Relatively few Jews ever earn their livelihood at manual work, and so are not handy at such things, and, in fact, are often appalled by the prospect of them.

Jewish people prefer stone or face-brick construction to wood. And, more than any other group, Jews are receptive to "contemporary" architecture, with its openness and modernity. They don't try to prove through their houses that they had ancestors in pre-Revolutionary Vermont, as one builder put it, because no one would believe them if they did try to.

Jews have their own upper class, and their own way of achieving high status within their group. Near Chicago there is a new development of "one-maid" split-level houses occupied primarily by young married Jews, many under thirty years of age. I'll call it Grandview. Most of the houses of Grandview are close together on plots of less than one-third acre. Houses nearby, just across the boundary from Grandview, which look very much like the houses inside Grandview, sell for around $45,000. The houses inside the Grandview border sell at prices ranging from $55,000 to $100,000. The land on which this high-priced development is built is flat and unwooded. Some of it is reclaimed swampland. Grandview has neither water view nor commanding view nor fine old trees to recommend it to the elite, yet some of the land, when broken up into lots, has been sold for as much as $50,000 an acre.

I have tried to indicate that, based on objective factors alone, these houses, while tastefully and carefully built, are no great prize at the price charged. Yet they are in tremendous demand, and the developer of Grandview does virtually no advertising. An envious Jewish builder, showing me this colony, explained why these houses were in such demand, "If you are a Jewish person, you have arrived if you get one of these homes."

He explained that those Jewish parents who, in recent years, have succeeded in an outstanding way financially, want their sons and daughters starting out in marriage to have the "best," and Grandview is believed by them to be the best. It has had an aura of social selectness around it from the beginning. My guide pointed out that residents of Grandview do not own Cadillacs, and do not send their children to private school. "They don't need to," he explained. "They've managed to get one of these houses." Later, he introduced me to Grandview's developer, who cheerfully acknowledged that Grandview homes were unsurpassed status symbols for a young Jew. The developer said, "There is a snob appeal in getting in here in the first place. The buyers like the idea of living in this general area because it has one of the highest per capita incomes in the country . . . and it is well known that I have an expensive house."

The role of the neighborhood in helping fix one's status with the status-conscious will be explored more fully in the following chapter.

CHAPTER 6

Choosing a Proper Address

A person who has lived twenty years in the same house, as many pre-1950 Americans did, usually will not bother to tear up his roots and move simply because the house no longer accurately reflects his status in the community. He has learned to love the place. However, with our greatly increased geographic mobility—more than 25,000 United States families move and face new neighbors every day—millions of Americans judge not only homes but neighborhoods much more carefully than before, if only at the subconscious level, in terms of status attached to them. And they strive, in their home hopping, to upgrade themselves with each hop as far as they dare.[1]

People at the management level working for a large company who move—or are moved—to a new community frequently find there is a design at work that dictates (or tries to dictate) where they will nest. It is just as dangerous to move into an area above their level as one that is below. They might, in fact, find themselves on the receiving end of some quiet organized discipline if they try to move into a neighborhood dominated by people from a clearly higher level than themselves in the hierarchy at the company.

Even when we go down the scale to the limited-success level, there still is a great deal of anxious concern about the status meaning of the particular home the family will have in a new neighborhood. People see themselves establishing a social beachhead, and the big question in their minds is whether they are going to be accepted.[2]

The W. Lloyd Warner group, studying Yankee City, found that the social meaning of neighborhoods was so important that people there used street names to designate social classes. The investigators found, for example, that people referred to as "Hill Streeters" often actually didn't live on Hill Street (upper class); and they found that people designated as "Riverbrook" people often didn't actually live in Riverbrook (lowest class). They concluded that these terms were oblique, "democratic" ways to indicate social-class designations without crudely specifying them.

Every city has its one area where there is an especially heavy concentration of upper-class people. Although New York City covers 315 square

---

[1] *The New Consumer, Chicago Tribune* Research Division, *Chicago Tribune,* Chicago.
[2] Ralph Bodek, *How and Why People Buy Homes* (Philadelphia: Municipal Publications, Inc., 1957).

miles, most of the rich and fashionable live in just one of these square miles: the area between Sixty-fifth Street and Seventy-eighth Street on the east side of Central Park, from Fifth Avenue to Third Avenue.[3] (Others argue that the north-south boundaries should be extended to Eighty-sixth and Sixtieth Streets with added tiny clusters along the East River.) In Houston, River Oaks, with its costly castles, is as fashionable an address as you can have. In Atlanta, it is the Buckhead section; in New Orleans, it is Bayou Liberty; and in Charleston, South Carolina, it is the wedge formed by South Battery and East Battery. While Philadelphia and Boston have several islands for the elite, the name Chestnut Hill, by coincidence, is unsurpassed for prestige in both.

And each community has its own way of deciding where the elite can be found. With many, elevation is the principal factor. As you wind your way up Lookout Mountain outside Chattanooga, Tennessee, the homes become more and more costly. A hillside in Waterbury, Connecticut, has mostly working people at the bottom and mostly elite at the top. Hundreds of people in the Hollywood movie colony live in the area of Beverly Hills, north of Santa Monica Boulevard. As you go up the very gradual rise from the boulevard, the yards become wider and the houses larger. By the time you reach the homes of Jack Benny and Desi Arnaz, they are very wide and very large indeed. Even within homogeneous developments (which, for economy reasons, are most often built in potato fields or areas bulldozed flat), prospects compete for the houses on high ground, and hold back (even when bargain prices are quoted) from buying low-lying homes others can look down upon.

In some communities, nearness to water is the prime determinant of elite residential location. Sociologist Ernest R. Mowrer of Northwestern University has been making a long-term study of the residential patterns of the Chicago suburbs. He points out that along the North Shore the towns, such as Winnetka and Wilmette, overwhelmingly are settled by executives and professionals. As you go back from the water, you find occasional islands of wealth, but in general you start encountering the lower levels of business people (small merchants and salesmen). By the time you reach Des Plaines, you find whole neighborhoods of skilled trades. Much the same pattern exists along Boston's North Shore.

Nearness to the golf course becomes the measure of eliteness of address in many other towns. In communities such as Lancaster, Pennsylvania, Wichita Falls, Texas, and Bel Air, California, many of the most-prized home sites face the golf course. A realtor who was showing an

---

[3] *New York Times*, March 4, 1957 (part of a series on "Society" of modern American cities).

executive's wife possible homes in Darien, Connecticut, received pretty explicit instructions on where to look. The wife said, "My husband recently became vice-president of his company. . . . We want to be in the club area."

To continue with the factors that make a neighborhood highly fashionable, in many towns an area becomes the most elite in town simply because the area's leading citizen decided to build or buy there. Sam G. Russell, Denver realtor, points out that all the houses in an area rise tremendously in value when that happens. The houses are "still the same houses" but "immediately there is a demand" for homes and home sites near the noted personage. Still other towns use the railroad track as the dividing line for separating the select from the non-select.

And in many cities the desirability of an address can be determined by its distance from the downtown business district. Most of the prize fighters are recruited from the lower, most hard-pressed segments of our society; and a sociological study of their origins has revealed that virtually all of those investigated came from the run-down, blighted areas next to the downtown business districts. In Chicago, for example, the fighters came from the Near South and Near West Sides.

Cities, like trees, grow by adding rings at their perimeters. As you move outward from the center, the houses tend to become progressively less aged, and (other things being equal) more desirable for those who can pay the higher prices. A few old high-prestige neighborhoods manage, by investing in paint and polish, to maintain their status; but most areas lose their elite status within thirty to fifty years. Their middle-aged mansions become funeral parlors or Moose lodges. Even Boston's long-elite Beacon Hill and New York's Riverside Drive are far past their prime.

The pressure is always outward. Members of minority groups who have managed to succeed financially as businessmen or professionals seek to move out from the blighted, overcrowded central area where their people have been confined. They hope to set themselves apart from their still-depressed lower-class neighbors and live in the better houses that they now can afford. Their new neighbors note only their East European–sounding names or their tan skins, and recoil in panic. They make no distinction between these successful, well-educated people, who by all objective socioeconomic standards are their own kind of people, and the masses who have the same foreign-sounding names or dark skins. (Some of the most beautiful modern buildings in America, for example, are being designed by Negro architects.) As the residents hasten to sell, before the inundation they have been led to fear sets in, real-estate values sometimes fall. This permits the poorer members of these minority groups to afford to move into the area, and soon the character of the neighborhood is transformed. Realtors have been known to encourage the panic by calling property owners and asking them if they want to sell before it is too late. The people who profit most from a fast turnover of a neighborhood, of course, are the realtors. They work on commission. A panic sale of 10,000 houses within a year can bring them $5,000,000 in fees. In one area of New York City, a public school within one year underwent a complete turnover from light-skinned to dark-skinned students. A large area of Chicago has undergone four virtually complete turnovers of population since 1940: from white-collar white to poor Southern white to Japanese to Negro.

One of the firmly held articles of faith among realtors and homeowners is that property values go down when a Negro family moves into a white neighborhood. This permits people to put discrimination on a we're-tolerant-but-you-gotta-be-realistic basis. The Commission on Race and Housing, which, with the help of social scientists from a dozen universities, spent three years investigating the residential problems of non-whites in mid-century America, looked into this assumption of a deterioration of values.[4]

It found that sometimes values go down, sometimes they remain stable, and sometimes they go up. The values usually go down only where the neighborhood is run down anyway, and the entry of non-whites simply provides "evidence" of the deterioration, or where the neighbors panic and glut the market with houses for sale. In such cases, the expectation of a drop in value thus becomes a "self-fulfilling prophecy."

When waves of settlers move out of the run-down residential area surrounding the business district, the void nowadays is typically filled not by immigrants from Europe, as in earlier decades, but by migrants from American soil: Southern Negroes and Puerto Ricans. In Buffalo, New York, for example, as medium-income whites moved to the suburbs, the white population of the city dropped approximately 13,000. This loss was more than made up by an influx of 14,000 Negroes. One Negro official has complained, "Before long most of the city will be Negro, the suburbs white. That's segregation all over again."[5] Undoubtedly, he was being overly pessimistic. Negroes constitute only 10 percent of Buffalo's population today, and the city planners are struggling valiantly to reverse the flow of whites across the city lines.

Meanwhile, the Commission on Race and Housing predicts that by 1970 "many cities" will find non-whites and Puerto Ricans constituting at least a third of their total population if their present city limits remain and if current trends in the circulation of people are not altered. We have recently been seeing the outpouring of tens of millions of people who can afford it (and who are acceptable) to suburbs mass-produced to house them. Many of these new communities are geared to specific economic levels and, in some instances, to people of specific religious and ethnic groups. And thousands of these development "communities" are—by dictate of the builders—100 percent white. Racial segregation is much more sweeping in new development-type towns than in established, old-fashioned-type communities. The Commission on Race and Housing charges that the mass builders have done much to intensify racial segregation in America.

The result of all this clustering by kind is the creation of many hundreds of one-class communities unparalleled in the history of America. Each mass-produced community has its own shopping center and community center. There is no need to rub elbows with fellow Americans who are of a different class. The more expensive of these one-layer communities, where homes cost $50,000, import their teachers, policemen, and store clerks from nearby communities in a lower price range.

Some of this homogeneous layering was dictated by the problem of mass production of houses. There is, however, another factor behind the growth of one-layer towns, which at least abets the developer's vested interest in homogeneity. That is our own habit of seeking out our own kind. The fact that we have recently become, in effect, a nation of strangers and near-strangers has aggravated this birds-of-a-feather tendency. In our insecurity we search for our own kind of people. Doctors start running with doctors, and so forth. Thus, within the relatively homogeneous economic layer of residents, symbols of status reassert themselves and class distinctions begin to reappear. These are, of course, based not on the usual classes found in a total society, which would be impossible, but in terms of different levels of status possible within the development's particular slice of society.

What happens to the personalities of people who live in communities where the houses for miles around are virtually identical, and the people seen are all from the same socioeconomic slice? It is too early to tell. From outward appearances, most people seem to find the atmosphere congenial rather than oppressive, although changes, as we'll see in Chapter 21, are appearing.[6]

[6] David Boroff, *The New York Post*, April 20, 1958.

Even more oppressive than the uniformity of these new one-layer town developments is the synthetic, manipulated quality of the community life found in many of them. A top executive of a development in southwestern New Jersey proudly related to me how his firm had helped generate a "tremendous community spirit." Employees of the firm "started" sewing groups, musicales, Girl Scouts, Boy Scouts, Brownies, and a Little League. He explained that these activities "interweave a fabric . . . tie a community together." Within seven or eight months, he said, his home buyers formed a civic association. "We helped guide it," he said. "We wanted the right people in charge, people oriented to our problems. You get a rabble rouser in and you have a very genuine problem."

This official mentioned he was currently trying to "sell" the Catholic diocese on the idea of building a Catholic school in the development. The aim, evidently, is to make the development more attractive to Catholics. He said his firm aims to keep a 50-50 balance between Jews and non-Jews, and turns down sales that threaten to upset the balance.

In general, residential barriers against Jews, long excluded in many areas by covenants and "gentleman's agreements," have been slowly melting. Polls have regularly been taken on the question: "Suppose a Jewish family moves in next door, how would you feel?" In 1950, 69 percent said it would "make no difference." By 1954, the "make no difference" figure was up to 88 percent. It should be noted, however, that amiability on the Jewish question declines as you go up the class scale. Whereas only 8 percent of the people in the working class say they "wouldn't like it" if a Jew moved in next door, that figure climbs to 35 percent by the time you reach the upper class.

Some of the elite residential communities near Detroit, favored by automobile-industry executives and other upper-class people, have very few or no Jews. I happened to show a Jewish Detroit builder a population breakdown of one of these towns. It stated: "Jewish—.8%." He was astonished and exclaimed, "That must be a janitor."

The twin trends toward the manipulated one-layer community and toward more straining for a fashionable address, taken together, offer a depressing commentary on our success as a civilized people. The home, I should think, should properly be a private and very individual haven. Progress would seem to lie in the direction of turning inward rather than outward for inspiration in the creation of one's homestead.

CHAPTER 7

Totem Poles of Job Prestige

Our occupational rank looms as a powerful factor in fixing our status in the public's mind. What is it that establishes the prestige or status rating for each of our thousands of occupations? Certainly some of the discrepancies in valuation we see result from whimsical or irrational forces. An example of irrational discrepancy is the fact that men typically are paid more than women for performing the same job, such as that of bank teller. Usually there is no pretense that men can do the job in question any better than women. In general, however, a logic of sorts is at work to try to assure our society, through differential reward and recognition, a sufficiency of the scarce talents our society needs or desires.

Typically, a half-dozen factors combine to establish the prestige ranking of any occupation. And this prestige rank of the breadwinner's occupation, in 'urn, as we've seen, plays a major part in placing his family in the social-class system. These are the six main bases we use in assigning prestige to an occupation:

1. *The importance of the task performed.* Raymond Mack, sociologist of Northwestern University, and an authority on social stratification, made an analysis of the social system of a United States Air Force base. He queried airmen in thirty squadrons at two Strategic Air Command bomber bases to get their ideas on the "best" and "worst" squadrons to be in. Men tended to upgrade their own outfits, but overall an unmistakable pattern of prestige emerged. Squadrons engaged in the primary SAC mission, that is, in manning bombers, rated highest in esteem. Those in command at wing headquarters rated next. These were followed, much further down in status, by the various squadrons providing support for the primary mission, such as armament maintenance. And finally, lowest in prestige were all the squadrons servicing the base, such as those in Medical, Air Police, and Food Service.[1]

2. *The authority and responsibility inherent in the job.* With the growing importance of large corporations in our economic life, there has been a demand for "generalists" (experts in decision-making) capable of deciding what to do with large work forces and million-dollar budgets. Doctors wield little authority, but we grant them life-and-death responsibilities.

---

[1] Raymond W. Mack, "The Prestige System of an Air Force Base: Squadron Ranking and Morale," *American Sociological Review*, Vol. 19, No. 3 (June 1954).

3. *The knowledge required.* Bernard Barber of Barnard College makes the point that to achieve high status one's knowledge must be of a special kind. It must be "systematized" and "generalized." A butcher, he points out, can be a storehouse of information about meat cuts, and yet doesn't have the kind of systematic knowledge of animal anatomy required of a biologist.

4. *The brains required.* Harvard sociologist Pitirim Sorokin has stated that the higher the intelligence called for in a task (along with the more social control involved) the higher we will rank its practitioners as a privileged group. Americans do not stand in awe of their more brilliant professors as most Europeans do, but up to a point they accept the notion that brains should not go unrewarded. "Brain" jobs offer more prestige, if not more money, than "brawn" jobs.

5. *The dignity of the job.* Hollingshead found in Elmtown that one of the leading financial pillars of the town's churches and a person of considerable wealth and power held an exceedingly low prestige position. She was Polish Paula, the town's leading madam. In contrast, a notoriously skinflint banker held perhaps the highest position in prestige. In many cities, bookies and racketeers are among the communities' wealthiest citizens, and are frequently leading contributors to candidates for high political office. They, too, rank low in most communities (but not in some Italian-American and Negro lower-class districts).

6. *The financial rewards of the occupation.* This undoubtedly is the most important of all in influencing us to assign high or low status, since it is, as I've indicated, more visible to neighbors than some of the other factors.

Our patterns of reward have been undergoing a profound change in the past decade. Occupations once thought to be highly rewarding are less so today, and occupations we once thought of as being poor sources of income are producing rewards far up the income scale. Seemingly startling inequities have developed. Some of these changes illustrate, at the same time, the great gains in income of many blue-collar groups in relation to white-collar groups.

It was only a decade ago that an economist, in explaining to congressmen the class and income structure of America, pictured a pyramid with a broad base of unskilled laborers at the bottom. Above that base he pictured ever-smaller layers upward in this order: semi-skilled, skilled, white-collar clerical and sales force, semi-professional and lower administrative positions, professionals and higher administrators.

That picture today is cockeyed. In fact, the long-favored concept of a pyramid is obsolete. Unskilled laborers no longer form a broad base. Their number is shriveling. Meanwhile, the better-paid blue-collar working people such as craftsmen and foremen are coming to dominate the middle-income position in our society. A clear majority of all families in the $4,000 to $7,500 bracket, long accepted as the middle-income range, now wear blue, not white, collars.

At the same time, groups such as policemen, bank tellers, firemen, clergymen, social workers, and, yes, income-tax collectors have been dropping to a lower relative position on the income scale.

Here are six conclusions I believe we can draw about the income pattern now emerging.[2]

Among the professions, your best opportunity, moneywise, is to be a doctor. In fact, when it comes to money, it is better to be an independent physician than just about anybody. General practitioners on the average net around $16,000 a year; surgeons average about $35,000. (Psychiatrists average only $17,000, perhaps because their patients individually take up more of their time than ordinary patients.) Most specialists average several thousand more. If your town has more than fifty doctors, the chances are excellent that at least one nets more than $75,000 a year. A few of the nation's more enterprising physicians net more than $200,000 a year.[3]

Medical people usually justify their income on the grounds that they require a long and costly training and that they work long hours. It should be noted, however, that they have not always had such an enviable edge over other professionals. In 1929, lawyers were in first place on the scale of professional incomes, engineers and scientists second, and medical people third. Lawyers are now a poor second, and engineers and scientists an even poorer third. A realtor in Taunton, Massachusetts, suggested a possible reason why doctors have pulled a good $5,000 a year ahead of lawyers: doctors in the town are in short supply and lawyers are over-abundant, more than sixty for a town of 40,000.

Dentists have not pushed incomes up as rapidly as physicians, but have gained faster than most other professionals, including lawyers. They net somewhat more than $12,000 annually.

As for engineers and scientists, the recruiting advertisements seeking them are misleading. We read a great deal about the high starting salaries for engineering lads fresh out of college. One advertisement for them cried: "CRAZY, MAN, CRAZY ARE OUR RATES." But while rates are high for

---

[2] Vance Packard, "How Does Your Income Compare with Others?" *Collier's,* November 23, 1956.

[3] Richard Carter, *The Doctor Business* (New York: Doubleday & Company, Inc., 1958), p. 85.

beginners, close to $5,000, engineers soon find themselves up against a ceiling.

As professions become less "practical" (and are less likely to be in demand by profit-making organizations) they command less and less money. The median annual income for an anthropologist with a master's degree is approximately $4,700. At the bottom of the professional scale are clergymen. Protestant ministers are paid less than factory workers (but many of them have housing provided without charge).

In contrast, men now beginning careers as doctors can look forward confidently to a lifetime income of more than a million dollars. Why have medical practitioners succeeded in pulling so far ahead of other professionals? A major answer seems to be that they have been exercising collective birth control on themselves. A scarcity—an artificial one, some charge—has been created. In spite of the increase in our medical needs over the decades, the number of doctors available in a typical community has been decreasing. In 1900, there was one licensed doctor for every 578 people. By 1940, the proportion of doctors had shrunk to the point where there was one for every 750 patients; or, if you consider only those still in active practice, there was one active doctor for every 935 persons.[4] President Eisenhower in 1957 referred to "the already acute shortage" of medical manpower. At hospitals at least 2,000 intern positions have remained unfilled.

Blue-collar skills are gaining on the lower white-collar skills in relative reward. In many cases, unionized working-class people, paid an hourly wage, have been earning more per week than the salaried, white-collared members of the limited-success class (or lower middle class) who identify themselves more with management and typically are not unionized.

While bricklayers were advancing to $150 a week, a major airline advertised for white-collared reservation agents. It said it wanted "university graduates" with sales experience and good voice and diction. The pay: $65 a week.

Private industries tend to pay much better than public-supported institutions. One reason for this, perhaps, is that the private industries are major taxpayers and so keep a sharper eye on signs of "waste" and "frills" in public institutions than they do in their own (where frills can be deducted on their tax forms as a business expense).

Young physicists with Ph.D.'s often start to work with private firms at higher pay than their professors back at the university are making, who

4 C. Wright Mills, *White Collar*, p. 119.

have been working more than twenty years—and who taught the neophytes most of what they know!

The farm is a hard place to make a living these days unless you own a large one. Although farmers began enjoying a rise in income during 1958, the fifties in general have been most discouraging, especially to small farmers. Cash net income of farmers dropped substantially in the decade beginning 1947, with farmers who grow cotton, wheat, tobacco, corn, and peanuts having a particularly difficult time.

One white-collar skill that is highly rewarded is salesmanship. The clerks who "wait on" people in a general-merchandise store average approximately $45 a week, whereas salesmen working for automobile agencies (where hard selling is called for) make nearly twice as much.

In this era of self-service, more and more attention is being paid to pre-selling products through advertising; and the experts in this highly competitive field of devising messages and imagery that will move merchandise are well rewarded indeed.

The best way to assure oneself of a six-figure income is to be a business manager or owner. Lower-range, or medium-responsibility, business executives (those above the rank of foremen, but below the policy-making level) have been averaging approximately $12,000–$13,000 nationwide. When you move up to the heads of companies the positions pay primarily on the basis of the size of the company. Bank presidents as a group average $25,000, but the heads of the larger banks typically earn more than $100,000 by salary alone. As for the top men of our largest industrial concerns, they may earn anywhere from $50,000 to more than $500,000.

While the big salaries went to the top executives of the large companies, it is, nevertheless, true that the fabulous fortune builders of our present high-tax generation are virtually all men who own or substantially control their own smaller firms. Such entrepreneurs, if highly successful, can end up with more income each year after taxes because, as already noted, they can have their profits taxed on the more favorable capital-gains basis. A few are managing to accumulate several million dollars in additional wealth each year. Even at the less grandiose level, successful individual entrepreneurs seem to be living more lushly than salaried executives of the large corporations.

Money, as they say, isn't everything—at least when it comes to social prestige.[5] Among professionals, for example, a world-famous scientist on

[5] Seymour E. Harris, "Who Gets Paid What," *Atlantic Monthly,* May 1958, pp. 35–38.

the payroll of a leading university at $10,000 a year may be the full equal in status of a corporation lawyer making $100,000. As Harvard's Talcott Parsons points out, the scientist "simply does not compete on the plane of 'conspicuous consumption' which is open to the lawyer but closed to him." And it may well be that the $100,000 lawyer's greatest ambition in life—now that he has his fortune and his yacht—is to walk, begowned, somewhere near the $10,000-a-year scientist in a Commencement Day ceremony that will culminate in the bestowal upon the lawyer of some sort of honorary degree.

Several investigators have attempted in recent years to arrive at an overall ranking of occupations by prestige.[6] One obvious way to do this is to ask people how they, in their minds, rank different occupations. Mapheus Smith, while at the University of Kansas, asked 345 evaluators to imagine they were arranging a formal dinner for a celebrity, and had to seat one typical representative from each of one hundred occupations. Aside from government occupations, such as that of United States Supreme Court justice, the seven occupations entitled to seats closest to the celebrity proved to be college president, banker, medical doctor, captain of ocean-going merchant ship, criminal lawyer, architect, author. And the bottom seven in prestige for this dinner table, in descending order, were peddler, scissors grinder, odd-job worker, scrub woman, garbage collector, unskilled migratory worker, prostitute.

Prostitutes, it might be noted, have their own fairly rigid hierarchy of status. Call girls, who consider themselves the aristocrats of the profession (to use the word loosely), shun even for socializing restaurants and bars frequented by street-workers or "house girls" or even "chippies" (promiscuous amateurs). And a $50-a-trick girl wouldn't dream of swapping telephone numbers of prospects with a $30-a-trick girl. Anyone charging below $20 a trick is regarded in the trade as "a common prostitute."

Status among prostitutes is based in large part on the customary fee the female can command. It is also based on appearance, address, political connections. Finally it is based to a large extent on the style in which she maintains her pimp or "old man" (assuming she can afford one).

Harold Greenwald, Executive Director of the Association for Applied Psychoanalysis, found in his study of a group of call girls that the pimp, far from being a harsh exploiter, typically functions as a status symbol. The

---

[6] C. Wright Mills, "The Middle Class in Middle-Sized Cities," from *Class, Status, and Power,* edited by Reinhard Bendix and Seymour Martin Lipset (Glencoe, Illinois: The Free Press, 1953), p. 206.

high-status prostitute will lavish upon her pimp (or kept man) fine clothes, first-edition books, and Cadillac convertibles in much the same way that a businessman may lavish upon his wife fine furs and jewelry as visible symbols of his success. Greenwald also makes the point that there is little inter-class mobility among prostitutes. A streetwalker doesn't work her way up to being a call girl (but an aging call girl may descend to being a streetwalker). The call girl starts out at that level. She comes typically from what he calls "upper or middle class" origin. Greenwald concludes that association appears to be easier when the class levels of customer and call girl are approximately the same. The overwhelming majority of call girls, he adds, are filled with self-hatred and are utterly unresponsive to the "Johns" who patronize them. Most have made suicide attempts.

The most imposing study of occupational prestige is that made by the National Opinion Research Center about a decade ago. It took a nationwide sample involving 2,920 people, who were asked to grade each of ninety occupations on their general standing. Again the job of being a Supreme Court justice ranked highest. Here are the rankings (in descending order) of twenty-five occupations that were scored above average in prestige and twenty-five that were scored below average in prestige.

ABOVE AVERAGE

	Relative rank		Relative rank
Physician	2	Sociologist	27
College professor	7	Accountant for large firm	28
Banker	10	Author	31
County judge	12	Army captain	32
Minister	14	Building contractor	33
Architect	15	Public-school teacher	36
Dentist	17	Railroad engineer	38
Lawyer	18	Farm owner	39
Large corporation director	19	Official, international labor union	40
Nuclear physicist	20	Radio announcer	41
Psychologist	22	Newspaper columnist	42
Airline pilot	24	Electrician	44
Owner of factory employing about 100 people	26		

UNDER AVERAGE

	Relative rank		Relative rank
Small-store manager	49	Night-club singer	75
Bookkeeper	50	Farm hand	76
Insurance agent	51	Coal miner	77
Policeman	55	Taxi driver	78
Mail carrier	57	Railroad section hand	79
Auto repairman	59	Restaurant waiter	80
Plumber	60	Night watchman	82
Factory machine		Clothes presser	83
operator	65	Soda-fountain clerk	84
Barber	66	Bartender	85
Store clerk	67	Janitor	86
Milk-route man	70	Street sweeper	89
Filling-station attendant	74	Shoeshiner	90

The NORC list above probably grants more prestige to academic occupations—and less to business executives—than people really feel. I suspect a distortion caused by people giving answers they think they ought to give, just as many people say they read high-prestige magazines when they really don't. We profess admiration for intellectual pursuits, but really reserve our highest envy and respect for successful businessmen. This is understandable, since our aspirations primarily are focused in the business world.[7]

Another impressive approach to establishing an overall rank order of prestige for occupations is that reported by sociologist Bevode McCall on behalf of the Research Division of the *Chicago Tribune*. In this approach, sociologists from the University of Chicago arbitrarily assigned a status rating to each occupation, based on the skill and responsibility involved. The occupations are more precisely defined than in any other listing I've encountered. The ratings were for occupations found in the Chicago area, and were arrived at after the sociologists analyzed data supplied by the *Tribune* on a sample census of 3,880 Chicago households.[8]

In this approach, approximately 300 occupations were given a status rating of from 1 (highest) to 7 (lowest). Here are examples of occupations assigned to each of the seven groups.

[7] Delbert C. Miller, "Industry and Community Power Structure," *American Sociological Review*, Vol. 23, No. 1 (February 1958), pp. 9–15.

[8] Bevode C. McCall, Research Memorandum, Report #3 on the *Chicago Tribune Sample Census*, February 15, 1956.

HIGHEST-STATUS GROUP

Licensed architects
Medical specialist
Executives, top level, large
    national concern
Stock brokers

Federal judge
Law partner in prestige firm
Flag-rank military officers
Bishop, D.D.

SECOND-STATUS GROUP

General medical practitioner
Editor of newspaper
Mechanical engineer
Top-level executive, local firm
City or county judge

Downtown lawyer
Colonel or Navy captain
College professor, prestige
    school

THIRD-STATUS GROUP

Bank cashier
Department-store buyer
Professor, small or municipal
    college
Advertising copy writer

Junior executive
High-school teacher
Minister (D.D.) from
    sectarian school
Office supervisor

FOURTH-STATUS GROUP

Bank clerk
Carpenter, small contractor
Clerk, prestige store
Dental technician
Railroad engineer
Grade-school teacher

Factory foreman
Insurance salesman
Chain-store manager
Staff sergeant
Office secretary

FIFTH-STATUS GROUP

Auto mechanics
Barber
Bartender
Carpenter, employed
Grocery clerk
Crane operator
Skilled factory worker

Hotel desk clerk
Telephone lineman
Mail clerk
Corporal
Policeman
Truck driver

SIXTH-STATUS GROUP

Taxi driver
Semi-skilled factory worker
Gas-station attendant
Plumber's helper
Spotter, dry cleaning

Stock clerk
Waitress
Watchman
Riveter

Hod carrier	Janitor
Dishwasher	Coal-miner, laborer
Domestic servant	Scrub woman
Gardener	Street cleaner

This ranking by status based on assessment by social scientists at least has the advantages of preciseness. All executives are not lumped together, nor are all teachers. Note, too, that the long-assumed status superiority of white-collar workers over blue-collar workers does not carry through in any definitive, straight-line way on the list. Bartenders reading this list can rejoice that sociologists, at least, rate them a notch or two higher than public opinion does, as revealed by the earlier NORC listing.

A few final observations might be made. The system of material rewards we have evolved for work skills seems to be to some extent out of kilter. If work roles are appraised objectively in terms of talent, training, and responsibility required, we seem in general to over-reward business-men and under-reward those in intellectual pursuits. We seem to be under-rewarding people working for our many non-profit institutions and over-rewarding those with the same skills working for profit-making in-stitutions. We seem to over-reward any occupational group that by col-lective action can control the flow of new, competitive talent into their field. Finally, if I may be permitted a bold suggestion, it would seem that any reward system that year after year pays a wailing crooner approx-imately one hundred times as much as the Chief Justice of the United States Supreme Court is somewhat out of balance.

CHAPTER 8

Pecking Orders in Corporate Barnyards

The headlong trend toward large organizational structures in America—not only in business but in government, labor, and education—has in the past decade produced new built-in stratification systems across the land-scape. Nowhere is this more apparent than in the great corporation, which can often impose its hierarchy of ranks—and symbols of differential status—upon the social structure of the surrounding community.

These hierarchical ranks are becoming as explicit as those of the United States Civil Service or those of the armed forces. Each corporation has its hierarchy of the "line" (first-line foreman, assistant general foreman, general foreman, assistant department superintendent, department superintendent, divisional superintendent, assistant plant manager, plant manager, and others responsible for production) and its vertically parallel hierarchy of staff specialists (such as designer, assistant supervisor, supervisor, general supervisor, assistant staff head, staff head). Topping these twin jungles of titles are the elect of "advanced management" or "elite nucleus."

One result of the growth of corporate bureaucracy is the intense preoccupation that has developed in the past decade with symbols of status. The *Wall Street Journal,* after a nationwide study of business trends, reported on its page 1: "At an increasing number of concerns, the corporate caste system is being formalized and rigidified."[1]

In a small company, everybody knows who is who, and where the power resides. An executive can charge about in shirt sleeves issuing orders and use a battered desk in an open room as his office. In my search for men who had made at least $10,000,000 in the last twenty years, I found that almost all made their fortunes by starting and running their own companies (which makes them look a little like dinosaurs in this modern managerial era); and I found the ways of operating of these lone wolves startlingly different from the hundreds of corporate executives I have interrogated, over the years, behind their neat, polished desks. Several of the entrepreneur-multimillionaires worked in such modest cubicles that I couldn't believe I had reached my destination when I faced them.

In the large corporation, just as in the Army, the executive feels a need for highly visible signs of his authority, even though he feels a need simultaneously to act out the American Creed by showing what a nice, regular fellow he is.

The result is that the office managers of many corporations are trained in the nuances of status and systematize the apportioning of "perks."

First, there is the physical problem of assigning office space. This is often done by rule. Crown Zellerbach Corporation, in planning its move to a new twenty-story building, has arranged walls so that offices for executives of equal rank can "all be built to within a square inch of one another in size."[2] In a typical corporation, the head of the hierarchy assigned to a floor gets the corner office with the nicest view, and the

[1] "Status Symbols," *Wall Street Journal,* October 29, 1957, p. 1.
[2] Ibid.

offices of his subordinates branch out from his corner in descending order of rank. Physical closeness to the center of power is considered evidence of status; and nobody wants to be put out "in left field."

Desks, too, typically are categorized by rank. Mahogany, of course, outranks walnut; and walnut outranks oak. The man who is entitled to wall-to-wall carpeting is likely to have a water carafe, which has replaced the brass spittoon as a symbol of flag rank, and also probably has a red-leather couch. An executive with a two-pen set on his desk clearly outranks a man with a one-pen set. At one broadcasting company, executives above a certain level—and only they—are entitled to electric typewriters for their secretaries.

Several of the automobile-making corporations have highly formalized systems for bestowing status symbols. Here is how the *Wall Street Journal* described the ascent of one former Ford executive: "As his position improved, his office grew larger, his furniture fancier, his name went on the door, he received a rug for the floor and a spot in the indoor garage. Then came keys to executive washrooms, country club membership at company expense, and finally a free car." One of the added benefits of gaining a key to the executive washroom was that in it he could enjoy showers and the use of electric shavers and free cologne. In the town of Darien, Connecticut, where executives tend to congregate, 65 percent of the membership fees of one local country club are paid by companies.

The private washroom, in many companies, is reserved for vice-presidents and up. Some have gold faucets. At a Midwestern oil firm, however, a fine line is drawn. The vice-presidents, like the president, have a private washroom; but it is literally that. Their washroom has no toilet, as the president's has.

An invitation to use the executive dining room is another "perk" that comes only when the employee passes a certain level on the company's hierarchical chart. At a steel plant I visited near Pittsburgh, there were two executive dining rooms side by side for different levels of executives. The one with tablecloths was for the higher group. A New York insurance company has, in its building, five dining rooms in ascending elegance, and personnel are assigned by rank. The democratic custom of eating with rank-and-file employees at a common dining hall has become so rarely observed by corporate executives that the president of a medium-sized company in Northeast City boasted to me that he did that. It helped morale, he felt.

The circumstances under which an employee arrives for work also are highly indicative of status. Does the employee have to punch a time clock or not? Does he or she come through the plant gate or the office door? At what time does he or she arrive in relation to others? Bosses typically make it a practice to arrive either earlier or later than their flock.

Perhaps the most precise assigning of status symbols—certainly the most visible to the general public—is seen in the way many corporations assign company cars. A large oil corporation divides its management people into five levels for the purpose of distributing all sorts of special "perks," including the company cars. A Class I person (division managers, etc.) is assigned a Cadillac or comparable limousine. A Class V person (salesmen, etc.) is confined in his choice to certain specific models of Chevrolet, Ford, and Plymouth.[3]

The privilege of going to a distant spa for an annual or semiannual free medical checkup that takes several days (you play golf in the afternoon) is granted only to those executives of high status. Rank-and-file executives can get their checkups at a local hospital. If you really rate, your wife goes along and gets a checkup, too. And you are permitted to put her on the expense account on company excursions. Wives, in fact, play a key role in all the pushing for the trappings of status at the office, because they need some way to indicate their husbands' importance when chatting with the girls; and it is easier to mention a free junket to a spa—or the number of secretaries a husband has—than it is to boast about how much he earns.

Behind the façade of elaborate courtesy shown one another by members of the management "team" of the typical corporation, a great deal of quite forthright elbowing for status takes place. Sociologist Melville Dalton of the University of California spent a great many months at three industrial plants studying the tensions within each hierarchy. He concluded that in all the plants the relations between members of management could best be described as "a general conflict system."[4] Two principal causes of the conflicts were the drives by many members to "increase their status in the hierarchy," and frictions between members of the two vertically parallel rank orders of officers: staff and line. This last source of conflict has been increasing because the trend is toward using more and more staff specialists—such as engineers, statisticians, public and personnel experts, chemists, and so on—who like to consider themselves agents of top management. They are typically younger, better educated, and smoother than the older "line" managers in charge of producing the goods. The latter may still have dirty fingernails and typically view the young "college punks," "pretty boys," and "chair-warmers" from staff with suspicion or annoyance; and they receive their most delicious pleasures

[3] David Knickerbocker, *New York World-Telegram and Sun,* February 25, 1957.
[4] Melville Dalton, "Conflicts between Staff and Line Managerial Officers," *American Sociological Review,* Vol. 15, No. 3 (June 1950).

from batting down or slyly sabotaging bright ideas staff men have for improving their own methods of operating. A young staff officer complained to Dalton, "We're always in hot water with these old guys on the line. You can't tell them a damn thing. They're bull-headed as hell!"

Upward progress within any corporate hierarchy of management depends, of course, in large part on talent. But a number of informal considerations—some of them social—often weigh heavily in promotions and hiring. In early 1958, the *Wall Street Journal* made another study of executives, and quoted one recently appointed vice-president as saying, "Naturally you have pride if you're socially accepted by your superiors. It does you an awful lot of good. You can have a wonderful personnel system, but the thing that determines where you go in the company is personal contacts."

Where your office is located also seems to be a factor of importance. Being on the same floor with the people at the "head office," so that you can be seen, helps. Other things being equal, you are far more likely to be advanced than a status equal whose office happens to be in another floor, another building, or (worse) another city.

Home life, too, is important. An advertising executive who stated publicly that he and his family couldn't live on $25,000 a year also stated why: "There is no denying that when a man starts to make a certain amount of money how he lives becomes a matter of concern to his employers. And the advertising business is an Ivy League, where clothes, manners, and gracious living are an essential part of doing business."[5] So, evidently, is the gracious wife. A top official of a Midwestern concern states: "Entertaining is one of the best ways to determine if the wife is good enough to enable a man to become a well-rounded executive."[6]

Who you are, in terms of religion, ethnic background, and politics, also is important in influencing your possibilities for progressing in many, if not most, corporate hierarchies. Melville Dalton, in a study of informal factors influencing the career achievement of 226 people within a managerial hierarchy, cited these criteria of success as apparently exerting influence: not being a Roman Catholic, being Anglo-Saxon or Germanic, being a member of a local yacht club (114 were), and being a Republican. Virtually all the 226 except a few first-line foremen were.

In Northeast City, which I investigated, the top managements of the major industries in town were heavily Protestant, even though the city was almost 50 percent Catholic. One president, an Episcopalian, confided,

---

[5] *Ladies' Home Journal*, February 1958.
[6] *Wall Street Journal*, November 13, 1957.

however, "Our treasurer is a Catholic . . . and it is hard for a Protestant to get a job in his office." Jews were even more rarely encountered among the management personnel of the larger companies of Northeast City's major industries.[7]

With the growth of more complex corporate hierarchies, we are seeing a growth in anxiety about status, partly because such systems call for superiors who are expert in applying pressure. And we are seeing a growing adoption of the military procedure of periodic ratings by immediate superiors. This latter forces every aspiring employee constantly to wonder how successfully he is impressing himself upon the superior. Unwittingly he may eagerly assume for himself the known prejudices of the superior, and even his mannerisms.

Those who reach the top level of hierarchies are, increasingly, those who have successfully shed their rough edges of individualism. As the businessman's magazine, *Changing Times,* has noted, the trend is toward an upper level of businessmen and technologists who are "highly trained technically and less individualistic, screened for qualities that will make them better players on the team. . . ."

Few men who hope to reach the top today can be indifferent to the opinion of associates, as Henry Kaiser or old Henry Ford[8] could be. The top power in modern business can be achieved only by those who are accepted by the members of the board and by the company's bankers as sound upper-class men like themselves. And even at the lower level of striving, the strain to prove oneself sound and amenable leaves its mark. Sociologist C. Wright Mills, in his study of white-collar people, made this disquieting point: "When white-collar people get jobs, they sell not only their time and energy, but their personalities as well. They sell by the week, or month, their smiles and their kindly gestures, and they must practice the prompt repression of resentment and aggression."[9]

Some of these members of the management "team" are never free, except in their dreams, when, as George Orwell put it, they have the boss in the bottom of the well bunging lumps of coal at him. Others, at the more sophisticated level, and who live in metropolitan areas not dominated by their company's shadow, manage to become rebels at night. They become wicked wits and flaming liberals in the safety of their patios and favorite bars.

Meanwhile, some more thoughtful corporate managers are uneasily

[7] William Attwood, "The Position of the Jews in America Today," *Look,* November 29, 1955.

[8] Henry Kaiser (1882–1967) and Henry Ford (1863–1947) were industrialists. — ED.

[9] C. Wright Mills, *White Collar,* p. xvii.

wondering if hierarchical growth has not got out of hand. The personnel director of Sears, Roebuck made a study of the impact of organization structure on employee morale and concluded: "We seriously question the necessity for much of our present high degree of over-specialization and over-functionalization."

The proliferation of hierarchy, of course, is not limited to private business. Our larger universities, where staffs number in the thousands, have developed social systems of their own, with low-status maintenance hierarchies and the higher hierarchies of faculty and administration.

With the growth of Big Labor, even labor unions, which once idealized the leather-jacketed, open-collared leader-worker, developed their own fairly complex hierarchies with many staff people in neckties, such as educational directors, publicists, and negotiators, who have rarely seen the inside of a factory or mine. And many of the union leaders began taking on the trappings of status favored by the industrialists they faced across the bargaining table.[10] They pressed for high salaries (a number are in the $30,000–50,000 range), built themselves kingly offices, demanded limousines or private planes for their travel, held their conventions in deluxe seaside hotels where they demanded the best rooms, lived in penthouses—and stopped putting their feet up on their mahogany desks. That extreme of the empire-building businessman–labor leader, the teamsters' James Hoffa, explained the fact that his union supplied him with not only a Cadillac but a private barbershop, gymnasium, and massage room by saying: "Just because I'm a labor leader, do they want me to go around in baggy pants, drive a three-dollar car, and live in a four-dollar house?" One labor leader who has tried to keep his own way of life, and that of his headquarter associates, not too remote from that of the workingmen they represent is the fiery Walter Reuther of the automobile workers. At this writing, his United Auto Worker salary is less than $20,000. He will ride only in a medium-priced automobile on business, prefers coach when flying. When he found himself attending a labor convention in a luxurious Miami Beach hotel, he showed how he felt about it by insisting on sharing a double room with an aide. He, however, is a lonely hold-out from a trend among labor leaders to high-status living.

It would seem appropriate for the leaders of our big organization structures in all fields, with their neatly ordered hierarchies, to cast a searching eye on the human cost of stratified bigness. If, more and more, bigness is judged to be irrevocably destined, perhaps, at the least, efforts can be made to check the withering of individuality of the "teammates."

[10] A. H. Raskin, "The Moral Issue That Confronts Labor," *New York Times Magazine*, March 31, 1957.

CHAPTER 9

Shopping for Status

Our excursions into specific stores—and particularly the excursions women make to fashionable clothing stores—indicate more than we realize about our status and our status aspirations. The clothing we buy says a good deal about our status. And, for that matter, the way we pay our bills for the clothing and other purchases varies to some extent depending upon our status in our community.

The *Chicago Tribune*'s study of shoppers and their habits in three homogeneous communities outside Chicago reveals that many women see the shopping trip to a prestige store (regardless of any purchases made) as a ritual which, if successful, reassures the woman of her own high status. The trip, the *Tribune*'s investigators found, "enables her to test her self-conception status-wise against the conception" others hold of her.[1]

Such women dress up for the shopping trip. They strive to look their most chic and poised, and if the trip is a success they feel "pride, pleasure, and prestige" in patronizing the store and in the satisfaction of "looking down on the customers of the lower-status store" (where women typically don't dress up to shop). Some women said it made them "feel good" just to go into a high-status store. The investigators concluded that "shopping at a prestige store enhances the status of the shopper and vice versa."

On the other hand, women who get beyond their status in their ventures into stores feel uncomfortable. There is a widespread feeling among women that store clerks endeavor to maintain what they consider to be the proper tone for their store by snooting customers who seem out of place. The wife of a research physicist in Stamford, Connecticut, told me that one day when she "ran" into a high-prestige store about a block from her home to buy a blouse that she needed she simply "threw" a babushka over her head and wore slacks. The clerks pretended not to see her. When she asked for a specific blouse in the window, the clerk frozen-face said it was sold. Next morning, dressed in her best, she went back to the same store, sought out the same clerk (who did not recognize her in her more elegant apparel), and without difficulty purchased the same blouse. Sweetly she gave the clerk a $100 bill. The clerk couldn't change such a large bill, and apologetically took the $100 bill to a bank a

---

[1] *The New Consumer*, p. 25. (See also "Class Is Open for Discussion" by Pierre Martineau in *Motivation in Advertising* [New York: McGraw-Hill Book Co., 1957], pp. 163–72.)

block away to get change. Our vengeful wife said she enjoyed every minute of the wait.

In the choice of any store for making an important purchase, we unwittingly seek out the store with a status image at or near our own status level. Pierre Martineau of the *Tribune* has found that many merchants are unaware of this. He asked a major Chicago retailer with a large store in the heart of the city about the socioeconomic character of his customers. The man replied proudly that the entire range of economic classes was his oyster. He said he drew people from all social classes. "But an analysis of his sales tickets," Mr. Martineau states, "revealed that nothing could be further from the truth!" Although he was centrally located, the vast majority of his customers were drawn from the lower third of the economic scale, with addresses in the South Side or southern suburbs.[2]

Now let us examine the status meanings of the clothing we buy in these stores.

The elite long viewed clothing as a way to demonstrate both its superior wealth and its habitual abstinence from any productive form of labor. Some examples of the latter: the high hats, patent-leather shoes, and fluffy white collars and cuffs of the males; the high spiked heels, hobble skirts, and bound feet of females. Developments of recent years, however, weakened the effectiveness of clothing for these two purposes. The mass production and mass marketing of fine fabrics—including nylon stockings—weakened the first function; and the lessening significance of leisure as a symbol of high status, due to the shorter work week, weakened the second one.

It develops, however, that class distinctions persist in more subtle forms. Sociologists Bernard Barber and Lyle S. Lobel made an analysis of clothing preferences of women at different social levels by analyzing fashion material in a number of women's magazines covering a twenty-year period.[3] The classes studied ranged from "old money" upper class down to lower middle class.

They found, for example, a significant difference in emphasis as you moved from the "old money" rich, or true elite, to the "new money" rich, or unseasoned elite. The women of "old money" families tend to be relatively indifferent to swings in fashion; and their taste is oriented more

[2] Pierre Martineau, "The Store Personality," *Harvard Business Review*, January–February 1958.

[3] Bernard Barber and Lyle S. Lobel, "Fashion in Women's Clothes and the American Social System," *Social Forces*, December 1952.

to that of the British upper classes than to the French. They like woolens and prefer a tweedy look to a daring look. All this, Barber and Lobel conclude, reveals a "concern for birth distinction and English heredity as against the distinction of occupational achievement." They respond to fashion messages that use such words as "aristocratic" and such phrases as "well-bred looks" or "a trumpet flare at the hip."

In contrast, the "new money" women are fascinated with high fashion, especially as it is dictated by Paris. They strive for a chic, sophisticated look while at the same time, with an eye on the goal of gaining acceptance from the "old money" rich, they strive for an appearance of quiet, assured elegance.

The objectives women typically have in mind when they dress also vary from class to class. Women who are really secure in their upper-class status may become fond of a really good outfit and wear it for years as a favorite costume. The fabulously well-dressed Mrs. Winston Guest recently took with her to Europe a suit she has been wearing for eight years. She was reported as explaining, "Good suits simply do not wear out if you hang them up." When you drop down to the semi-upper-class level, however, you find a great deal of striving to demonstrate variety of wardrobe.

Social Research, Inc., has found that lower-middle-class women (limited success), on the other hand, dress primarily to make a nice impression on other people, particularly other women. And the lower-status woman, it found, likes to dress up for still a different reason. She wants most the fantasy of the experience. She is eager to get away from the drudgery of housework and children, and wants to become a Cinderella and so escape for a moment from her troubles. She doesn't dress particularly for men because most of the males she sees at parties are her relatives and in-laws.

Men, too, despite their resistance to attempts to change their styles, exhibit certain distinctive modes of dress as you move from class to class. Upper-class males are much more likely to wear vests than males of any other class. Many grown men would feel uncouth if they ever had to appear in public without their Brooks Brothers suit. They've been buying them ever since their own boarding-school days. The importance of the upper-class label and "look" to males can be seen in the fact that a Third Avenue merchant in New York has developed a highly successful business selling cast-off "snob label" clothing, for around $35 a suit, to men who have momentarily come upon hard times.

Perhaps the most visible differentiation between males of the upper cluster of classes and those of the lower classes is the elaborate casualness of the upper-class dress for most occasions outside work and the faith in formality of those in the lower groups. A now famous Hollywood actor still reveals his lower white-collar origins every time he sits down. He pulls up his trousers to preserve the crease.

In clothing as in other matters, the really rich prize age, whereas men well below them in status prize newness. The New England aristocrat clings to his cracked shoes through many re-solings and his old hat.

The shape of our clothing varies in another interesting way by class. As you go up the class scale, you find an increasing number of fat men. Among women the opposite is true. You rarely see a really plump woman on the streets of the well-to-do suburbs surrounding New York. The slim figure is more of a preoccupation with women of the two upper classes. As you go down the scale, the married women take plumpness more calmly.

The way we spend our money and pay our bills—for clothes and other items—also is to a considerable degree a reflection of class-induced attitudes. William Foote Whyte found in interviews with Chick and Doc, two contrasting young men from the Italian slums of a New England city, that attitude toward money has a lot to do with the possibility of rising in the social scale. Chick went on to "Ivy University" and law school to become a successful lawyer. Doc, in contrast, made little progress, continued to hang out nightly with the street-corner gang. Whyte concluded: "The college boy must save his money in order to finance his education and launch his business and professional career. He therefore cultivates the middle class virtue of thrift." In contrast, Doc, to maintain his prestige as leader of his street-corner gang, had to be a free spender. "It is not possible," Whyte said, "to be thrifty and yet hold a high position in the corner gang."[4]

Aside from the lowest class, the worst credit risks in America appear to be the upward strivers of the semi-upper class. The *Chicago Tribune* study of "The New Consumer" quotes a dweller of its high-status community, Golf, as explaining: "You must spend just a little more than you can afford to progress high in life."

As you go up the class scale, you find that people tend to develop, as a status right, a more delaying attitude toward monthly bills. A workingman's wife who neglects to pay a bill by the fifteenth is likely to find her credit cut off at the butcher's and, if delinquent more than a few days, to find a collector on her door step. A semi-upper-class wife, in contrast, is

[4] William Foote Whyte, *Street Corner Society*, pp. 106, 258.

likely to consider it "plebeian" to pay bills promptly and expects trades-people to maintain a patient, hat-in-hand attitude. The man and wife are much too busy with larger matters to bother with bills. Actually, of course, they often are strapped.

In the real upper class, you are likely to see a monumental casualness about bills. The local tradespeople pretend that money really is a nuisance and often make a point of seeming negligent and offhand about submitting bills. And the customers frequently take three or more months to pay. When you reach the higher levels of the upper class, the casualness about bills becomes a source of wonderment. Gloria Vanderbilt recalls, in her autobiography, which she wrote with her twin sister, her surprise at learning that the family butcher bill had reached $40,000.

CHAPTER 10

Behavior That Gives Us Away

While Americans are ceremoniously egalitarian in their more conspicuous behavior patterns, they reflect, sometimes wittingly and often unwittingly, their class status by the nuances of their demeanor, speech, taste, drinking and dining patterns, and favored pastimes.

In the matter of demeanor, the upper-class ideal is one of cool, poised reserve. This demeanor serves the double purpose of rebuffing pretenders and demonstrating one's own competence to carry the torch of gentility. The model of genteel behavior is the pre–World War II British aristocrat, who wore a wooden mask and, in the male version, cultivated a mustache to hide any emotional twitchings at the mouth when the owner was under stress.

In speech, too, the upper-class members copy the British model, at least to the extent of striving for a cool, precise diction, and by pronouncing the "a" of *tomato* with an "ah."

With Americans, choice of words is more indicative of status than accent, although the New England boarding schools nurturing future upper-class boys have long fostered the Harvard, or Proper Bostonian, accent. In general, both the upper classes and the lower classes in America tend to be more forthright and matter-of-fact in calling a spade a spade (for example: organs of the body, sexual terms, excretory functions, etc.) than people in between, members of the semi-upper and limited-success classes. In this respect, at least, we are reminded of Lord Melbourne's lament: "The higher and lower classes, there's some good in them, but the middle classes are all affectation and conceit and pretense and concealment."[1]

Sociologist E. Digby Baltzell of the University of Pennsylvania has compiled a table[2] of upper-class and middle-class usage of language as he found it while making a study of Philadelphia's elite. Here are a few examples:

UPPER CLASS	MIDDLE CLASS
Wash	Launder
Sofa	Davenport
Long dress	Formal gown
Dinner jacket	Tuxedo
Rich	Wealthy
Hello	Pleased to meet you
What?	Pardon?
I feel sick.	I feel ill.

When members of different classes address each other, we see a recognition of the differences in the language used. Ostensibly, we use first names with each other because first-naming is symbolic of equality. Actually, it is a little more complicated. Anyone is uncomfortable if his expectations are not met, and a social inferior expects his superior to act superior. However, it must be done in a nice, democratic way. The superior calls the inferior, democratically, by the first name; but the inferior shows deference in responding by addressing the superior more formally. Amy Vanderbilt, the etiquette authority, for example, advises me that even though the wife of a boss may address the wife of a subordinate by her first name, the subordinate's wife should not address the wife of the boss by her first name until invited to do so.

Now we turn to other areas of behavior where characteristic class patterns emerge.

Drinking habits. Social Research, Inc., made a comparative study of patrons of twenty-two cocktail lounges and twenty-four taverns in the Chicago area, and found that they represented different worlds socially.[3]

[1] Peter Griffith, *The Waist-High Culture* (New York: Harper & Brothers, 1959).

[2] E. Digby Baltzell, *Philadelphia Gentlemen* (Glencoe, Illinois: The Free Press, 1958), pp. 50–55.

[3] David Gottlieb, "The Neighborhood Tavern and the Cocktail Lounge," *American Journal of Sociology,* May 1954.

The cocktail lounge is primarily an upper-middle-class institution serving primarily mixed drinks made of hard liquor, and operating in a commercial district primarily between the hours of 12 to 8 P.M. In contrast, the tavern is a neighborhood social center, and operates from early morning till late at night. Its patrons are almost entirely from what I call the supporting classes, the lower three. As you go down the scale, the number of hours that people who frequent drinking establishments spend in those establishments increases. Upper-lower-class people (essentially working class) who frequent taverns spend fourteen to twenty-three hours a week there.

As might be surmised from the foregoing, patrons of the tavern see the tavern as a place where they can obtain social and psychological satisfactions—and not just a fast drink. Most of the patrons live within two blocks of the tavern. Each tavern has its own social system. "Regulars" come in at the same time every day; they have their own rules about who is acceptable as a member of their in-group, and what constitutes proper and improper behavior in a tavern.

In general, the preferred drink of tavern habitués is beer. A glass of beer can be nursed a long time and, further, it is less likely to threaten self-control. Pierre Martineau, in mentioning this fact, referred to beer as a "drink of control." He went on to say that the tavern customer, usually a solid workingman, has a "terrible fear of getting out of control and getting fired." You find the least concern about self-control, he added, at the top of the social structure. People there don't worry when they drink. They can do no wrong.

In this connection, the attitude of Jews toward drinking might be noted. Among Jews, drunkenness is unforgivable. It is viewed not simply as in bad taste for a Jew to become drunk but degrading and sinful. An older Jew will rarely drink anything at all except an occasional sherry. The younger Jew, if he lives in a Gentile area, will serve martinis to guests before dinner, and may even, to be congenial, have a bar in his house. However, if he lives in a predominantly Jewish area, he drinks very sparingly; and if a Gentile visits his home he is, out of habit, more likely to offer food than drink as a refreshment.

Two considerations seem to account for the Jewish aversion to drinking. The first is the Jew's tremendous respect for intellectual accomplishment. Drunkenness, of course, undermines—at least for a time—one's intellectual capacity. More important, perhaps, Jews see alcohol as a threat to self-control. Historically, Jews, as a persecuted group, have had to be alert constantly to threats to their family and their life. Drunkenness has seemed to make about as much sense for them as it would for an antelope in lion country.

Dining patterns. Tastes in food vary considerably from one end of the social scale to the other. In general, conceptions about what foods best serve as treats become more elaborate as you go down the social scale. Bakeries in working-class neighborhoods sell birthday cakes that exhibit spectacular creations with a variety of flowers made in icing and a figure standing in the middle. Hors d'oeuvres will most likely consist of little sandwiches covered with a bland, green cream cheese and decorated with roses. I once saw an upper-class group, accustomed to casual hors d'oeuvres such as peanuts, blanch when offered a tray of decorated sandwiches at a party. Patrons of metallic diners — most of the patrons are from the three lower classes — can have their choice of pie or cake but all will be buried in whipped cream.

Finally, acceptance of strange, offbeat foods is much more common with the two upper classes than with the three lower supporting classes. The average person of the lower group feels anxious in the presence of strange foods, and considers them fraught with danger. A Midwestern society matron reports her astonishment to find that her maid will not touch many of the very costly foods she serves the guests, such as venison, wild duck, pompano, caviar. Even when these are all prepared, steaming and ready to eat, the maid will cook herself some salt pork, turnip greens, and potatoes. They are the foods she knows.

Foods also become cherished by the social elite as they become more expensive, rare, or difficult to prepare. Social prestige derives thus from knowing the difference between a burgundy and a claret, or serving caviar, abalone, or lobster. Harriet Moore of Social Research, Inc., states: "As a person strives to gain entree into a more sophisticated social group, he will almost invariably be alert and receptive to food preferences and dietary habits of its members. Failure to do so may well mean failure to get 'in.' " They learn, for example, to prefer to have their coffee served in demitasse cups. An acquaintance relates that he recently attended a supper given by socially elite wives for their town's volunteer firemen (largely drawn from the three supporting classes). The firemen were fascinated with the dinky cups placed before them by the ladies, but later seemed chagrined when their tiny portions of coffee were poured. The person striving to gain entree into a select social group also soon perceives that one never asks for ginger ale with his whisky (a favored drink at the limited-success level).

Games and pastimes. Interest in developing perfection in dancing skill goes down as social status rises. If you drive along the lower-income stretches of Chicago's Archer Avenue, you will note large establishments, conspicuously advertised, devoted to teaching dancing. They promise high levels of skill not only in ballroom but also "toe, tap, ballet, and acrobatic" dancing. Working-class parents, particularly those of East or South European backgrounds, have been persuaded that helping their children acquire grace through dancing will help them escape to a higher class, and so is worth considerable financial sacrifice. On the other hand, if you look in on a higher-class dance, say at a New England boarding school, you are struck by the dancers' lackadaisical, offhand approach to dancing. Some, in fact, shuffle like zombies.

The magazine *Mademoiselle* has found, in a comparative study it made of the lives of women who went to college and those who didn't, that college-educated women are seven times as likely to play golf and eight times as likely to play tennis as women who never went to college. On the other hand, the non-college women are more likely to go bowling, fishing, and boating.

Others have noted that bridge playing is largely confined to the upper two classes, and bingo playing to the lower three classes. While poker playing cuts across class lines, some of its most passionate devotees are Negro "society" women. They talk about their latest game for hours over the telephone, and some even stake their automobiles on the turn of a card. Sociologist E. Franklin Frazier, in exploring this phenomenon, sees their obsession with poker as an attempt to escape the frustrations (sexual and other) of their lives. One woman said that winning at poker was in some ways similar to the release of sexual orgasm.

Entertainment and "culture." Although most United States families now have television sets somewhere in their houses, television was originally most enthusiastically embraced (and still is) by people in the lower classes. When television was an innovation, the percentage of class members buying a set rose with every move down the social-class scale. At one stage, nearly three-quarters of the members of the two lower-class families had television sets, while only one-quarter of the upper-class families had them.[4] One explanation — taste aside — for the greater popularity of television with people of the lower classes is that they are more confined to the house. They have no country club to go to.

A similar descending growth in popularity exists in the pattern of attendance at motion pictures, sports events, and other "spectator" types of recreation. In contrast, members of the two upper classes show a marked preference for active, creative activities such as playing tennis, visiting friends, and carrying on programs of serious reading. The upper

[4] Saxon Graham, "Class and Conservatism in the Adoption of Innovations," *Human Relations*, Vol. 9, No. 1 (1956), pp. 91–99.

classes read non-fiction as well as fiction. The lower-class members who read books at all strongly prefer fiction.

The old class lines that preserved "culture" as a monopoly for the aristocrats, it might however be noted, have slowly been crumbling with the growth of literacy, democratic forms, and mass-production processes. Opera is being marketed in the hinterlands, and reproductions of art masterpieces are hanging on the walls in tens of thousands of American homes. The result has been the emergence of "mass culture," which Dwight Macdonald[5] calls "a debased form of High Culture." Mass culture, he points out, is imposed from above: "It is fabricated by technicians hired by businessmen; its audiences are passive consumers, their participation limited to the choice between buying and not buying."

Magazine reading. The editorial content of any magazine pretty much selects its audience. We are drawn to the magazines where we can find self-identification with the situations, characters, or authors presented. Social Research, Inc., found this to be true in terms of class in its study of blue-collar vs. white-collar wives. As I indicated in Chapter 1, it found an "invisible wall" between the ways of life of the two groups. This carries over, it was found, into their selection of magazines. The blue-collar or Wage Town wife, who reads the "family behavior" magazines (sometimes called "romance" or "confession" magazines), very rarely reads the "women's service" magazines such as *Good Housekeeping.*

The report by MacFadden Publications, on Social Research's findings, states: "You might find a story about a truck driver and a diner waitress in either *True Story* or a women's service magazine. But in the service magazine the atmosphere is apt to be light and airy, the characters even treated as faintly comic. In *True Story*, these people are hero and heroine. . . ." (And the hero or heroine, if I may intrude a thought, is usually caught in some ghastly dilemma involving sexual waywardness on someone's part.) Here are examples found of typical contrasts in title treatment between the white-collar "service" magazines and the Wage Town "behavior" magazines:

SERVICE MAGAZINES	BEHAVIOR MAGAZINES
Young love	
"To Catch a Man"	"I Want You"
Bigamy problem	
"One Wife Is Enough"	"Which Man Is My Husband?"
Eternal triangle	
"Remember He's a Married Man"	"Lovers in Hiding"

[5] Dwight Macdonald (1906–1982) was an influential political and cultural critic. — ED.

The "behavior" magazine article typically is illustrated with photographs, rather than drawings, to enhance the reader's feeling that this is an honest-to-gosh true tale.

Instinctive differences of behavior patterns by class will probably always be with us. Watching for the differences can in itself be a game that challenges our perceptiveness.

CHAPTER 11

The Sociology of Sex Appeal

Persons in the upper classes tend to assume that sexual behavior becomes more and more promiscuous as you move down the social scale. They often express shock and disgust at the way the lower classes, wed or unwed, make love like "animals," to employ a frequently used word. On the other hand, people in the lower classes often express shock at what they feel to be the "wild," depraved love-making habits of the upper classes.

It might be fruitful to examine what each group considers to be shocking in the other group's behavior. Much of the general disapproval springs from the fact that people in the different social classes have distinctive courtship patterns; tend to marry within their own class; and develop distinctive patterns as far as stability, fidelity, and dominance are concerned after marriage. Many of the differences that seem so shocking, it should be noted at the outset, develop from the single fact that marriage is delayed more and more as you go up the class scale. Girls in the lower classes start marrying soon after their mid-teens, whereas girls in the two upper classes are usually well into their twenties before they marry. They are waiting for men who must complete their higher education and launch themselves in careers. The years of delay after both the girls and men are physiologically ripe for marriage force them to develop inhibited rituals of courtship that will still supply them with token gratifications.

August B. Hollingshead, in his study of the high-school-age youth of Elmtown in Illinois, concluded that at the high-school age the "sex mores were violated far more frequently" by adolescents in the two lower classes than in the upper and in-between classes.[1] Girls in the lower classes also talked more openly about sex, and were believed to be more "full of sex."

[1] August B. Hollingshead, *Elmtown's Youth*, p. 239.

The boys in the lower classes who had already dropped out of school derived much of their prestige among their peers from their skill in "making" girls. The boy who had not "made" a girl was likely to lie and say that he had, because failure to do so made him a "pansy" with his clique mates. However, he was subject to severe condemnation if he fell into "trouble," either by "knocking a girl up" or "getting a load" (venereal disease).

As for the girls of the lower classes, many had learned to develop an expectation that affectionate responses to physical advances were the natural and reasonable *quid pro quo* for their acceptance of material favors such as a movie, a ride, a gift, or candy. Many considered all this as "having some fun before settling down." The girls insist that they be "treated as a lady," but they interpret this quite broadly as "not being manhandled" in a muscular way by boy friends. A lower-class boy who really treats a girl as a lady, Hollingshead pointed out, is not respected by the girls and is hooted at by the boys.[2]

As one aspect of its investigations, Indiana University's Institute for Sex Research has been analyzing sexual behavior encountered at different class levels (on a ten-class scale).[3] It has found that the boy destined to become a semi-skilled worker later on is fifteen times as likely to have intercourse by the time he reaches his mid-teens as the boy destined to go to college and become a professional or "upper white-collar" person. The Institute reports that in some lower-level communities it had been unable to find a single male who had not, by the time he was seventeen, had sexual relations. And, in such lower-level communities, the occasional boy who had not had such relations proved to be either physically or mentally handicapped, homosexual, or a bright, ambitious lad destined to go to college. Premarital intercourse for males is accepted as such a normal and natural occurrence at the lower social levels that some lower-level clergymen, according to the Institute, preach against profanity, smoking, drinking, gambling, and infidelity, but will not include premarital sex in their listing of sins to guard against. Even in the matter of extra-marital sex relations there is general, if bitter, acceptance that, although such activity is disapproved, boys will be boys.

When we turn, however, to the behavior of the girls of the lower

[2] See also William Foote Whyte, "A Slum Sex Code," *American Journal of Sociology*, Vol. 49 (July 1943), p. 24.
[3] A. C. Kinsey, W. B. Pomeroy, and C. E. Martin, *Sexual Behavior in the Human Male* (Philadelphia: W. B. Saunders Co., 1948); same authors plus Paul H. Gebhard, *Sexual Behavior in the Human Female* (Philadelphia: W. B. Saunders Co., 1953); and report in *McCall's*, March 1958, on the findings of the Institute for Sex Research on pregnancy and abortions.

classes, quite a different morality prevails. This contrasting morality is supported by the men who take it for granted that a double standard should prevail. Although the young men at this level are almost unanimously experienced sexually, 41 percent of them insist that they wouldn't consider marrying a girl who wasn't a virgin!

Whatever the reasons, girls in the lower educational classes show just about the same restraint in waiting as girls in the upper classes. The girls not going beyond high school who transgress the moral code are likely to start their transgressing earlier than the girls who go on to college. On the other hand, the girls going on to college have a much longer wait before marrying after the onset of puberty than the girls with grade-school or high-school educations. That presumably helps account for the seemingly contradictory fact that, among girls who do not go beyond the lower-grade school, 70 percent are virgins at the time they marry whereas the proportion drops to 40 percent for girls who go to college. The girls at the lower educational levels show somewhat more proneness to become pregnant before marriage; but this may derive from the fact that their transgressions occur while they are at a younger, more naive age.

The upper classes, viewing much of the sexual behavior of the lower classes as morally abhorrent, often consider it their moral duty to impose their own code, as far as possible, on people in the lower classes under their domination or influence. So let us look at the sexual behavior pattern of the two upper classes.

Unmarried males of the upper educational and vocational levels certainly do show more continence than males at any lower level. On the other hand, they engage in many expedient practices the lower classes consider to be unnatural if not perverted. Two-thirds of the upper-level men going to college masturbate, according to the Institute for Sex Research's investigation, while fewer than a third of the men the same age at the lower level do. The contrast is even more extreme in the matter of petting to orgasm.

A lower-level male may have intercourse with dozens of girls he casually encounters and not kiss any of them, at least more than superficially. In contrast, the college-level male, while continent as far as intercourse is concerned, engages in deep or tongue kissing with dozens of girls. Nearly nine-tenths of all college men are tongue kissers, according to the Institute, and yet many of these same men would recoil at the thought of sharing a common drinking glass. Lower-class people consider such wallowing about at the mouth as filthy and unsanitary.

Similarly, upper-level males show considerably more fascination with the female's breasts, both as objects of beauty and as objects for manipulation during intimacies, than males from the lower classes. The latter tend to associate them more with their feeding function.

When the upper-level people marry, their sexual behavior again often seems odd to people at the lower level. Perhaps the upper-level people just have livelier imaginations. At any rate, they are more experimental in their love-making: they make love in the nude (a thought that appalls many in the lower level) and they occasionally make love in the light (an even more appalling, indecent arrangement in the eyes of people of the lower level).

While upper-level couples devise a variety of ways, before marriage, to handle their impulses short of coitus, there is some evidence that after marriage they feel less urgent concern about the sexual side of their union than lower-level couples do. Certainly the husbands are less demanding. Many have restrained themselves so long—more than a decade after puberty—that they are far less likely than lower-level males to be sexually unfaithful after marriage. Not only are they inhibited sexually, but they wouldn't know how to go about plotting and carrying through a seduction.

Furthermore, there is evidence that a sizable proportion of men who have gone to college are relatively unaggressive as partners and love-makers.[4]

When people of different class levels marry, they face a considerable problem in adjusting themselves to a mutually agreeable mode of expressing love for each other. And that is just one area where there are deep differences between the social classes. Two social scientists of the University of Chicago, Julius Roth and Robert F. Peck, who have investigated the problem of cross-class adjustment in marriage, found the differences "deep enough to make it relatively hard for two people of different classes to live together happily as man and wife." To illustrate, they cited the adjustment problems of an upper-level man dedicated to accumulating an estate for the future marrying a lower-level girl who has always been taught to believe that money is meant to be spent, and as quickly as possible. Because of such difficulties, these two investigators found, "cross-class marriages . . . are a poorer risk than same-class marriages." Low happiness scores, they added, are particularly common in cross-class marriages in which the wife is conspicuously superior to the husband in education.[5]

    [4] Robert F. Winch, *Mate Selection: A Study of Complementary Needs* (New York: Harper & Brothers, 1958); MacFadden Publications research report, *The Invisible Wall* (New York: 1957).
    [5] Julius Roth and Robert F. Peck, "Social Class and Social Mobility Factors Related to Marital Adjustment," *American Sociological Review*, Vol. 16, No. 4 (August 1951); Richard Centers, "Marital Selection and Occupational Strata," *American Journal of Sociology*, Vol. 54 (1949).

Our dating and marrying is even more clearly compartmentalized by the vertical stratifications of religion, national background, and, of course, race.[6] In some American cities, the overwhelming majority of marriages take place within the boundaries of religion or national background. Two studies of marriages in New Haven, Connecticut, emphasize this.[7] One showed that 91 percent of all white marriages were within the same religious group. Another showed that two-thirds of the marriages took place within the same national-background group. Nationals who intermarry tend to do so within the boundaries of religion. Protestants with British, German, or Scandinavian backgrounds intermarry; Catholics from Ireland, Italy, and Poland form another intermarrying group; and Jews of whatever background marry almost completely among themselves.[8] In recent decades, the Irish-Catholics in New Haven have been marrying more and more Italian-Catholics, because the prestige of Italians in New Haven has been rising rapidly. In some other Connecticut cities, however, the Irish have tended to remain aloof.

Intermarriage rates between Catholics and non-Catholics have been considerably higher in cities less conspicuously ethnic than New Haven. In a city such as Raleigh, North Carolina, where barely 2 percent of the population are Catholic, three-quarters of all Catholics enter into mixed marriages. On the other hand, in a city such as Santa Fe, where the majority of people are Catholic, less than 10 percent of the Catholics enter into mixed marriages.

Barriers in the form of intense public disapproval prevent all but a very few whites and Negroes from establishing relations of courtship and marriage. Casual sexual relations, however, are quite a different matter. Here the barriers work in some complex and peculiar ways.

Sexual barriers affect only half the adult Southerners in a mandatory way. White women and Negro men are sternly prevented from amatory pursuits across the caste line. White men and Negro women know that the taboo does not apply, at least strictly, to them. In 1958, newspapers featured a story from North Carolina that, in one paper, was entitled: "Negro Boy Jailed for Kissing White Girl." It is most unlikely that a white boy would be jailed for kissing a Negro girl, or vice versa.

Some years ago, Yale's social psychologist John Dollard explored these barriers while studying in depth Southern Town. Officially, Dollard found, it was only the no-good poor white or "red-neck" males who went prowling with sex in mind in the Negro section of Southern Town after dark.

[6]W. Lloyd Warner, *Democracy in Jonesville* (New York: Harper & Brothers, 1949), p. 75.
[7]August B. Hollingshead, "Trends in Social Stratification."
[8]R. J. R. Kennedy, "Single or Triple Melting Pot? Intermarriage Trends in New Haven, 1870–1940," *American Journal of Sociology*, Vol. 49 (1944), pp. 331–39.

Dollard heard from informants of both races, however, that some of the highest-class males in town had consorted with Negro women, and that a great many of the local white boys began their sexual experience with Negro girls.

One white woman, who believed that most white men in the town "had to do" with Negro girls, told Dollard of one of her own unforgettable courtship experiences. She was in love with a white boy and gave him a very warm farewell kiss. An older woman observing this admonished her afterward never again to kiss a boy so warmly. She said such a kiss might inspire him to go to "nigger town" afterward.

That incident illuminates the dual attitude many Southern white men have toward women. They have idealized the Southern white women to the point where many come to regard them as untouchable. At least this was so at the time of Dollard's researches. Negro girls, then, become the lightning rods for their unsublimated sexual feelings; and in their fantasies the white men often picture the Negro women as seductresses who live for the moment of sexual expression. Needless to say, many Negro women, particularly the educated ones, deeply resent this concept and have had to learn to be forthright with amorous white males who have come to believe their own fantasies.

With the recent economic upheaval and the great movement of population into, and out of, the South, Southern men appear to be moving toward the American norm in their attitude toward women. They seem to be breaking away somewhat from the tradition that the white girl must be placed on a pedestal and left there to be admired from a distance until the veil of marriage is lifted.

Relations between the sexes at all levels and in all areas have distinctive characteristics that deserve our sympathetic interest. These distinctive patterns are not the result of whim or "wildness" but of fairly fundamental facts in the people's lives. Professional people who seek to guide or regulate relations between the sexes, in particular, I feel, would be well advised to act only after achieving a breadth of understanding of our mores.

CHAPTER 12

Who Can Be a Friend?

The people who ask us back to dinner are almost always those who regard us as approximate equals in social prestige. I'm referring here to the social evenings that are relaxed and spontaneous. For better or worse, most people feel more at ease with their own kind. An early sociologist, F. H. Giddings, developed a concept to explain this, which has become known as "consciousness of kind." Certainly it is true that many people find that trying to socialize across class barriers can be a strain, because ingrained habits, outlooks, tastes, and interests, especially if they are people of low curiosity, typically differ by class.

Furthermore, most of us confine our socializing to members of our own social class because we feel that status is attached to the act of socializing. What will people think if we are seen at so-and-so's house? People a notch higher than we are, socially, may hesitate to come to our house, despite all our charming qualities, because someone might interpret this as meaning they had slipped down to our social class. Thus it is that we usually end up confining our socializing to our own kind of people.

Perhaps the most illuminating study of friendship patterns is that conducted by Bevode McCall in a study of the social structure of his Georgia Town.[1] He concluded: "The way people choose their friends is a part of the functioning of social class." In his Georgia Town, at least, few mutual friendships crossed the lines of the classes he found there. McCall asked more than 2,000 persons to name their "three best friends." Many people named one of two bank presidents as their best friend. A druggist and an eighty-year-old lady also were named as "best friend" by many people. With the exception of the very bottom class, the people in each class named as "best friends" more people in their own class than in any other.

Altogether, McCall had 5,200 choices listed for "three best friends." He sorted out all the cases where a "best friend" was named across a class line. Then he checked the list of the persons named to see if the feeling was mutual. (Often it was not.) He found only 140 cases out of the 5,200 where there was a mutual choice across class lines—or less than 3 percent!

The stratification of our socializing patterns is seen most vividly in situations that parallel the company town. I have in mind those socializing

---

[1] Bevode C. McCall, "Social Class Structure in a Small Southern Town" (doctoral dissertation, University of Chicago Library).

systems confined to employees of one company, or to people of a military base, a university campus, or a one-industry town such as Hollywood. Let us look at examples of the four in order.

Company entertaining. Management officials of a company, living in the same area, will almost always devote most of their home entertaining to one another. Partly, perhaps, this is "consciousness of kind" at work. Partly it results from a deliberate encouragement by management of off-hour socializing to promote, it hopes, team spirit. Also, it reflects an anxiety on the part of the officials to keep an eye on one another even during off hours. And much of it is a reflection of ambition. One account of Neil McElroy's rise up through the echelons of Procter & Gamble states that he and his wife, both ambitious for higher things, "limited their entertaining primarily to important P & G people. . . . "[2]

Recently, *Nation's Business* carried an article, "Friendship Can Ruin Your Business," by a business writer who cautioned executives to keep a sharp eye on fraternization patterns developing around the office to prevent fraternization from becoming "excessive." He cited positive values such as "group spirit," but his concluding paragraph pointed out that precautionary watchfulness "will prevent an up-and-coming manager from carrying around his neck a millstone of personal commitments, loyalties, and friendships . . . " and help him perform his job better.

Below the management level of companies, you find somewhat similar stratification in entertainment. Although members of the white-collar force may work only a few yards from blue-collar workers, they almost never intermingle with them, either on or off the jobs. As for the blue-collar workers, they apparently just want to get home. They rarely invite their colleagues to come to their houses for supper; and most of them wouldn't dream of asking their foreman to their houses. It is not that they would be afraid to. The idea simply would not occur to them.

Military towns. Officers in the regular services, of course, are accustomed to putting the business of behaving according to one's rank openly and precisely on the line. They aren't inhibited by the requirement imposed on corporate officers to maintain, ostensibly, democratic forms. Actually, there is quite a bit of unofficial intermingling at the casual level across the lines of rank. In any social event of consequence, however, the lines are drawn firmly by rank; and seating is by date of rank. An invitation that comes from a higher-ranking officer, or his wife, has the force of a command. And, if it is a large affair where both tea and coffee are to be poured, the officer's wife invited to pour the coffee must outrank the wife invited to pour tea.

[2] *Time,* January 13, 1958, p. 12.

University towns. For all their broad-mindedness, college professors are almost as careful about observing rank in social matters as the most anxious corporate executive. They have their own tight hierarchical structure for socializing, especially if the college dominates the community. Associate professors, on many campuses, are people who still haven't arrived; assistant professors are a big step further away from arriving; and teaching fellows at the bottom of the scale have no status at all. They might as well be janitors.

A former faculty member, who served as an associate professor at Michigan for some years, told me he made several overtures to seek membership in a "discussion and drinking" faculty club on the campus. More than two hundred faculty members belong. He kept receiving evasive responses to his overtures. Finally, a friend, a full professor, advised him: "You need to be a full professor, or the equivalent in status, to belong."

Even the full professor has his social limitations. He would not invite a dean to his house socially, or the president or the vice-president. However, he might invite a department head if it was a large affair. At larger, more official, parties, where a dean is the top ranking guest invited, he or she will be careful to be the last to arrive and the first to leave.

Students, too, at the universities are evidently showing keen interest in being seen only with the right people. *Parade* magazine quotes one of the biggest men on campus at Iowa State University as stating: "You have to be careful not to associate with the wrong clan of people, an introvert group that isn't socially acceptable, guys who dress in the fashion of ten years ago, blue serge suits and loud ties. These people are just not accepted. And if you associate with them, you're not accepted either." This man, who was on the Student Council, said he aspired after college to go to work for a large corporation. As for the secret of his success in becoming a campus leader: "You've always got to be in there pitching and smiling."

Hollywood. My informant here is a high-ranking, creative artist who has been in Hollywood more than twenty years, and has attended "hundreds" of Hollywood parties. "Hollywood is the most class-conscious place in the world, and getting worse," he said. "It's brutal." Suprisingly, to me, it is not the stars who throw their rank around. They tend, he said, to be rather naively democratic. He called them "jay walkers." Rather, it is the movie makers (producers, writers, technicians, and staff people, etc.) who draw the lines. A $120-a-week secretary would not think of associating with a $70-a-week one. "A $1,000-a-week writer will not associate with a $2,000-a-week writer," he said. "If they associated when they both made $1,000, they stop associating. The man being promoted in income may associate once or twice after the promotion with his old $1,000 friend—he doesn't want to seem an utter heel—but no more." All creative artists, such as composers and writers, who are permitted to work at home, are automatically of higher status than those who are expected to report in regularly at studios.

Anyone giving a party in Hollywood, he said, draws the guests from his social level. He indicated four of the major levels by listing the kind of people you inevitably see at the parties of each of the four levels:

First level: "Your party here will be made up of directors, producers, a couple of stars (probably of pre-1940 vintage), a famous columnist, perhaps the wife of a famous writer, now dead. You will never find a cameraman, important as he is, at this level, nor a set designer unless he is awfully famous, brought in especially for a film from New York."

Second level: "Most of the composers, writers, top cameramen, set designers. I'm at this level. I've been to hundreds of parties and I've never seen a cutter, even though he makes more money than many of us, and can be terribly important—some say the most important—in making or breaking a picture. He's not 'creative.' "

Third level: "The cutters, top electricians who handle the lights, skilled technicians of all kinds, the 'effects' men who make the miniatures. When the Oscars are handed out each year, these effects men are the two little guys who run up early in the evening, when no one is paying any attention, to get their prize."

Fourth level: "The lower levels of prop men, the higher level of secretaries, etc."

As with the faculty people of universities, the Hollywood motion-picture people, from top to bottom, socialized almost exclusively within their own fantasy-building world. The outside butcher, brakeman, and candlestick manufacturer may pass them every day, but are seen only as blurred figures.

To return to the overall view, ideas about what constitutes a good party vary from class to class. At the upper-class level, the cliques tend to prefer a good deal of relaxed informality, with the emphasis on sociability laced with whisky rather than show. Food typically is offered casually. There may be amiable and fairly open flirting, and talking. Weaving figures may offer toasts. Other parties at this level are carried on with quiet decorum. It depends on the personalities. Publicity, in the newspapers, in either case is not sought. It is considered a sign of social weakness to seek publicity. The people having the party at the upper level usually aren't trying to prove anything.

At the semi-upper-class level, members of the cliques frequently are trying to prove something, and it shows. More thought and effort go into decorations and food preparation. Allison Davis and Burleigh B. and Mary R. Gardner, describing party life in a Southern town they studied, noted that, at the upper-middle-class level (as they call it), there was a great deal of vying to serve the most unusual delicacies, and a great deal of pre-occupation with decoration and display of status symbols.[3] There is less emphasis on drinking or flirting. There may be card playing, or some cultural treat such as a Tchaikovsky recording just acquired. The hostess will often see to it that news about her party will somehow reach the attention of the local society editor.

Clique parties in homes of the still lower limited-success class are likely to be even more decorous, if less ostentatious. These are the people who show the greatest fondness for church suppers, and when they have parties at their homes prefer the same type of festivity. Frequently, at least in smaller communities such as Elmtown, each couple will bring a dish. They call it "potluck," but when the hostess gets around to writing her piece for the local paper, as she is very likely to do, it will become a "covered dish party."

At the working-class level, most of the socializing is done with siblings, siblings-in-law, or very near neighbors, and is quite random. The parties are often spur-of-the-moment affairs. In fact, the clique, as we've known it in the above classes, a pack of people running together, virtually dis-appears at the working-class level. A study of fifty working-class couples in the New Haven area disclosed that only two out of the fifty couples belonged to a clique of non-relatives who took turns giving parties. And two-fifths of these working-class couples confined their intimate friendships entirely to kinfolk. At this level we see, too, the beginning of a tendency of the sexes to split up in their socializing. The women have their auxiliaries and their "hen" circles. The men get away from their wives by chatting or drinking with male friends and relatives.

The real-lower-class people depend even more than the working class on relatives for companionship. Their idea of festivity is to idle on Main Street Saturday nights, chatting with people they know, or to congregate in the taverns. In any case, the tendency for the sexes to split up in their chatting becomes even more marked.

[3] Allison Davis, Burleigh B. and Mary R. Gardner, *Deep South* (Chicago: University of Chicago Press, 1941).

One interesting way people reveal their class status in a simple act of socializing is the way that two married couples, on their way to a festivity, get into an automobile. If they are from one of the two lower classes, the men will climb into the front seat together and the women in the back. If they are from the limited-success class, where respectable behavior is cherished, each man will typically get in beside his wife. If they are from one of the two top classes, each husband will most likely, with a show of gallantry, get in with the other man's wife.

We shall explore in the following chapter the more organized aspects of socializing.

CHAPTER 13

Clubs, Lodges, and Blackballs

With the rise of national opulence permitting plumbers to drive limousines and foot doctors to buy mansions, the private club has looked more and more attractive to status-minded people as a place to draw lines. In the private club, you can sit, as in a fortress, in judgment of pretender-applicants. They can pound the wall in vain if you have your blackball and a good, sound membership committee in front of you to do the preliminary screening.

One thing you'll want to see from an applicant is the list of his other clubs. Has he achieved membership in clubs of comparable prestige? Lacking that, has he served time (or better still, did his father serve time) in one of the proper waiting-room clubs?[1] Every city has its elite clubs and its waiting-room clubs. In fact, there is usually a well-understood hierarchy of clubs. Among the men's city clubs of New York and Philadelphia, you have at the pinnacles of prestige the Knickerbocker Club in New York (favored by several Rockefeller brothers, etc.) and the Philadelphia Club in Philadelphia. Just slightly below them in prestige are the Union Club (New York) and the Rittenhouse Club (Philadelphia). Below them, in both cities, are the waiting-room Union League and University Clubs; and at a level

[1] Waiting-room clubs were ones that someone joined while waiting for membership in a more prestigious one. — ED.

below these, at least in these two cities, are the Athletic Clubs. And below these are many others of varying prestige. An informed clubman can, by a glance at any applicant's list of clubs, place him just as surely as he could by reading a long biography of the man that included his present position and income.

While I was exploring the elite structure of Northeast City, I talked with two dozen business and social leaders who were described to me as the "real powers" of the city. Most of them talked with considerable pride about their clubs. And they were in substantial agreement on the prestige meaning of each club. The "real aristocracy" of the city's business and social life belongs to two clubs, the Pioneer's Club (city) and the Gentry Club (country). Most of the current aristocrats or their families belonged to waiting-room clubs during their rise to power, and may or may not continue membership in them, along with their membership in the elite clubs, depending on their inclination to be status-lenders. The lowest-prestige bank president I saw (a newcomer in the smallest major bank) had just been accepted finally for membership in the Pioneer's Club, and in talking with me he said he "used" to belong to the lesser-status University Club. Evidently he still felt so precarious in his new role that he feared to remain in the University Club, which is well recognized in Northeast City as a waiting-room club. Another city club generally recognized as a waiting room is the Downtown Club.

The elite individuals I consulted were quick to deny that there was any significant relationship between club membership and their success in business. The clubs, they said, were "just social." And most of them saw no handicap to Jewish businessmen, who are barred from most of the leading city and country clubs of the area. The Jews, they kept saying, have their own country club. The main city club accepting Jews, the Downtown Club, is considered more "business" than "social." In other remarks, however, these people revealed that their club memberships did make important contributions to their business effectiveness.

The women of Northeast City, I should add, have their hierarchy of clubs, too, topped by the Martha Washington Club, housed in a remodeled old mansion. It is highest in prestige and is composed of older women from the older first families. There is also the Cheerio Club for the younger wives of comers. This dual pattern seems to be typical in metropolitan centers across the nation.

Dixon Wecter sums up the greater appeal of the men's social club, with its mahogany paneling, mellow leather chairs, and vast fireplaces, in these words: "Here is his peculiar asylum from the pandemonium of commerce, the bumptiousness of democracy and the feminism of his own household."[2] The Philadelphia Club has permitted female guests inside its premises only rarely. During a recent one-hundred-year period, women were permitted inside on an average of once every thirty-three years.[3] The Athletic Club of Milwaukee requires women to use a side door. A few years ago, one lady created a scandal by fortifying herself with stimulants, and brazening her way right through the front door.

More alarming than the invasion of women to many older club members is the growing commercialization of the town clubs. Many no longer are social sanctuaries where congenial fellows relax over cards and billiards but rather are luncheon clubs where corporate executives take clients for business talks on the expense account.

The Piedmont Driving Club sponsors a Halloween Ball every year at which the debutantes of Atlanta's leading families are presented. The men's Idlewild Club in Dallas performs the same function of unveiling the properly reared daughters of proper Dallas families. Dallas also has a "Party Service" for the debutante-age set, made up of society people, which maintains eligibility lists for society's whirl of winter parties.

Society, in most United States cities, supplements the private "coming-out" debutante parties with at least one mass ball that stamps a girl with the imprimatur of Society. This has become necessary, especially in Texas, because so many ambitious, new-rich, free-wheeling mothers have tried to bring out daughters with flossy parties, sneeringly called "climbers' balls," without anyone's permission.

To assure a proper launching into society, a girl needs, as a first requirement, a father with plenty of money or a high business position. As a second requirement, she needs a mother with a good deal of shrewd-ness, persistence, and, if she is slightly weak on the money requirement, a good deal of aggressiveness. At the very latest, the mother must start mapping plans by the time the girl is ten years old. Age six is preferable. The girl must be enrolled in the acceptable schools (see Chapter 16), because they become the key to everything in many cities. She must also be enrolled in the right dancing school. As the girl fulfills these require-ments she must be invited to the right sub-debutante parties. To achieve this, in the New York area, the mother must send a letter of application to the invitations committee of each dance she wishes her daughter to attend, along with three letters of recommendation from people who are personal friends of three different members of the committee. This is

[2] Dixon Wecter, *The Saga of American Society* (New York: Charles Scribner's Sons, 1937).
[3] E. Digby Baltzell, *Philadelphia Gentlemen*, p. 337.

where the climbing mother must display her social skills on the telephone and at parties. She must win commitments to write letters from insiders without seeming guilty of gall and aggressiveness.

When the girl of proper background approaches marriageable age, she and her mother start the maneuvers necessary to win an invitation from the local Junior League. Among old families, these tend to be handed down unofficially from mother to daughter. Daughters of families that have been in the community less than a generation face a challenge. You don't just apply. That would be unforgivable. You must be proposed by a member and seconded by another member. This often takes persuasion because members must hoard their proposing and seconding privilege. They are restricted to using each only once a year. Once the proposal is made, your qualifications are most carefully examined on such points as "congeniality" by a screening committee. New members must be between eighteen and thirty-four. Those accepted must face the prospects of spending considerable time not only at high-level play but in engaging in charity, worthy causes, and other good works.

In Los Angeles, a well-established socialite caustically commented on the large number of new groups dedicated to worthy causes that have appeared there by saying, "I know of some cases where the groups were formed before they found a disease to work for." The aspiring socialite knows that the way to recognition is to work like fury on a minor subcommittee for some worthy cause. Eventually the day will come, if her social credentials are adequate, when she will achieve an important committee post and have her picture taken for the newspapers beside the socially eminent status-lenders heading up the drive. And all this tireless striving, it should be noted, does indeed raise money for worthy causes, and it does get bandages wrapped. Daughters of the well-to-do are taught from girlhood that proper people devote themselves to proper causes. An extremely wealthy father on Chicago's North Shore, who had sent his daughter to Northwestern University, was trying to explain to a friend one area of her course of study. He said, "She's taking some handicraft courses. . . . You know, to prepare herself for volunteer work later."

Social clubs and associations that offer their members prestige usually stress how exclusive they are. To be exclusive you must exclude. Some exclude on the basis of undesired character traits, or lack of money, or failure to attend proper boarding schools. Whatever other bases they use, most exclude on a religious basis.

The most elite clubs, such as the Knickerbocker in New York, the Somerset in Boston, or the Pacific Union in San Francisco, are so particular on this point that an applicant not only has to be a Protestant but the

right kind of Protestant—usually Episcopal. When you get down to the
mass of non-elite country and city clubs, however, where Lutherans and
Catholics are not necessarily excluded, the exclusiveness regarding religion is typically limited to one specification: no Jews. We shall explore later
what seems to be behind this aversion of the upper and semi-upper
Gentiles toward Jews as club members. At this point, we shall merely note
that it is a nationwide phenomenon involving thousands of clubs. Some of
the more elite New York clubs draw no line on religion at all; but in most
American cities the line is quite firmly drawn. Atlanta is an example of a
city where most of the country clubs and city clubs are either 100 percent
Gentile or 100 percent Jewish.

With the help of a Rockefeller grant, two Cornell professors, Robin M.
Williams, Jr., and John P. Dean, directed a study of social discrimination
that reached into 248 cities, small and large. In each city they made three
tests of social acceptability: admission to the Junior League; admission to
the country and city clubs; and admission to exclusive residential areas. In
more than eighty cities—or one-third of them—Jews were denied admission to all three. In only 20 out of 248 cities were even some Jews
accepted in all three of these categories.

These investigators note a paradox on a nationwide basis that I noted in
Northeast City. Many cities welcome and encourage Jews to work with
Gentiles in the leadership of programs for community improvement and in
community fund-raising drives. Many of the Gentile leaders in Northeast
City told me admiringly of the wonderful way all religions worked together
to better the community. Yet in Northeast City—and throughout other
cites in the country, according to the Williams and Dean study—the social
barriers against Jews are in full force. In fact, there seems to be an odd,
inverse relationship. Dean states: "The communities that score *low* on
social acceptability of Jews score *high* on Jewish participation in community
affairs." The situation undoubtedly is not only perplexing, but discouraging, to Jews. Dean quotes one Jewish community leader as saying, "I
sometimes feel like a prostitute. They'll call on me to lead their Community Chest campaign. . . . But when it comes to the country club, I'm not
good enough for them."

Until this point, we have been examining club life at the higher level of
the larger metropolitan areas and their suburbs. Tens of thousands of the
nation's clubs, of course, are in the small towns: service clubs, garden
clubs, Optimist clubs, secret fraternal orders, women's clubs, veterans'
posts, union clubs, and so on. Americans are tremendous joiners, especially among the three higher classes. Some of this joining, unparalleled
in the world, is a symptom of our gregariousness in the face of growing

loneliness. And, possibly, it may reflect a growing inability of Americans to draw upon their own inner resources. Much of it, however, clearly represents an effort to improve one's social standing.[4]

When these club-joining habits of Americans in typical towns are subjected to class analysis, we see that the primary split—as in many other areas of life—is between the two upper classes and the three lower classes. Until recent years, we had social associations such as fraternal orders that covered the spectrum of our classes. Today, the two upper classes have substantially abandoned all associations, such as the lodges, that would bring them into contact with members of the three lower classes.

The two upper classes in their joining habits today prefer clubs that are by invitation only. This is especially true of the upper class, which participates primarily in social and charity clubs. The upper-class person in our smaller cities and towns is likely to belong to the country club (as a status-lender). The woman will belong to the garden club. In Jonesville, the W. Lloyd Warner group found that virtually all the upper-class women belonged to one of these three: a charity club to support the local hospital, the local chapter of the Daughters of the American Revolution, and a social club called the Monday Club. All three, it should be noted, have devices for restricting membership.

At the semi-upper-class level—or upper-middle, if you prefer the conventional terminology—you have the bulk of the country-club membership. In Elmtown, Hollingshead found that 85 percent of his Class II members[5] belonged to the local country club. Some country clubs in the smaller communities, for economic survival, draw members from the lower, limited-success class. This is a fact widely bemoaned by the members of the two upper classes.

A major purpose of the semi-uppers today in their joining, however, is to prove to the world—and particularly to the upper class they aspire to—what fine, sound-minded, reliable citizens they are. Their clubs are devoted to local uplift. The women have their Woman's Club, and the men their Rotary and other civic luncheon clubs, where they rejoice in their own solidarity, receive inspirational addresses, tell dirty stories, and map plans for community or business betterment. In the larger towns, where you find more than one civic club, the clubs are usually well understood to have differential prestige. Rotary typically draws the cream of the commu-

---

[4] Max Lerner, *America as a Civilization* (New York: Simon & Schuster, Inc., 1957), p. 636.

[5] Packard generally adopted Hollingshead's social class scale in formulating his own, so the class designations mentioned here are similar to those discussed by Packard. — ED.

nity leaders. The Lions, when in the same town with Rotary, sometimes draw members from a more modestly successful level.

Now let us drop from the elite to the level of the three supporting classes to examine their joining habits.[6] At the supporting-classes level, the clubs joined are mainly of the patriotic and mystical type with a higher mixture of secrecy and emotional symbolism than the upper classes consider to be dignified these days.

The fraternal orders reached their peak of popularity in the 1920's, when most of the adult males of America belonged to one or more. Their secrecy and rituals and costumes may seem a bit juvenile today, but these orders did make one important contribution to democracy. Like the Roman Catholic church, they embraced the span of the American social order. The lodge hall was an excellent place for people of all classes to become acquainted, and to understand each other's problems and aspirations. Such an opportunity to make oneself known to people of the superior class is an essential precondition to winning acceptance into their class, in case one has ambitions. The fraternal orders performed, at least, that vital function of providing a common ground for intermingling. A generation ago in Jonesville, W. Lloyd Warner points out, "every important man in the community was a Mason, and often an Odd Fellow or a Woodman."[7] And the man who managed to become a high-degree Mason was taking a long, sure stride toward social success. Today, the situation has changed abruptly not only in Jonesville but throughout America. The members of the two upper classes have abandoned the lodges almost completely in favor of their exclusive civic-type groups; and, typically, the lower classes have not been able to follow them into these. Nowadays, the Masons and the Knights of Columbus draw their membership predominantly from the limited-success class; and the Woodmen of the World, the Odd Fellows, Eagles, and Redmen draw a very large part of their membership from the workingman class.

Even among the three lower classes the fraternal orders have lost much of their fascination. In Northeast City, I was told, the Moose were having a "hard time," and were running what amounted to restaurants. Other towns have Elk headquarters that seem to be frequented primarily as restaurants or taverns. Many men at the lower levels keep up their lodge affiliations because of insurance and other advantages. Oddly, while the male lodges have, in general, been declining, their feminine auxiliaries (and here, again, we see the sexual apartness common at the lower-class levels) have been thriving.

---

[6] W. Lloyd Warner, *Democracy in Jonesville*, p. 138.
[7] Ibid., p. 119.

To summarize, it would seem that our socializing patterns, both informal and organized, are characterized by a confinement to one's own kind and a carefulness to avoid or exclude those who might be construed to be of lesser or different status. The example of our leading national folk hero, Abraham Lincoln—who relished mingling with all kinds of people and enjoyed pricking the pretentious—is evidently no longer considered relevant by a very large proportion of our people.

CHAPTER 14

The Long Road from Pentecostal to Episcopal

America, we keep reading, is undergoing a tremendous religious renaissance. Membership is growing by a million a year, and is now up to more than 104,000,000. Per member contributions are up. Nearly a billion dollars' worth of new structures are going up in the United States each year.

In the face of all this, we see some puzzling bits of evidence. In the study of Elmtown's youth, it was found that religion was remote from the lives of the great majority of them. And the exceptions were mostly youngsters from Norwegian and Lutheran families. To most students, Hollingshead concluded, "the church is a community facility like the school, the drug store, the city government, and the bowling alley."[1] And this is in the heart of the so-called Bible Belt. Many of the youngsters attend church functions regularly, but carry their status feelings with them, often in a most un-Christian manner. He said that a socially select gang of girls attending the Sunday night "Fellowship" meetings at the most elite church (Federated) "deliberately make any girl of whom they do not approve feel so uncomfortable" that she will not attend again.

Going to church is a deeply felt, soul-searching experience for many millions of Americans. And religious faith still dominates and guides the lives of millions of people, some of whom may not be regular churchgoers. Many still kneel in fervent prayer at night. For the majority of American Christians, however, going to church is the nice thing that proper people do on Sundays. It advertises their respectability, gives them a warm feeling that they are behaving in a way their God-fearing ancestors would

[1] August B. Hollingshead, *Elmtown's Youth*, p. 246.

approve, and adds (they hope) a few cubits to their social stature by throwing them with a social group with which they wish to be identified. And even those who take their worshiping seriously often prefer to do it while surrounded by their own kind of people.

The status implications of attending a particular church are especially perceivable among the Protestant churchgoers. In our frontier days, the Protestant churches outside the settled coastal towns and cities were institutions where brotherhood often truly prevailed. I remember, from my own boyhood and young manhood—long after all the frontiers were settled—attending Protestant churches that drew their congregation from virtually the entire community. Today, such churches are becoming harder and harder to find. The trend toward more rigid stratification in the Protestant churches is proceeding apace with the general trend in that direction. This is perhaps not surprising, because, as Liston Pope, Dean of Yale Divinity School, points out, "every American community . . . has some pronounced pattern of social stratification, and religious institutions are always very closely associated with this pattern."

In earlier days, people who moved to a new community typically chose the church that came closest to harmonizing with their own doctrinal viewpoint. And these doctrinal viewpoints were often passionately felt and held. Today, the doctrinal meaning of joining a particular church is far less important in the decision than the social or business meaning.

Let us then look at the social meanings—from the most elite downward—of the various Protestant denominations. There are, of course, variations, particularly in the South, and churches, like country clubs, draw their members from a band that covers more than one class. Also, it should be noted that individual churches built more than twenty years ago may find that, while they start out as high-status churches, population shifts have left them in a sea of lower white-collar or working-class homes. Actually, every denomination if not the individual church has some members from all the social layers. With those qualifications, there does seem to be a definite prevailing pattern in the ratio of distribution of church preferences among the various classes.

The upper class in most United States communities is drawn more powerfully to the Episcopal church than to any other.[2] The upper-class fascination with the Episcopalian church seems to stem, at least in part, from its close kinship ties with the Church of England.

Three other denominations strongly favored by the two top social

[2] David L. Hatch and Mary A. Hatch, "Criteria of Social Status as Derived from Marriage Announcements in the *New York Times*," *American Sociological Review*, Vol. 12 (August 1947); Mabel Newcomer, *Big Business Executive*, pp. 47–48.

classes of America are the Presbyterian, Congregationalist, and Unitarian. As you go north into New England, the Presbyterians tend to become Congregationalists. The Congregational churches can be found in mill towns. And in many New England villages they have congregations that represent the entire church-going population. But, in larger cities and growing suburbs, these churches tend to be especially appealing to people from the higher socioeconomic and educational levels. The Unitarian church, tiny in total number, outranks all denominations in the number of eminent Americans who have claimed it as their church.

Whatever the denomination, care is taken, in many American churches having a strong element of wealthy socialites in the congregation, to see that the socialites are visited, in the church's annual canvass, by someone of their own social standing rather than by a volunteer chosen at random from the general committee. Also, care is sometimes taken to see that downright lower-class people don't wander in on a lovely Sunday morning. The W. Lloyd Warner group reports that, in Yankee City, the two churches with the heaviest upper-class membership "devised a method of limiting the number of persons from the lower parts of the class hierarchy." St. Paul's Church (Episcopal) and the Unitarian Church established branches in the lower reaches of town that served as missions for people of the two lower classes.[3]

Sociologist E. Franklin Frazier reports finding that some Negroes in professional occupations maintain two church memberships. They will maintain their colored Baptist or Methodist membership as they themselves move up the social ladder because most of their clients are still in those churches. This, Frazier points out, has financial advantages. At the same time, they may affiliate with Episcopal, Congregational, or Presbyterian churches, usually colored, "because of their social status."

As we drop down the social scale, we come to the denominations that have the largest (and usually the most enthusiastically active) followings. Methodism probably comes closer to being the choice of the average American than any other. There are 12,000,000 Methodists in the United States today. It has many elite churches, especially in the South, but overall it has only half as many upper-class members, on a percentage basis, as the Episcopal church. Nearly two-thirds of all Methodists are either farmers or manual workers, according to an analysis made by the Federal Council of Churches of a nationwide sampling (Office of Public Opinion Research).[4]

---

[3] W. Lloyd Warner and Paul S. Lunt, *The Social Life of a Modern Community* (New Haven: Yale University Press, 1941), p. 358.

[4] *Information Service*, 27, Part II, May 15, 1948, Federal Council of Churches.

A shade below the Methodists, in the Federal Council analysis, are the Lutherans. The Lutheran church is particularly strong with farmers and skilled workers of Scandinavian or German backgrounds. And somewhat below the Lutherans come the Baptists. In many communities, and especially in the South, the local Baptist church is the highest-prestige church in town; but, nationally, it is predominantly a workingman's church. At the bottom of the social scale you find few churchgoers. They suspect—and correctly, Hollingshead found in Elmtown—that they are not wanted by the congregations of the so-called respectable churches in their town, and often not by the ministers.

Increasingly, in the past quarter-century, Liston Pope reports, people in the lower classes have turned to the new Pentecostal and Holiness sects. They represent, on the one hand, he says, "a protest (couched in religious form) against social exclusiveness, and, on the other, a compensatory method (also in religious form) for regaining status, and for redefining class lines in religious terms."[5] Other studies have shown that a dominant theme in some of these new lower-class revivalist and fundamentalist religions is that faith and righteousness make their adherents holier-than-thou; and will entitle them, when they get to Heaven, to sit in the high places (and be waited on by servants). At the same time, however, their ritual typically says, "Have mercy upon us, miserable offenders."

While the lower-class religions offer consolation for failure, many (but not all) upper-class churches tend to generate the pleasant feeling that everything within the social system is pretty fine just as it is. As you go up the social scale, services become less emotional and evangelical, and more intellectualized and restrained.

Now let us move on, for a moment, from the Protestants to the other major United States religions. The Federal Council found that the distribution of Jews in the three-class scale is quite similar to that of Episcopalians. One reason for this, undoubtedly, is that few Jews ever become manual workers or farmers. Viewing Jews on the basis of their occupations, they lead all religious groups in the proportion of their total engaged in "business," "professional," or "white-collar" occupations.

Jewry, too, has its denominations: Orthodox, Conservative, and Reform. And they are differentiated somewhat by social class. Lower-class Jews tend to remain in Orthodox synagogues. The upper-class Jews,

---

[5] Liston Pope, "Religion and the Class Structure," *The Annals of the American Academy of Political and Social Science,* March 1948.

especially those with higher educations, tend to move on to the Conservative and Reform denominations. The Roman Catholic church, of course, does not have denominations, and so has escaped the trend to stratification by social classes that is becoming so conspicuous in the Protestant churches. Catholic parishes are organized on a geographic basis, and each parish is expected to minister to all Catholics in its area. The more conspicuous divisions within the Catholic church, if they might be called that, are on the bases of vertical ethnic divisions rather than horizontal economic divisions. Thus, in adjoining parishes, you may have churches—because ethnics tend to cluster in their home addresses—that are predominantly Irish Catholic, Italian Catholic, French Catholic, or Polish Catholic.

As for the social-class profile of the Catholic church as a whole, it resembles that of the Baptists more than that of any other Protestant denomination. The explanation for the predominantly working-class composition of the Catholic church is easy to find. A large proportion of its members are descendants of immigrants who, as a group, arrived later on this continent than the national groups, especially English, that largely make up Protestantism in the United States.

One interesting current development in the Catholic church is its mild success in recruiting Negro converts. This has several explanations, including this church's continuing desire to minister to all who declare themselves members of the faith. In addition, a real-estate factor has been making a contribution to this trend in some areas, such as certain sections of Chicago. As children and grandchildren of Irish, Italian, and Polish immigrants have prospered and moved out of the working-class districts into suburban developments, Negroes, also prospering at a lower level, have been leaving their confines of the slums to replace them. The parish churches have, of course, been unable to follow the flocks. They have welcomed the incoming Negroes.

To date, the proportion of Negro church members who are Catholic is small, about 1 in 25. At least one-third of them are affiliated with mixed parishes. The rest are in segregated churches. But even that record of integration is far higher than that of the Protestant churches. Until a few years ago, barely 1 percent of the Protestant congregations with white members had any Negro members. By a variety of techniques, about as gracious as that of the white waitress who spills soup in their laps, the white members have succeeded in making those Negroes who have ventured to approach white churches feel unwelcome. When a Negro persisted in coming to a church in one Kansas town, the minister took him aside and said that, of course, he was welcome but wouldn't he be happier in his "own" colored church of the same denomination on the other side of town, a mile's walk from his home? While great strides were made during the 1940's in lowering the color bans in business, sports, politics, entertainment, and education, Protestant churches did little, actually, and remained 99 percent Jim Crow.[6] For the last few years, however, Liston Pope tells me, considerable progress has been made in reducing the segregation in the Protestant churches. This forthright and courageous dean has been in the forefront of those seeking to pierce the color barrier in the churches. The proportion of Protestant churches that now have at least a few Negro members is approaching 10 percent. A Congregational church in the Boston area has recently had a Negro Sunday-school superintendent of a mixed congregation. Among Protestant churches, the Congregational and Episcopal churches have been particularly active in seeking an end to racial barriers in the churches. Relatively few Negroes belong to those two denominations, even on a segregated basis, and those who do belong—just as among whites—are the more educated, sedate, and prosperous.

All of the foregoing indicates, I believe, that Christianity in mid-century America shows a sizable gulf between practice and preaching. It may reasonably be argued that some of the social stratification of Protestant churches arises from the composition of the neighborhood surrounding the churches. A minister in Levittown, Long Island, has little opportunity to broaden the social reach of his church. His stratification is built in. Also, it may be argued that some people can worship more serenely and at ease if they are surrounded by their own kind.

But still the question persists: Should one be worshiping in a setting that makes a mockery of one of the core values of Christianity: the brotherhood of man? At present, the brotherhood of man is in danger of becoming merely a nice intellectual concept.

---

[6] *Jim Crow* was the phrase used to refer to systematic patterns of racial segregation that existed in the South from the late nineteenth century until well into the 1960s. — ED.

CHAPTER 15

A Sociological Peek
into the Voting Booth

Our attitudes toward the world around us are to a very large extent shaped by our particular standing in the social structure. This is perhaps most conspicuously evident in our political predispositions. More and more, our voting habits are determined by status factors within ourselves rather than by specific issues and party programs at stake in an election campaign. Increasingly we vote as our friends, neighbors, and business associates vote.[1]

One of the candidate's most challenging problems thus is to pull together—by such acts of symbol manipulation as eating pizza pies—a winning combination of status groups from within his particular electorate.

Have you ever wondered how someone is going to vote in a coming election—or what his "politics" really is? What follows is a handy guide that, while perhaps not as accurate as a Univac[2] machine, will in most cases whir up the right answer for you. (Also, if you have any doubts, it can probably whir up how you are going to vote yourself.) Because of the fact that there are still a few rugged individualists left in our society who persist in the old-fashioned habit of voting cerebrally—conceivably you may be one of them—100 percent accuracy is not guaranteed. Also, it should be noted, Southerners are regulated by a somewhat different set of factors. With these qualifications, let us proceed.

Five factors in the average voter's life pretty much determine how he votes and thinks on political issues. They are:

1. *The money factor.* It is hardly news that upper-class rich people tend to be conservative, show a reverence for the status quo, and prefer the Republican party; and that working people tend to be liberal or radical and to show a bias in favor of the Democratic party. However, two facts are noteworthy about the money factor. One is the precision with which political attitudes change as you move down the stratification scale of occupation. The other is the fact that this tendency is increasing.

Richard Centers, who analyzed the political attitudes of 1,100 Amer-

---

[1] Paul Lazarsfeld, "The People's Choice," from *American Social Patterns*, edited by William Petersen (New York: Doubleday & Company, Inc., 1956), p. 129.

[2] UNIVAC, which stood for Universal Automatic Computer, was a commercially successful computer put into operation in 1951. — ED.

icans in a nationwide sample, concluded: "There exists some fairly convincing evidence in the data obtained from this survey that the political alignments of our population are shifting steadily in the direction of cleavage along stratification lines."

He compared the political preferences of the 1,100 people interviewed with those of their parents. "The parents' voting habits do not show so great a difference along stratification lines as those of the younger generation," he said, and added, "The cleavage has grown."[3]

Centers asked his subjects a series of questions designed to uncover their position on a radical-conservative scale. (Wanting change vs. wanting to keep things just as they are.) Here are the results by seven major occupational groups:

	CONSERVATIVE OR ULTRA CONSERVATIVE	RADICAL OR ULTRA RADICAL
Large business	87%	2%
Professional	70	11
Small business	74	8
White collar	56	16
Skilled manual	39	27
Semi-skilled manual	21	49
Unskilled manual	23	38

These columns, you will note, follow a fairly regular progression as we descend Centers' occupational scale. There are two mild (and interesting) distortions, and both can be accounted for. Professionals tend to be somewhat less conservative than small businessmen. Although professional men typically have relatively high incomes and status, they typically don't feel as much of a stake in preserving the status quo as businessmen, big or little. The other distortion is that semi-skilled manuals rather than the unskilled at the bottom are our most radical group. Presumably the explanation here is that the semi-skilled are more likely to be organized and militantly led by labor unions.[4]

One interesting paradox on the rich-poor axis of American politics is that the sons of fabulously wealthy families who aspire to high office have usually appeared as Democrats. The names of Roosevelt, Harriman, Biddle, Lehman, and Kennedy[5] come to mind.[6]

[3] Richard Centers, *The Psychology of Social Classes*, p. 66.
[4] Paul Lazarsfeld, "The People's Choice," p. 123.
[5] Franklin D. Roosevelt (1882–1945), W. Averell Harriman (1891–1986), Francis Biddle (1886–1968), Herbert H. Lehman (1878–1963), and John F. Kennedy (1917–1963) were Democratic politicians from wealthy and prominent families. — Ed.
[6] Leo Egan, "Can Rockefeller Save the GOP in New York?" *The Reporter*, October 30, 1958.

2. *The ancestry factor.* There is a strong tendency for descendants of early arrivals in America to be Republican and the descendants of later arrivals to be Democratic.

According to the Federal Council of Churches analysis of the 1944 elections, Catholics were 12 percent more Democratic than the nation as a whole. And Jewish voters were 33 percent more Democratic. Centers found Catholics to be more inclined to radical solutions to national problems than the United States norm. The official Catholic policy, of course, has been vigorously anti-Communist.

Among the Protestant denominations, according to the Federal Council study, only the Baptists produced more Democratic than Republican voters. Methodism produced a slight preponderance of Republicans and the Lutherans a substantial preponderance. The massive majorities of Republican votes were produced by the Presbyterians, Episcopalians, and Congregationalists.

There has been a growing tendency in recent years for the two national parties to play politics with the ethnic blocs. They have set up divisions and committees to play upon the dissatisfactions of the various major ethnic groups. In this the Democrats, because of the ancestry factor, have had the best of it. But there have been exceptions. The Republicans were able to make sizable inroads with Italian-Americans after the Democratic Administration declared war on Italy in World War II. And, in 1952, the Republicans won many Polish, Czech, and Hungarian votes by indicating that liberating Communist-held Poland, Hungary, and Czechoslovakia would be one of their first concerns.

3. *The distance-from-center-of-city factor.* In general, the closer one's home is to the center of a metropolitan area, the more likely he is to be Democratic. And the farther out you go toward exurbia (to use A. C. Spectorsky's phrase) and surrounding farmland, the more likely a person is to be Republican.

Two forces appear to be at work to account for this. The first is economic. The poorest houses, as we've seen, tend to be those ringing the downtown area; and the value and desirability of houses tend to increase every quarter mile as you move outward. Also, home owning, in contrast to renting, increases. Nothing makes a person a Republican faster than acquiring a mortgage. As the waves of prospering urban masses from Democratic precincts move outward into Republican country, they tend to become Republican.[7]

---

[7] William H. Whyte, Jr., *The Organization Man* (New York: Simon & Schuster, Inc., 1956), p. 300.

The second force that seems to be at work to produce more Republicans and fewer Democrats as you move out from the center of a metropolis is the farmer vote (although in the late fifties this was becoming less and less assuredly Republican). Farmers have traditionally voted Republican. Partly, perhaps, this is family habit. Partly it is the farmer's faith in going it alone vs. the city dweller's conviction that many of his problems are beyond the power of singlehanded solution and require unified action. This tendency shows up even among Negroes. Although preponderantly Democratic, rural Negroes tend to be distinctly more conservative in their outlook than city Negroes. Farmers in recent years have had to do a great deal of rationalizing to square their traditional faith in the leave-me-alone approach with their eagerness to receive federal support for farm prices in our now more-or-less chronic times of glut. There is a growing suspicion that the foxy farmers are rising above tradition and playing power politics in their voting. They have found they can apply more leverage on farm policy if they make sure that the same party—whether Republican or Democratic—is not in control of both the Administration and Congress.

4. *The egghead factor.* If the person you are trying to diagnose politically is some sort of intellectual, the chances are 2 to 1 he is a Democrat. The intellectuals constitute the great exception to the money factor. Many are at least moderately well off, earning $5,000 to $20,000, and yet do not turn Republican.

Why? Republicans are likely to say it just proves how muddleheaded, visionary, and impractical they are. The eggheads themselves, of course, like to think their choice is the result of intellectual deliberation. Possibly so, but other factors also seem to be at work. Some of the eggheads subconsciously resent the fact that they seem as bright as (or brighter than) the prosperous businessmen who are so fond of the GOP image but make much less money. Also, the eggheads can be more carefree on matters of public spending because they are not, as businessmen like to say, meeting a payroll.

Personality factors also undoubtedly play a part. Intellectuals tend to glorify traits that are the opposite of those reflected by leading Republicans. The Republican, wherever you find him, is likely to cherish such traits as orderliness, respectability, practicality, self-achievement. And he is fairly likely to take a wary view of the outside world. Eggheads, in contrast, tend to cherish such traits as nonconformity, playfulness, worldliness, bias for the underdog, and even untidiness. Observers who have spent a great deal of time visiting Republican and Democratic campaign headquarters around the country find the Republicans' characteristically more neat and businesslike.

The four factors thus far cited—money, ancestry, distance of home from center of city, and eggheadedness—can, viewed in combination, give you an excellent hunch as to the way 9 out of 10 Americans will vote. If most of the factors point in the same direction, your chances of coming up with a correct guess are especially good. Lazarsfeld found in a study of voting in the Sandusky, Ohio, area that 90 percent of the Catholic laborers living within the city limits voted Democratic while 75 percent of prosperous Protestant farmers voted Republican.

As Catholics prosper and rise on the economic scale, they tend to become Republican. Many affluent Irish and German Catholics are Republicans. Still, Catholic executives with $15,000 salaries, while far more likely to be Republican than Catholic steelworkers, are not as likely to be Republican as Protestant executives sitting in the next office and also earning $15,000. According to one study, while only 30 percent of Protestants above the working-class level are Democratic, 45 percent of Catholics above this level are Democratic. Perhaps we can summarize this situation by saying that Catholics have to become richer than Protestants do before they suddenly realize that they are not Democrats at all but really Republicans at heart.

When you see a person of clearly upper-class economic status who is a liberal politically, the chances are high that he is not fully accepted socially by the upper classes. He is not accepted because of the handicap of ancestry or other complicating factors.[8] This phenomenon, which sociologist Gerhard E. Lenski calls "low status crystallization," helps account for the strong liberal tendencies, previously noted, of Jewish people. If you judged them by their economic position alone, they should be mostly on the side of Republicanism-conservatism.

Thus we see counter-pressures pushing people one way and the other on the conservative-liberal scale. The four factors I've thus far cited will, in most cases, suggest a definite political inclination that can be accepted as a reasonably safe assumption. When the counter-pressures of status balance out so neatly that the person is left near the center of the political spectrum in his inclinations, a final factor can usually resolve the confusion as to which lever the hand will firmly grasp.

5. *The frustration-boredom factor.* This final element, although not a status factor, arises largely from the voter's own life, and is becoming more significant with each campaign. It works to the disadvantage of any party in control of the national Administration for more than two years. The atomic stalemate helps account for the frustration part of it.

[8] Gerhard E. Lenski, "Social Participation and Status Crystallization," *American Sociological Review*, Vol. 21, No. 4 (August 1956).

American voters and columnists alike bemoan the "eternal shilly-shallying over foreign policy," to use the phrase of one columnist. With the world split into two massive camps, this shilly-shallying is likely to continue—short of a generalized nuclear searing of the planet—into the indefinite future. Americans are accustomed to setting disagreeable situations straight in a hurry. Since this is no longer feasible, our foreign-policy makers, whoever they happen to be at the moment, are likely to be the butt of our irritations. The result is a yearning—more intensive with each year an Administration stays in office—for a housecleaning and new faces.

Another factor conditioning the public to yearn for "new faces" is the growing tendency of voters to be bored with any face they've seen around on the billboards before. Advertising has conditioned the public to expect new models and to desire to trade in the old.

The tendency, then, is for those voters near the center of the political spectrum, as a result of a balancing of status factors, to vote for the appealing face, and to vote against the party that has been in control of the Administration, faces being equal. And the longer the party has been in power, the more compelling this urge becomes.

Both parties, it is being frequently observed, are coming to look more and more alike to the voter. This is because both know victory lies in swaying the political neuters in the middle of the spectrum. (Most frequently, these neutral voters tend to be members of the limited-success class—skilled workers and white-collar workers.)

In their soliciting, both parties—and especially their public-relations consultants—are convinced they must offer these swing voters a new look and fresh personalities to counteract the boredom-frustration factor. Even the Democrats after the 1958 landslide[9] agreed, according to *Newsweek,* that they would do well to pin their faith on new faces. It also appeared more and more obvious that sex appeal should be taken into account because of the larger women's vote. *Life* magazine, commenting on the Democratic sweep, noted that the plus qualities of the Democrats at the polls were the youthful look and sex appeal of candidates. It described one Democratic victor as looking like a "blond Greek god." Another was reported to be hard on the "hormones" of ladies. And it quoted one woman voter in Wyoming as saying she got a "buzz" just from watching the handsome young Democrat running (successfully) for governor. With television becoming such a decisive factor, candidates with lean, young faces were favored because TV tends to fatten and age a face.

---

[9] In the elections of 1958, the Democrats picked up forty-seven seats in the House and thirteen in the Senate, giving them control of both houses of Congress. — ED.

James Reston of the *New York Times* reported after the 1958 votes were in that the professional politicians were starting to show an "almost pathological fascination" with any candidate who is "good" on television.

As the situation now stands in mid-century America, former successful candidates who lacked the toothpaste-ad look such as Abraham Lincoln, John Adams, George Washington, John Calhoun, William Howard Taft, and Herbert Hoover would find campaigning a pretty discouraging business.

While at the University of Wisconsin recently, I came upon the trail of a political-science major, Jim Wimmer, who has earned a reputation in the Midwest as a "political prodigy." Talking of the evident new trend of voters to vote for personalities rather than issues, he states: "I think probably the most important thing a politician can do, under our present system, is to establish a public personality, rather than establish a set of issues."

As for the long-glorified typical American voter and his recent surge to the polls in record-breaking numbers, Wimmer stated: "I believe that the American voter is not interested in the issues of today; he is as sluggish as the political system. Larger numbers of the voters turn out, not because of interest, but rather because the mass media have constantly drummed into their heads the notion that they *should* vote."

In short, they vote pretty much as they go to church. It's the thing to do.

And they have, for the most part, accepted Groupthink while posing as the thoughtful, issue-weighing voter-citizens so glowingly depicted on the billboards. I think we could feel better about the democratic process as it is practiced in the United States if voters in general would start looking beyond personalities and predispositions, and make searching analyses of the core issues involved and the commitments of the candidates.

CHAPTER 16
The Molding of Tender Minds

Class differences begin in the cradle. White-collared mothers are likely to make quite a personal drama of being a new mother and lavish their baby with protective love. The working-class mother is likely to have mixed feelings. She'll be matter-of-fact with occasional spontaneous expressions of joyous love.

Interviewers for the *Chicago Tribune* in a motivational study asked young mothers to state the first thought that leaped into their minds when the interviewer said the word "baby." Women in the upper half of the population would make such exclamations as "darling," "mother," or "sweet." Those in the lower half were more likely to say "pain in the neck" or "darling but a bother."

During the first years of life when, psychiatrists say, our personality is largely molded, youngsters in the lowest class learn to do what comes naturally. They are breast fed whenever they feel in the mood for a nip. They learn bowel and bladder training in a permissive way. As you move up into the higher levels of the working class and into the limited-success class, you encounter much more effort to exert control and guidance, according to studies made by a number of sociologists at the University of Chicago. For example, mothers of these classes begin to train their babies in bowel control at the age of about seven and a half months, or nearly three months before the lower-class mothers do.

The more success-conscious mothers at the somewhat higher level also begin earlier than women in the lower level in trying to wean their babies. These mothers at the higher level also work much harder at training their children to restrain their emotions and to accept responsibilities around the house. Training to "make good" begins early.

One result of all the training is that at least the middle-class child appears to be more orderly, organized, and inhibited than his counterpart in the lower classes.

When toddlers grow into youngsters, the class differences become more clear-cut. Three sociologists focused their scrutiny on a one-half-square-mile area in Chicago that was chosen because it included the whole class gamut of families from real lower to real upper. All the youngsters thus had access to the same community facilities: movies, libraries, playgrounds, Y.M.C.A., Boy Scouts, parks, churches, settlement houses. All children in three grades (fifth to seventh) in a local school were asked to keep diaries of their daily activities. An analysis of these diaries revealed that, out of school, the youngsters from the lower classes lived in a world largely different from that of the so-called middle classes.[1] After school they went to the clubs and centers specifically designed for the so-called underprivileged. They spent much time at the movies, and they tended to have considerable freedom to roam and to come and go at home.

In contrast, youngsters at the higher level spent much of their time at self-improvement activities such as taking lessons and reading, indicating the future-mindedness of themselves and their parents. And they took part in great numbers in Y.M.C.A. and Boy Scout activities.[2]

In the disciplining of children, class differences also appear. Among the lower classes, the youngster deemed to be guilty of serious misbehavior is flogged or deprived of privileges. And the punishment is most likely to be administered by the father. When you get up into the so-called middle classes, the mother is likely to dominate in the disciplining. Father, who typically gets home late from business, is likely to busy himself trying to prove in the few fleeting moments available with children that he is a real pal. At this level, the punishment most commonly inflicted is withdrawal of love.

Penn State's sociologist Arnold W. Green relates that he spent several years in a predominantly Polish-American industrial town in Massachusetts. The streets of dilapidated row houses rang with the screams and wails of youngsters being flogged by fathers trying to enforce obedience upon children contemptuous of their parents' Old World ways. Yet, Green points out, "those children do not become neurotics. Why? Because parental authority, however harsh and brutal, is in a sense casual and external to the 'core of the self.' "

Green points, in contrast, to the incidence of neuroses among youngsters reared in "Protestant, urban, college-educated middle-class" homes where a hand may never be laid on the children in anger. Such children, he points out, often find their personality absorbed by their parents. There is often a "physical and emotional blanketing of the child, bringing about a slavish dependence on the parents."[3]

The mother, in particular, may "absorb" the child's personality as her life may be dominated by care of the child. In cases where the child actually

[1] M. Macdonald, C. McGuire, and R. J. Havighurst, "Leisure Activities and the Socio-Economic Status of Children," *American Journal of Sociology*, Vol. 54 (1949), p. 505.

[2] James West, "Learning the Class System of Plainville, U.S.A.," from *Readings in Social Psychology*, edited by Theodore M. Newcomb and Eugene L. Hartley (New York: Henry Holt and Co., Inc., 1947), pp. 475–77.

[3] Arnold W. Green, "The Middle Class Male Child and Neurosis," *American Sociological Review* (February 1946).

is a bother and a burden to a man and wife because it interferes with their dominant values and compulsions—career, social and economic success, hedonistic enjoyment—withdrawal of love occurs for prolonged periods, or indefinitely. The child is thrown into a panic and develops guilt feelings. Other investigators point out that parents of the major white-collar classes continually seek to arouse in the child a fear of losing parental love as a technique in training the child.

"In such a child," Green points out, "a disapproving glance may produce more terror than a twenty-minute lashing in little Stanislaus Wojcik."

Growing youngsters, we should also note, develop different life values, according to their class. The most impressive investigation in this regard is a study of the personalities of Harvard freshmen conducted by Harvard psychologist Charles C. McArthur. By using thematic apperception tests, he sought to find if there was a fundamental difference between upper-class boys coming from private schools and boys from the "middle classes" coming from public high schools.

The public-school boys—reflecting the dominant success culture of America—saw their father as a figure they were expected to surpass occupationally. These boys were oriented to *doing,* to accomplishing. To them, the significant time dimension is the *future.* They see college as a road to success.

The upper-class, private-school boys, in contrast, were oriented to *being* rather than doing. They expected to be evaluated for what they already were. And in terms of time, the important dimension was the *past.* Such a boy accepts his father as a model who probably was so successful that there is no point in striving to surpass him. Going to college, to this boy, offers the opportunity to live out his predetermined life role of a gentleman. And his collegiate interests center around the club and around congenial friends he will find there. As for collegiate study, his goal in marks is likely to be "the gentleman's C," which shows he is above striving. He knows that, for him, college grades have little relevance to his future career.

Psychologists, meanwhile, are finding that the lower classes are oriented to the *present,* the here right now. The people in the lower classes are the hedonists. They show little interest in thrift. They live for living's sake because tomorrow, if it ever comes, will probably be tougher. This contrasts with the prevailing white-collar youth's attitude of proper behavior and straining to make a nice impression. In surveying these two states of mind, Lee J. Cronbach, one of the nation's leading educational psychologists, asks of our educators:

"Can the school be sure that punctuality and self-control and effort are better values than casualness and self-expression and enjoyment of the moment?"[4]

With that blunt question in mind, let us turn to the role of our educational system in creating and nurturing and coping with class differences. First, the public schools.

America's public schools are often said to be a force for democracy. And when compared with private schools, they undoubtedly are. At the elementary level, the public schools often are class melting pots, particularly in old-fashioned-type communities that embrace the spectrum of income groups. But as Bevode McCall points out: "It is a fallacy to say that we have mass education in this country." Even the public schools reflect the class feelings of the teaching staff, parents, and school board.

By the time youngsters reach the senior-high-school level, two of the five major social classes have pretty well disappeared from the picture. The youngsters from the upper class have to a large extent gone off to private schools (particularly in the East). And virtually all youngsters from the real lower class — and in many towns most of the working class — have quit school. Only a little more than half of all adolescents ever complete work for a high-school diploma.

Youngsters, by the time they reach the fifth or sixth grade, have absorbed the social-class origins of their playmates, and know whom they shouldn't associate with, except on a polite basis. Awareness of the social status of one's classmates becomes more intense as the youngster gets into junior high school and starts dating. The lower-class youngster, almost universally looked down upon, often becomes a "problem" student, and typically counts the days until he can legally quit. Once he quits, of course, his class status is likely to be frozen for life. The Institute for Sex Research, for example, has found that the level at which one terminates one's formal schooling is the most precise single indicator of social level.

With most of the upper class gone off to private schools, the student bodies of our high schools are dominated by the semi-upper- (or upper-middle-) class youngster. And as McCall points out: "Teachers tend to kowtow to upper-middle-class children." Middle-class parents tend to be firm allies of the teachers because they are eager for their children to get ahead. Being human, the teachers like this. In contrast, lower-class parents tend to view teachers as authority figures and approach them, if they must, warily. The teachers, again being human — and often untrained in class behavior patterns — react negatively.

In many schools, the youngsters from the higher-prestige families form

[4] Lee J. Cronbach, *Educational Psychology* (New York: Harcourt, Brace & Co., 1954). See section on class differences.

tight cliques. An eighth-grade teacher in a Connecticut school voiced to me her discouragement because she had in her home room "a snippy little clique of girls" from the upper level of classes "who outlaw everyone who doesn't seem to belong to their group and do what they do." One girl in the clique fell by the wayside because her parents neglected to send her to dancing school. "She was dropped from everything," the teacher relates.

The public schools of America are in general not only dominated by upper-middle-class thinking but make intensive—if unwitting—efforts to reinforce values cherished by such classes. Efforts are made to hammer proper grammar into the minds and speech of the lower-class youngster even though his use of such proper language in his own neighborhood will cause neighbors to snicker and call him a sissy. The school, as Cronbach points out, also stresses that all right-thinking citizens concern themselves with social problems, government policies, and world affairs. Typically, the father of a lower-class youngster takes either a dim or indifferent view of all such preoccupations.[5]

Of America's 39,000,000 school-age youngsters, about three-quarters of a million (or 2 percent) go to private schools rather than public or parochial schools. The private or "independent" schools that are near the family home are called "day schools" and cost about $650 a year on the average; those to which the youngster is sent away are known as "boarding schools" and cost about $2,000 a year. The exclusive private school offers a student social polish, somewhat more individual attention than in a public school, discipline, and an education that is sometimes superior but very often inferior to that available free of charge at a good public school.

The United States sociologist who has looked most searchingly at the private school is E. Digby Baltzell. He is himself a graduate of St. Paul's, one of the most elite of New England's Episcopal boarding schools.

Baltzell states that the private schools—along with the Ivy League universities—"serve the sociological function of differentiating the upper class in America from the rest of the population." They acculturate "the members of the younger generation, especially those not quite to the manor born, into an upper class style of life."[6] As American cities have expanded over the decades, it has become harder and harder in metropolitan areas for a wealthy family to establish eliteness on the basis of family

[5] On these issues, see August B. Hollingshead, *Elmtown's Youth*, p. 148; W. Lloyd Warner and Paul S. Lunt, *The Social Life of a Modern Community*, p. 363; Mary Jean Schulman and Robert J. Havighurst, "Relations between Ability and Social Status in a Midwestern Community, IV, Size of Vocabulary," *Journal of Educational Psychology*, Vol. 38 (1947), p. 437.
[6] E. Digby Baltzell, *Philadelphia Gentlemen*, p. 293.

lineage (as it can still be done in smaller cities where everybody knows who is really who). One result of this is the growing importance of going to a proper private school. Baltzell makes the point that the fashionable schools have become in a sense family surrogates or substitutes dedicated to training a national upper class. The private school is coming to loom larger than the family coat of arms in determining whether a young person is qualified to be accepted in the real upper circles.

What kind of families feel impelled to pay the extra $2,000 a year to send their growing youngster away from the family hearth at a relatively tender age to boarding school? Baltzell found that a majority of the young lads at St. Paul's in a recent year were descendants of alumni. We might refine the situation somewhat. While boarding-school youngsters come from all sorts of homes—including a few humble ones, for seasoning—the vast majority of students who are accepted appear to fall into one of these six categories:

1. Descendants of wealthy alumni.
2. Descendants of once-prosperous alumni who have come into difficult times.
3. Offspring of the new rich, too successful to be ignored. These youngsters need to be given a proper background so they can be a credit to the upper class.
4. Maladjusted or emotionally threatened youngsters from upper or semi-upper homes whose parents are separated, quarreling, or frequently away from home.
5. Exceptionally promising youngsters from moderate-income families who live in districts served by public schools that are poorly staffed or that draw most of their students from the two lower classes.
6. Children of ambitious semi-upper-class families seeking to improve their status or put it on a permanent basis.[7]

Interestingly, the really rich—the families who count their dollar wealth in the tens of millions—favor public schools for their children, perhaps to keep in touch with reality. *Fortune* magazine found in a survey of the super-multimillionaires that 41 percent of the very rich used public schools for their children while 36 percent used private ones. (The rest used both.)

There appear also to be regional variations in the likelihood of families

[7]John R. Seeley, R. Alexander Sim, and Elizabeth W. Loosley, *Crestwood Heights* (New York: Basic Books Inc., 1956), p. 307.

sending children to private schools. Prospering families in the Northeast who wish to indicate their good breeding tend to think that a private-school education for their children is almost mandatory. (They typically explain the move, however, on the grounds that local public schools are inadequate for their child.) On the other hand, virtually all the upper-income families of the North Shore above Chicago send their children to the very fine local public schools. The wealthy families in Palm Springs, California, likewise virtually all send their children to the local public schools.

There are about three thousand private schools in America. Each city has its fashionable day schools for the early ages. Baltzell found in his investigation that the following sixteen leading Protestant boarding schools for young men "set the pace and bore the brunt" of criticism received by private schools for their so-called "snobbish" and "un-democratic" values, at least as of the focus period of his study:[8]

NEW ENGLAND — EPISCOPAL

St. Paul's	St. George's
St. Mark's	Kent
Groton	

NEW ENGLAND — NON-DENOMINATIONAL

Exeter	Choate
Andover	Middlesex
Taft	Deerfield
Hotchkiss	

MIDDLE AND SOUTHERN STATES

Lawrenceville	Episcopal High School
Hill	Woodbury Forest

Another school that probably should be included in the list of leading boarding schools is Milton Academy.

The five Episcopal schools plus Middlesex are considered most fashionable in most circles. They are sometimes jovially referred to as "St. Grottlesex." They tend to be paternalistic and their staffs supervise most of the details of the lads' lives. In contrast, Baltzell points out, the two oldest and richest schools, Exeter and Andover, are least exclusive socially, and stress self-reliance. Interestingly, Exeter graduates tend in overwhelming number to go to Harvard University while more graduates of Andover go to Yale.

As for the girls, those who hope to move into proper social circles must

[8] E. Digby Baltzell, *Philadelphia Gentlemen*, p. 306.

by any means necessary become accepted at a school acceptable to local society. In the East, among the schools carrying the greatest social authority are these ten: The Masters in Dobbs Ferry, New York; St. Timothy's in Stevenson, Maryland; Ethel Walker in Simsbury, Connecticut; Westover in Middlebury, Connecticut; Miss Porter's in Farmington, Connecticut; Foxcroft in Middleburg, Virginia; Abbot Academy in Andover, Massachusetts; Chatham Hall in Chatham, Virginia; Baldwin in Bryn Mawr, Pennsylvania; the Madeira School, outside Washington, D.C.

At the private schools—for males or females—the students are taught how to dance and dress and talk and comport themselves. On the school rolls and announcements, a boy is not Rudy Sandringham as he might be listed in a public school. He is Rudolph Culbrith Sandringham III. Arrangements are frequently made by the school staff to see that heterosexual contacts are of the impeccable type. The entire student body of a proper boys' school may be invited to the dance or play of a girls' school.

Non-proper outsiders often have the notion that students who go away to fashionable private schools live there in pampered luxury. That is hardly the case. The emphasis typically is on the simple, austere life. Girls often are required to wear some sort of graceless uniform, or at least a jacket. Several investigators suggest this is to remind the girls that they are serving a sort of cocoon-like apprenticeship before they burst forth as butterflies of femininity to challenge their mothers. At the schools, much is made of the "democratic" atmosphere. Everybody is equal in this segregated or hothouse-type democracy. The ostentation and status striving and snubbing that might be encountered at a public school are frowned upon. Worldly possessions such as a car or radio frequently are banned. You can't tell a millionaire's son from a billionaire's. The students may even be required to sleep on hard mattresses.

Many prep-school students tend, when they go on to college, to be uninspired students despite the cramming they have got in the prep schools. Unmotivated to study, they have been content with the gentleman's C. (Also, many have been so intensively supervised at prep school that they haven't learned the self-discipline and self-starting required to excel at a college where they are on their own.) This has created a problem for the Ivy League colleges, which have traditionally favored the qualified sons of alumni, who mostly attend prep schools. This favoritism is probably reasonable since, being private institutions, they are to a large extent dependent upon gifts of wealthy alumni. In recent years, with the great rise in collegiate admission standards resulting from the growing demand for college facilities, the Ivy League colleges have taken more and more of the bright, success-oriented "hustlers" from the nation's public high schools. In 1958, Princeton finally became a predominantly public-school-educated institution. The public-high-school graduates tend to do better scholastically than the private-school graduates. One explanation given is that private-school graduates, not motivated to strive, frequently do not live up to the promise of their college-board examinations.

Whether you are a public-school boy or a preppie, there are clear advantages to going to an Ivy League college (rather than to just any university). Baltzell puts the advantage in overwhelming terms for people who aspire to the upper class. He says: "It is more advantageous, socially, and economically, to have graduated from Harvard, Yale or Princeton with a low academic standing than to have been a Phi Beta Kappa at some less fashionable institution."[9]

Ernest Havemann and Patricia Salter West put the advantage of going to one of these Big Three in dollar terms. In their study of 10,000 graduates of American colleges, they found that graduates of these three colleges (then averaging $7,365 a year) were earning $1,200 more a year than graduates of other Ivy League schools, $2,000 more than the gradu-ates of seventeen technical colleges, $2,200 more than graduates of the Big Ten, and $3,000 more than graduates of "all other Midwest col-leges."[10] (The fact that the Princeton-Yale-Harvard men were frequently the sons of wealthy businessmen to start with presumably helps account for their enviable income position.) Havemann and West also noted that, whatever the university, the students who are supported in college by their parents tend to end up with higher-paying jobs than the poorer boys who have to work their way through college.

The Ivy League schools, it should be pointed out in fairness, produce more per 1,000 graduates who become listed in *Who's Who* than any other group of colleges. However, as a group, they are outranked by several individual small Eastern colleges (Amherst, Wesleyan, Swarthmore, Hamilton, and Williams) and are pressed hard by several distinguished but less publicized non-Eastern colleges (Oberlin, De Pauw, Carleton, Reed, Knox, Wooster, Lawrence, Park, and Occidental).

Whatever school a poor boy chooses, his chances of getting ahead in a gratifying way will depend to some extent on the career for which he is studying. West has pointed out that a professional career (such as that of a scientist) offers much more opportunity to the poor-but-talented boy than a business career in a corporation. In business, she says, "there is a greater chance that your 'background' may defeat you." In some of the

[9] Ibid., p. 319.
[10] Ernest Havemann and Patricia Salter West, *They Went to College* (New York: Har-court, Brace & Co., 1952), especially Chapter 15.

professions, in contrast, good college grades are far more likely to be decisive.

Even in the professions, however, there has been a sharply growing separation of the poor from the well-off as far as specific professions are concerned. West states that the students who must work their way through college now increasingly go into the lower-paid professions such as the arts, education, and the ministry; whereas the students who are family-financed during college increasingly tend to go into the more lucrative professions such as medicine, dentistry, and the law.

Clubs and fraternities play a role in helping sons and daughters of the elite to develop their sense of unity among themselves and apartness from the general run of students. These clubs are valued at some of the Ivy League schools because of the influx of public-school graduates onto the campuses. C. Wright Mills points this up vividly when he describes how young men are sized up in proper adult circles: "Harvard or Yale or Princeton is not enough. It is the really exclusive prep school that counts, for that determines which of the two Harvards one attends." The clubs and cliques at college are made up of people who went to the proper private schools. "One's friends at Harvard," Mills explains, "are friends made at prep school. That is why in the upper social classes it does not mean much merely to have a degree from an Ivy League college. That is assumed; the point is not Harvard, but which Harvard? By Harvard one means Porcellian, Fly, or A.D.; by Yale one means Zeta Psi or Fence or Delta Kappa Epsilon; by Princeton, Cottage, Tiger, Cap & Gown, or Ivy. It is the prestige of the properly certified secondary education followed by a proper club in a proper Ivy League college that is the standard admission ticket to the world of urban clubs and parties in any major city in the nation."[11]

It might be noted that merely winning a degree from Yale, Princeton, or Harvard does not entitle one to join the local Yale, Princeton, or Harvard club in his city. One must be proposed, seconded, and approved.

At Harvard, the "right" Harvard (as Mills would put it) consists of only 15 percent of the student body. The rest of the students are free to develop the Harvard ideal of an intellectual elite regardless of background. (For this, Harvard has earned, and justly deserves, a worldwide reputation.) The elite 15 percent are typically sifted out at the sophomore level by the Hasty Pudding Club. Then, in the final years, if one survives the sifting, one may be invited to one of the dozen "final" clubs such as Porcellian.

[11] C. Wright Mills, *The Power Elite* (New York: Oxford University Press, 1956), p. 67.

Princeton has the appearance of a more democratic arrangement in its eating clubs. After a revolt of the sophomore class in 1949–50, it was agreed that every Princeton sophomore would receive an invitation to one of the seventeen eating clubs. What could be more democratic? Furthermore, every club began taking Jewish students into membership. Status lines, however, have reappeared. I have found Princeton students able to list with impressive unanimity the status ranking of the clubs, from the highest down to the seventeenth. Ivy, Cottage, Cap & Gown, and Colonial were the first four, and Prospect was Number 17.

At many universities including the great state universities—with students coming from a wide range on the social scale—the fraternities play an important role in helping the more elite in background to protect their social rank. Certain types of "undesirable" students are often barred by national policy of fraternities at campuses having local chapters. Sometimes the exclusionary national policies are written, but more often these days they are unwritten or softly written since *some* college administrations have been cracking down on fraternities with too blatantly restrictive clauses such as those specifying that only students of "Aryan blood" are acceptable. Today, if there is any written restrictive policy, it is likely to be couched under such carefully chosen words as "socially acceptable."

Exclusiveness of fraternities and sororities is frequently based on family background, social poise, and the "right" racial characteristics and religious background.[12] In general, the mood of most students is toward less arbitrary exclusion of groups because of race or religion. It is the alumni dominating the national fraternity councils and their paid officers who mainly are fighting to keep exclusionary policies.

There have been a number of moves in recent years to judge possible fraternity members solely on the basis of personal worth rather than by such gross categorical basis as ethnic background. But institutions focusing on personal worth and character (and not spurning people by categories) still tend to be exceptional. The national officers of a number of Greek-letter fraternities have resisted the idea of removing all restrictive policies, and have stubbornly opposed in most cases the idea of allowing each local chapter to set its own admission standards. Some have recoiled in horror at such a preposterous notion.

The situations I have pointed to in this chapter suggest, I believe, that our educational system is still a far-from-perfect incubator of democracy. If

---

[12] Alfred McClung Lee, *Fraternities without Brotherhood* (Boston: Beacon Press, 1955), p. 15.

democracy is to be a reality in our nation, it should start in our schools. Further, I think we should all bear in mind that the meanness of class distinctions is more painfully felt during school years than during any other period of people's lives.

CHAPTER 17

Gauging Social Position

We have seen during the course of this book that a host of factors carry weight with the status conscious. The six that sociologists have found most readily measurable on scales—occupation, education, income source, dwelling area, house type, and amount of income—work best when applied to a specific community. When any application is attempted on a national scale, they become at best crude indicators. This is particularly true of the last three. Conditions vary from town to town and the size-of-income factor is complicated, as we have noted, by a variety of anomalies.

What follows is an indication of the kind of scales the sociologists use to estimate the social position an individual holds in his community. I will list four scales. (I've eliminated from the six listed above the final one on size of income and have combined the two home factors, #4 and #5.)

Since some of the seven-point scales are believed to be more accurate indicators of status than others, those are assigned more weight. The status score on each scale would be multiplied by the weight assigned to that scale. These are weights that might well be used: the "occupation" score would be multiplied by 5; the "education" score would be multiplied by 4; the "source of income" score would be multiplied by 3; and the "kind of home" score would be multiplied by 2. Thus, if on the "occupation" scale the subject's status level is 4, that would be multiplied by 5 for a score of 20 for that scale. The lower the score, the higher the status.

STATUS LEVEL	OCCUPATION
1	Major executives of large firms or successful licensed professionals with advanced degrees.

2	Major executives of small firms; middle management executives of large firms; moderately thriving licensed professionals; faculty members of the better colleges; editors, critics, commentators, and other opinion molders.
3	Minor-responsibility business jobs; white-collar supervisors; professionals without licensing protection; high-school teachers.
4	Supervisors of manual workers; skilled white-collar workers; technicians; high-responsibility blue-collar employees.
5	Salaried manual workers; semi-skilled white-collar workers; semi-professionalized service workers.
6	Semi-skilled manual workers; white-collar machine attendants.
7	Casual laborers, domestic servants.

STATUS LEVEL	EDUCATION
1	Professional- or graduate-school attainment.
2	Graduate of a four-year college.
3	Graduate of a two-year college or at least one and one half years of college (but without a degree).
4	High-school graduate plus "trade school" or "business school" education or attendance for a year or less at a regular college.
5	High-school graduate.
6	Attended high school but did not graduate.
7	No more than eight grades of schooling.

STATUS LEVEL	SOURCE OF INCOME
1	Most of income from inherited wealth.
2	Most of annual income from investments and savings gained by earner.
3	Most of income from profits of business or fees from practice of profession.
4	Most of income from salary of job or commissions on sales.
5	Most of income from hourly wages from job or piecework.
6	Most of income from private assistance (friends, relatives, etc.) plus part-time work.

7	Most of income from public relief or non-respectable sources such as bootlegging.
STATUS LEVEL	**KIND OF HOME**
1	Own two homes, both with fashionable addresses.
2	Fine, large, well-kept home in "nicest" part of town; or live in high-status apartment building with doorman and tastefully decorated foyer.
3	A good, roomy house in one of the better sections of town or countryside; or live in a modern, well-kept apartment building.
4	A small, modern development house costing less than $15,000; or a plain, non-fashionable larger one in a nice but non-fashionable neighborhood; or live in an adequate but rather plain apartment building.
5	A double house or row house or an old walk-up apartment building where cooking odors and garbage are likely to be noticed in the hallways.
6	A small, plain, run-down house or apartment, badly in need of paint or redecoration, in one of poorer sections of town.
7	A dilapidated house or apartment in the poorest section of town.

The total score—when the weighted scores for each scale are added—can range anywhere from 14 to 98. For most people, a score of 25 or under would indicate they are members of the real upper class. A score of from 26 to 43 would typically indicate a semi-upper status. Those scoring between 44 and 61 would probably fall in the limited-success class. A score of from 62 to 79 indicates a working-class status. A score of 80 or more means the person would probably be considered to have a real-lower-class status.

III. Strains of Status

CHAPTER 18

The Price of Status Striving

The strainers of America can be seen on many streets: people who have accepted the American Dream of limitless opportunities, but are having personal difficulty in making much headway toward achieving the dream. Inhabitants of some of our homogeneous suburban developments are often caught up in a particularly dangerous kind of straining in their consumption patterns.[1]

Many people, on the other hand, do resist the temptation to strain in emulative consumption. Working-class men who manage to set up their own small enterprise and prosper often continue to live pretty much in the workingman's style of life and in the same neighborhood. Engineers, also, tend to live contentedly, and relatively frugally, within their means. Anyone who lives among people who have a little less money than he does has a better chance of achieving contentment and avoiding strain.

In general, however, Americans outside the blue-collar group are strivers. A substantial number have difficulty adjusting to swift upward mobility; an even larger number have difficulty adjusting to the frustration of little or no mobility; and quite a few have difficulty adjusting to the assumed humiliation of downward mobility. Americans have difficulty accepting the fact, but a stairway can be tumbled down, as well as climbed up. This is especially true for those who have brief moments of glory, high esteem, or high prosperity, such as beautiful actresses, oil wildcatters, advertising account executives, television comedians, and star athletes.[2]

Many socially declining or downward-mobile people turn to alcohol or

---

[1] William H. Whyte, Jr., *Organization Man*, p. 207.

[2] S. Kirson Weinberg and Henry Arond, "The Occupational Culture of the Boxer," *American Journal of Sociology*, Vol. 57 (March 1952), pp. 460–69.

drugs for support. Some become promiscuous. They often become known as troublemakers, with chips on their shoulders. Even their best friends become perplexed as to how to approach them without being snarled at. Wives find them disagreeable as mates. Such declining males are gloom-ridden, and those becoming seriously disturbed emotionally tend to develop sadistic-masochistic (destructive or self-destructive) attitudes.

The people who succeed in moving up the class scale in a conspicuous way must typically pay a price, too. As we have indicated, they feel impelled to take on new habits, new modes of living, new attitudes and beliefs, new addresses, new affiliations, new friends—and discard old ones. The resolute striver is a lonely man making his way on a slippery slope.

Often the upward striver is resented and rejected by the group he is leaving. Sociological studies in the Army have revealed that, when an individual begins "bucking for a promotion," he alienates himself—at least at the enlisted level—from his own group. His own group, in fact, may begin making "sucking and kissing noises" when the striver is sighted.

An effort to climb that fails can put the person involved into a particularly precarious position. Some time ago, a boy from an aspiring, moderately well-to-do Fairfield County, Connecticut, family "went away" from the local high school to Choate, a high-prestige boarding school. In a few months he was back at the public high school. He had flunked out of Choate. Many of his old public-school classmates seemed gratified by his humiliation. More interesting, the lad, in scrambling to be re-accepted by his old public-school acquaintances, became loudly and almost continuously contemptuous of the whole private-school setup.

If an upward striver does succeed, however, and goes on to become a conspicuous success, his old associates left behind forget their old resentment and brag fondly of having known him when.

The person who succeeds dramatically in moving up the class scale tends to be, to begin with, relatively rootless. He or she has become isolated from the way of life that the average young person has with his neighborhood. W. Lloyd Warner, in his study of Yankee City, Jonesville, and of America's big-business leaders, was struck in each instance by the role that neighborhood ties play in hindering upward mobility. He was impressed by the odd fact that among the relatively few big-business leaders of lower-level family origin—sons of laborers, white-collar workers, farmers—a large proportion were of immigrant backgrounds. Their rootlessness, he concluded, gave them an advantage.[3]

---

[3] W. Lloyd Warner and James C. Abegglen, *Big Business Leaders in America* (New York: Harper and Brothers, 1955), p. 193.

Warner concludes that, for mobility to occur, the many emotional and social obligations and engagements holding a man to his place must be broken. William Foote Whyte reached much the same conclusion after studying the college boy—who moves upward—and the corner boy—who does not—in Cornerville. Both are anxious to get ahead. "The difference between them," Whyte decided, "is that the college boy either does not tie himself to a group of close friends, or else is willing to sacrifice his friendship with those who do not advance as fast as he does. The corner boy is tied to his group by a network of reciprocal obligations from which he is either unwilling or unable to break away."[4]

The restless, migratory habits of many Americans, then, appear to be an asset for those aspiring to move upward. The moving van, in the words of Louis Kronenberger, is "a symbol of more than our restlessness; it is the most conclusive evidence possible of our progress."[5] Executing an end run by moving to a strange community has its advantages. A study of migration from Kentucky showed that sons who left their home communities tended to show more of a balance in favor of upward mobility than the sons who stayed home. The man who manages to make a spectacular advance within his own community must face across the class lines the past he has left behind. To some this is embarrassing.

A person who becomes adept at isolating himself from his past, and taking on the coloration of what he hopes is the future, may unwittingly take a manipulative attitude toward individuals around him. He can be charming, and yet he may seem to lack warmth. Such a person is wary of emotional involvement, and may even reach the point where, as Warner puts it, he "arouses a feeling of unpleasantness in others."

Among women, at least, there is further evidence indicating that the upward-mobile career woman is often driven by attitudes generated by humiliating childhood experiences. A study of mobile vs. non-mobile career women in Montgomery, Alabama, showed that the upward-mobile ones had at one time been rejected by their community. Some of these, as children, had also been neglected by parents who obviously favored a sister or brother.

Upward mobility also can put a severe strain on a marriage if the wife is less skilled than the husband in taking on new habits, attitudes, and friendships. Marriage is, as one sociologist put it, "a mutual mobility bet." Leland Gordon, economist of Denison University, cites the classic kind of situation where one partner is the loser: "When a bright young clerk in a chain store moves into a position as manager of a branch store, it is

---

[4] William Foote Whyte, *Street Corner Society*, p. 107.
[5] Louis Kronenberger, *Company Manners*, p. 175.

imperative that he join the country club set. But sometimes his salesgirl wife has not grown up with him. As he moves up and out, she is left behind. Many become alcoholics." Children, too, often find living with a rapidly upward-mobile couple a strain. They tend to feel isolated and insecure; and many compensate by becoming chronic talkers.

Both upward- and downward-mobile persons tend to be more prejudiced in their attitudes toward Jews and Negroes than people who are not in motion, socially.[6] Perhaps it is because they are insecure in their own status.

The tension, insecurity, and rootlessness characterizing many zealous upward strivers make them prone to certain emotional disorders. The mobility appears to increase mental strain. Hollingshead and his associates at Yale found that, when the social mobility of mental patients was compared with that of a control group of non-patients, the psychoneurotics and schizophrenics both showed clearly a record of more upward mobility than the normal control group.

Hollingshead makes a distinction between "climbers" (who achieve at least some success in their aspirations) and "strainers" (who achieve little success despite their very considerable efforts). The climbers, he finds, often encounter their first serious trouble when they try to crash the highest social level, and are rejected as upstarts. They typically react with depression, severe anxiety, and, occasionally, suicide attempts. In contrast, the strainers are dreamers and schemers rushing from one pursuit to another. (James Thurber's *The Secret Life of Walter Mitty*, Hollingshead finds, is a quite accurate fictional portrayal of the typical strainer.) Hollingshead has found that many psychoneurotics and psychotics in the limited-success class were haunted by occupational frustration that they blamed on education. In one sample, more than 90 percent of the psychoneurotics in that class felt handicapped by the amount of education they had received. Many, also, had aspirations that were far above their accomplishments. The growing barrier, based on education, between people of the limited-success class and those in the semi-upper class evidently has been making wrecks of some of the lower-level people without college education who still believe in the American Dream of unlimited opportunities.

Membership in each social class tends to impose its own kind of strain on people in it. There seems to be general agreement that the most severe strain (or the least capacity to withstand strain) is in the bottom class. People of that category have twice as many psychiatric breakdowns

---

[6] Joseph Greenblum and Leonard I. Pearlin, "Vertical Mobility and Prejudice: A Socio-Psychological Analysis," from *Class Status and Power*, pp. 480–90.

as they should have if mental illness were distributed evenly over the population. A team of sociologists and psychiatrists at Yale University, headed by August B. Hollingshead and Frederick C. Redlich, made an exhaustive study of the relationship between mental illness and social class.[7] These investigators found that a person in the bottom class was eleven times as likely to suffer from schizophrenia as a member of the top class.[8]

What is more startling, perhaps, is the discrimination shown against persons of the lower classes by psychiatrists, both in private practice and at the free or low-cost clinics. This discrimination, as we will note later, arises in large part from the inability of upper-class psychiatrists to communicate with lower-class patients; so that the patients are not regarded as good prospects for extended individual treatment.

The Yale team found that, even at the outpatient clinic where cost is no factor, "the higher an individual's social class position, the more likely he was to be accepted for treatment, to be treated by highly trained personnel, and to be treated intensively over a long period."[9] (Students treated the lower classes, residents-in-training tended to be assigned to middle-class patients, and the senior staff members took the higher-class patients.) It was found that these clinics spend eight times as much money treating an upper-middle-class patient as they do treating a working-class patient. There is a tendency to give individual psychotherapy to the higher classes, and administer shock treatment, drugs, organic therapy, etc., to the lower-class patients.

Hollingshead and Redlich report that this finding of discrimination "came as a 'bolt out of the blue' for the men who determined the policies of this clinic. It was certainly not planned. A similar situation is found in the public mental hospitals, where, also without regard to the ability of the patients' families to pay, the acute schizophrenics in class III are more likely to get psychotherapy than class IV and V patients in the same disease group who entered the hospital at approximately the same time."[10] The working-class or bottom-class schizophrenic, they added, may receive one or two series of organic treatments in a public hospital. If these do not succeed, "the patient drifts to the back wards where, in stultifying isolation, he regresses even more into a world of his own."

[7] August B. Hollingshead and Frederick C. Redlich, *Social Class and Mental Illness.*
[8] August B. Hollingshead and Frederick C. Redlich, "Social Stratification and Psychiatric Disorders," *American Sociological Review,* Vol. 18, No. 2 (April 1953); see also Joseph A. Kahl, *The American Class Structure,* p. 192.
[9] Jerome K. Myers and Leslie Schaffer, "Social Stratification and Psychiatric Practice: A Study of an Out-Patient Clinic," *American Sociological Review,* Vol. 19, No. 3 (June 1954).
[10] August B. Hollingshead and Frederick C. Redlich, *Social Class and Mental Illness,* p. 351.

CHAPTER 19

The Special Status Problems of Jews

One of the persistent puzzles of American life is the tendency in thousands of communities to erect barriers against Jews. Jewish people are singled out more than any other white ethnic category for such fence building.

This persistent treatment of the Jews in America as a group apart has become a question of mounting economic urgency. With the great growth of bigness in business organization, the Jew is seeing his world of opportunity shrinking. In the past, the Jews have survived by being able, in many cases, to prosper in their own enterprises. This assured them that they would not be at the mercy of a prejudiced Gentile employer.

Now, however, many Jews face the economic necessity of working within the hierarchy of the large corporations. The individual entrepreneur, at the producing level at least, is becoming more and more the lonely exception. Bigness is the mode of the era. And it is the rare large corporation that considers Jews on their qualifications alone in filling all its ranks. Some corporations shun Jews almost entirely. This is particularly true in insurance, banking, automobile making, utilities, oil, steel, heavy industry. Others profess hospitality to Jews; but then it often turns out that Jews are really welcomed only in the "inside" jobs requiring high intellectual capacity such as research, creativity, actuarial skill, etc. The "outside" jobs, calling for contact with clients or the public or with stockholders, are primarily reserved for Gentiles.

Another problem facing the Jew in the corporation is the five-o'clock shadow. Jew and Gentile may work amiably together all day in the corporate hierarchy, but, come five o'clock, the Gentile may go off to one of the city's elite clubs, and the Jew cannot follow. Or the Jew may have his own firm and see his biggest rival go into the town's elite club at five o'clock. And the elite social club, as we have noted, is becoming more and more the place where important business decisions often tend to jell.

It is hoped that what follows may offer both Jews and Gentiles some illumination on this curious aspect of our community life.

While I was in Northeast City talking with people who were identified as the "real powers" of the community, my primary, announced purpose was to study the elite structure of their city. I went into this quite thoroughly with each of them; and they were most co-operative and informative. I also had a second, unannounced purpose, and that was to draw them out, spontaneously and confidentially, on the subject of Jews. In this I was looking for insights that might explain why the lines were drawn against Jews at many points in the city's social and business life, especially at the elite or upper-class level. I was curious to know, in the face of the frequently stated great respect for Jews, why few Jewish names appeared among the officers of most of the banks, utilities, and large industrial firms. (Mostly, the leading Jews were merchants, lawyers, or textile-plant operators.) Also, why were there either no Jewish names or few Jewish names listed as members of the elite men's club (Pioneer's), the elite women's club (Martha Washington), and the three leading country clubs? And why was it, I wondered, that Jews and non-Jews worked wholeheartedly together on civic fund-raising projects, but went their separate ways socially? (All names of clubs and individuals cited in Northeast City, I should add, have been altered and are fictitious.)

I did not ask any of these questions directly and bluntly. That would have endangered the free flow of communication. Instead, I sought to lead my informants—after they had become relaxed by talking about the city's elite clubs, churches, etc.—into a general discussion of the role of Jews in American life and in the city's life. Subsequently I guided them into the desired areas. I made it clear I was simply trying to unravel a situation that reappears in city after city, and was not peculiar to Northeast City, which is a representative middle-sized United States metropolis. And I sought to create a permissive atmosphere by expressing keen interest in whatever they said about Jews. In a few cases I experimentally raised arguments against their viewpoints. This, invariably, drove them into a more cautious, proper tone. Typically, they became quite voluble on the subject of Jews. The only one who was ill at ease throughout was a man on the membership committee of the most elite country club (Gentry). (Since conducting these interviews, which took place in November and December, 1957, I have conducted similar but less intensive probings with a score of upper-class individuals in Fairfield County, Connecticut, and the later findings have illuminated but not modified the impressions I gained in Northeast City. Altogether, I have sounded out forty-five upper-class non-Jews, confidentially and with seeming casualness, on the subject of Jews.)

I suppose I should declare at this point that I am a Gentile. That puts me in what Jerome Weidman calls "the enemy camp." On the other hand—to declare my biases as far as I know them—I have had the conviction, based on my personal encounters with Jews as neighbors and colleagues, that it is a pity more non-Jews don't get to know Jews as friends.

The elite informants in Northeast City were certainly not as hostile to Jews in their conversations as you would assume from all the barriers that have been put up against Jews in their city. In fact, several seemed a little ashamed of the barriers as hardly worthy of as civilized a community as they liked to think Northeast City is.

In the social life of Northeast City, at least at the upper level, there is virtually no intermingling between Gentile and Jew. When I asked Mrs. Smyth, a First Family socialite, about the degree to which Jewish families take part in the city's club life, she said: "They have their own lovely club." With that, she gave me a broad wink.

The only city club where there is much intermingling is the Downtown Club. And, as I've noted, several of my informants repeatedly made the point that it was a "businessman's club." The more restrictive Pioneer's Club, in contrast, was considered a "social" or "community" club. Even at the Downtown Club, I was told by two informants, the Jewish membership has been "under control."

One well-known sociological force at work in causing many Gentiles to isolate Jews undoubtedly is that of status striving through exclusiveness. As the early sociologist, Max Weber, put it: "Status honor always rests upon distance and exclusiveness." To be exclusive, you must build fences to exclude those you like to think are not as elite as yourself. You can do this on personal worth, but it is much easier to exclude whole categories of people, such as Jews.

Another sociological factor at work in Northeast City and elsewhere is status protection in the face of threat. Entrenched old guarders need a mechanism to put challengers in their place. Jews, being perhaps the most enterprising of all American ethnic groups, are commonly viewed as most challenging.

The influential Gentiles I consulted in Northeast City offered a great variety of explanations for the local social and business barriers. Some of the explanations, undoubtedly, are rationalizations. They have been developed to explain a situation that violates the American Creed and so is embarrassing.

In sifting through the explanations offered for the barriers, these ten contentions stand out. I will list them in the order of frequency with which they were raised.

1. *The alleged "clannishness" of Jewish people.* This assumed clannishness, of course, where it exists, is quite probably the Jews' response to discrimination. Anyone who is being discriminated against feels better if he is among others in the same boat. No one likes to face discrimination alone. At any rate, ten Gentile informants in Northeast City cited this

clannishness as an explanation for the fact that there was little social intermingling with Jews.

Mr. Wallace, the realtor, said: "Jews are the most clannish, integrated people there are. They've always been segregated so they stick together now." Two informants cited a situation at a local high school to support this point. It seems that school authorities became concerned because fraternities and sororities were developing along religious lines, and formally banned them. The Gentile sororities and fraternities, according to my informants, were disbanded, but the Jewish ones have continued underground with strong support from Jewish parents, who reportedly do not want their children seriously dating Gentiles.[1]

This alleged clannishness of Jewish people, to the minds of my Gentile informants, not only helps explain the apartness that exists, but is a factor in convincing them that the apartness should continue as long as Jews lead their own social life. In Northeast City, they felt the assumed clannishness posed an inundation threat to any Gentile club that lowered its barriers. Mr. Ross, an industrialist, said: "When they clan up within a club it is not good."

There is no good evidence that modern Jews are any more clannish than Gentiles. Studies among children, in fact, indicate that Gentile children are more clannish than Jewish children.[2] More to the point, perhaps, is the discovery that the same people who accuse the Jews of being standoffish also accuse them of trying to be too eager to integrate with non-Jews.[3]

Whatever the precise situation is in this area, beclouded with irrationality, it seems clear that any easing of the barriers would be aided by a reduction of the self-segregating tendencies of both groups.

Historian Max Lerner feels that the cohesiveness of Jews may have intensified during the thirties and forties as an instinctive response to news of Hitler's persecution of the Jews, and of the trials of Jewish people abroad in building their new Israeli state. He states that the "emphasis within the American Jewish group shifted away from assimilation toward a sometimes overmilitant assertion of their uniqueness and separateness as a historical community."[4] Apparently, however, the trend has now been

---

[1] John P. Dean, "Patterns of Socialization and Association between Jews and Non-Jews," *Jewish Social Studies*, Vol. VII, No. 3 (1955).

[2] A. Harris and G. Watson, "Are Jewish or Gentile Children More Clannish?" *Journal of Social Psychology*, Vol. 24 (1946), pp. 71–76.

[3] T. W. Adorno et al., *The Authoritarian Personality* (New York: Harper & Brothers, 1950), pp. 66–75.

[4] Max Lerner, *America as a Civilization*, p. 510.

reversed. The American Jewish Committee made a study of a community called "Riverton." This reveals that younger Jews are twice as eager to participate socially in their general community as older Jews.[5]

2. *The alleged assertiveness of Jewish people.* This sometimes came up, from Northeast City informants, in back-handed references such as: "He's not aggressive like some Jews." A highly admired Jewish lawyer was referred to as being "aggressive, but not in a way that bothers." Among the elite Gentile informants, nine made some comment that assumed that assertiveness was a Jewish trait.

This image of assertiveness, psychologists find, is the kind of stereotype nurtured by a great deal of selective remembering and selective forgetting. A non-Jew will remember the assertive Jew and not think of the modest, self-effacing Jew in terms of Jewishness. Similarly, he may encounter brashness in dozens of Gentiles without thinking of brashness as being a Gentile trait.

3. *Jewish people are seen as different.* This feeling, frequently expressed, probably reflects the "consciousness of kind" factor at work. Many people apparently can't rise above their primitive birds-of-a-feather flocking impulse. Mr. Green, partner in one of the city's most elite law firms, said many of the city's leading Jews didn't seem to catch the Northeast City "spirit." He wasn't able to explain what that "spirit" was, with any clarity.

Partly, the sensing of differentness in Jewish people probably has a religious basis. Partly, it may spring from the physiognomy of some Jews. One bank president in Northeast City, Mr. Williams, talked at length about facial differences, real or imaginary, he had perceived in German Jews as distinguished from East European Jews. He mentioned a prominent, widely respected Jewish lawyer in town and said, as if in wonderment, "To look at him you wouldn't know he was Jewish." And, partly, the sensing of differentness may spring from the fact that traditionally Jews have been city people and are indentified in people's minds with the cosmopolitanism of the city. (They were long excluded from owning land.) Harvard psychologist Gordon W. Allport suggests that people who felt hostile toward cities may unwittingly have transferred their hostility to Jews.[6] In some small American towns where there isn't a single Jewish resident, anti-Semitism has been found to run high.

4. *Jewish people are "smart."* Six of the prominent Northeast City

---

[5] John Slawson, "Social Discrimination," American Jewish Committee, New York City.
[6] Gordon W. Allport, *The Nature of Prejudice* (Cambridge, Massachusetts: Addison-Wesley Publishing Co., Inc., 1954), pp. 250–51.

Gentiles made references to this in one form or another; and it is difficult to assess how much of this is admiration and how much of it is envy or apprehension.

5. *Some Jewish people behave in ways that bother some Gentiles.* The reverse also, of course, is true.

Mr. Potter, the banker, in talking of the exclusionary policies of clubs, said: "Anyone would want Joe Goldstein in the club. He is soft-spoken. The fact is, however, that a percentage of Jewish people are considered to be noisy. They don't have the good fortune I have of having a weak voice." And another banker, Mr. Williams—who has no Jews in his organization—said: "Certain traits stick out. They have a certain manner of speech, they are argumentative and wave their arms."

There may be a differentness between Gentile and Jew in temperament that has some basis in fact, as generalizations go. The Jewish home builder in Chicago, in talking of his Jewish homeowners, described them as "explosive" and eager for new experiences. He attributed this to the pressures under which they live. A sociologist in Chicago, in talking of Jews, said they tend to be more "volatile" than Gentiles. The wife of a playwright mentioned that predominantly Jewish audiences tend to be more excitable than Gentile audiences. She attributed this to the fact that many "are geared so high."

6. *Jewish people tend to be individualists.* This was usually cited by Northeast Gentiles to explain why Jews were not found among the executives of the major corporations in town. Individualism is a trait traditionally cherished in America; but in the modern era of corporate "team playing" we are seeing a conflict between ideal and practicality.

7. *In business, Jewish people are bold and impatient.* Mr. Whitcomb, head of one of the city's larger corporations and a civic leader, said: "The bright Jewish fellow isn't temperamentally inclined to take the long haul of working twenty-five years to get to the top of a company. Sidney Klein and I were good friends. [Sidney Klein was for long the city's most successful Jew.] Sid worked in a cigar store as a lad. He couldn't see it when I went to work for Consolidated Corporation. He said he would rather get in a small company and get there faster. He would chide me about my $2 raises, while he was already making big money. The Jews know you can make it faster in a small company." In short, this is the old-fashioned American spirit of risk-taking so insistently glorified in public statements by our Gentile industrial statesmen, who cautiously manage their own corporations by committee, with the counsel of survey makers and Univac machines.

8. *Some Gentiles feel Jewish businessmen are impersonal and not "fair-minded."* Several Northeast City businessmen said they would feel uneasy if they got in a jam and had to deal with Jews. One asked: "If this plant got into trouble, would Jews back us up as much as non-Jews if they saw a loss coming up?"

This attitude of the Gentiles would appear to be merely an illustration of "consciousness of kind" again at work. If a person gets into a jam, he feels he will receive a better break from his "own kind" of person, who should feel a group loyalty to be nice to him. Jews presumably feel the same way. (Very often, it should be added, the treatment one gets, in a showdown, from his "own kind" leaves him wishing he had left his fate to an objective outsider.)

9. *Many Jewish businessmen are felt to be money-minded.* When I reviewed the notes of my interviews on the Jewish situation in Northeast City, I was struck by the frequent use the Gentile informants made of the words "money" or "dollars" in talking of Jews. This was so common that I suspect the word "money" has become imbedded in the Gentile's image of Jews.

Here again we appear to be in the misty area of stereotype and projection. According to a study by Dorothy T. Spoerl, Jewish students being tested showed no more preoccupation with "economic value" than did Protestant or Catholic students.[7] Another study showed that the same people who deplored the money-mindedness of Jews were the ones who agreed overwhelmingly with the questionnaire statement that "financial success is an important measure of the man" and that "every child should learn the value of money early." As for the widespread image of Jews as "international bankers" and "Wall Street brokers," this amuses even the Wall Street folks. The truth is that there are relatively few Jews in either category.

10. *The wives of Gentile and Jew often create the barrier.* Mr. Ross, the industrialist, felt that Gentile wives are often more likely to be "petty and narrow" about Jews than their husbands. He said the wives are more concerned "about social status, and more apt to become intense about the Jew." And Mr. Kyle, the contractor, said, in trying to explain why most of his clubs excluded Jews: "In choosing new members for a club, you scrutinize not only the man but his wife. A man may be fine, but his wife may not get along with other women. Women are more isolated. And there is bound to be some jealousy on the part of our women if the Jewish women have mink coats and our women do not."

[7] Dorothy Spoerl, "The Jewish Stereotype," *Yivo Annual of Jewish Social Science,* Vol. 7 (1952), p. 268.

In many communities, there is far more self-segregation of both Gentiles and Jews at the wife level than at the husband level. And, significantly, it is the wife, rather than the husband, who makes most of the
social arrangements for a family. John P. Dean found, in his study of
Elmira, New York, Jews, that the women were much more likely to be
self-segregating than their husbands. He found that while only 12 percent
of the Jewish men confined their community activities to purely Jewish
organizations, 48 percent of the wives did. Whatever the reason for this
greater isolation, it would indicate that the wives have fewer personal,
friendly contacts with Gentiles than their husbands do.

The foregoing seems to represent the broad outlines of the barrier in
Gentile outlook separating the higher-status Gentile and Jew in a representative American city. Much of it, as indicated, is evidently just a picture
in the minds of Gentiles produced by lack of personal contact with real-life
Jewish people that might correct the distortions.

The Northeast City businessman who seemed to have had the most
first-hand contact with Jewish people was Mr. Wallace, the realtor. And he
made what was perhaps the most accurate summary of the situation. He
said: "Jews are just like everybody else—good, bad, and stinking."
Perhaps I should add that I talked with three leading Jewish businessmen
in Northeast City. What particularly impressed me, in view of what I had
been hearing, was that all three men were the complete reverse of the
stereotypes. They appeared to be restrained, responsible, soft-spoken,
fair-minded, patient, subdued in their tastes, and very proud of their city.
They acknowledged the barriers. In fact, they seemed philosophically—
almost good-humoredly—resigned to them as handicaps that had to be
accepted. Still more interesting, they spoke with warm respect of several
of the Gentile leaders who had, when pressed to account for the barriers,
uttered derogatory stereotype comments about Jewish people.

The kind of Gentile attitudes I have cited, whatever their substance,
seem to represent the state of mind that must be modified before any
effort to produce substantially more intermingling between Gentiles and
Jews will be really successful. This state of mind seems to stand as a
challenge to both Gentiles and Jews of good will.

The Gentile informants, I should stress, were far from unanimous in
their support of the barriers or in being critical of Jewish people. Several,
during the long and frank talks, never once uttered a remark that could be
construed as critical of Jewish people. They seemed to feel the barriers
were archaic hangovers.

It is my impression that the most important step to be taken in any community to reduce business and social barriers between Gentile and Jew is to develop a broader base of informal, friendly intermingling. Successful Jews who would like to belong to elite clubs now dominated by exclusionary Gentiles should examine their own socializing habits for self-segregating tendencies. They can't expect to be comfortable in a club with Gentiles if they haven't gotten to know these people first, through informal home entertaining and friendly intermingling in community affairs. And the latter typically don't require invitation. The same applies to Gentiles who would like to see a reduction of barriers.

It was a woman in Northeast City, the socialite Mrs. Carlson, who seemed to offer the best insight on how to reduce barriers. A lovely, gracious young mother, she is a former national officer of the Junior League. When I asked her what the Junior League practice was on barring Jewish women, she said: "Some clubs do, and some don't. I found that the local policy is usually determined by the local pattern of socializing. Jewish members will be found in those towns where the young Jewish and Gentile women travel back and forth a good deal in each other's homes, where they have gone to school together, have many things in common, and actually know each other as friends. This genuine basis of friendship seems to be the most important factor."

In the few cases I encountered where Gentile informants in Northeast City were sponsoring Jewish individuals for membership in their clubs, there was already established a genuine basis of friendship. They had come to have a high regard for each other as a result of working together on community or business projects and had entertained each other's families often in their homes. Personal friendship appears to be a more powerful motive than any abstract sense of justice in getting barriers removed.

And friendship can take root only where there is informal intermingling. Gentile families might well think back over their entertaining of the past year. If they have a number of Jewish acquaintances and did not include any of them in their home entertaining, it is quite probably not an accident. They have probably been accepting, wittingly or unwittingly, their Jewish neighbors as a segregated group.

Jewish families, too, might well scrutinize their home entertaining of the past year. They have perhaps confined themselves entirely to other Jewish families because they did not wish to take the risk of creating embarrassment by inviting someone who is possibly hostile to Jews. Such an apprehension is becoming more and more unrealistic. The barriers that persist today persist more out of habit than hostility. There has been a notable drop in hostility in the past decade. An official of the American

Jewish Committee made the point, in a recent chat, that the protective shells Jewish people have acquired in the past are today much thicker than necessary.

In any community, the prevailing climate of segregation or intermingling is largely the total of what individual families are doing in their socializing.

IV. Trends

CHAPTER 20

Nine Pressures Toward
a More Rigid Society

American ideology has strongly supported the notion that the United States is unique in the world as a place where a poor boy can start at the bottom and become a great captain of industry. Furthermore, according to the prevailing ideology, these opportunities for modern poor boys have been growing.

Both assumptions deserve scrutiny.

Certainly it is true that opportunities for upward mobility for the lower classes are greater in the United States than in most of Latin America, where class lines and class distinctions are still quite firmly drawn. Italy, too, to cite another example, offers relatively much fewer opportunities to the upward striver than the United States.

Highly industrialized Western nations, however, are a different matter. Sociologists, such as Seymour M. Lipset of the University of California, who have made comparisons between the United States and other industrialized nations in regard to mobility, find the situations have recently been quite similar. When the occupations of sons are compared with their fathers' in the various countries, the amount of upward shifting (measured on the arguable basis of shifts from manual to non-manual occupations) is approximately the same in the United States, Western Germany, France, and Sweden. Studies at Harvard have found that the upward mobility in the Soviet Union has recently been about the same as in the United States.

As for the second, more crucial proposition—that the opportunities for the boy of the lower classes are growing—a great body of evidence adds up to the conclusion: not proven. It is true that such a boy who is bright enough and fortunate enough to get a college education has a good chance for upward mobility, although not as good a chance as a boy with the same education from a well-to-do family. However, for the boy who goes to work for a company without the benefit of the college education, the prospects for upward progress are distinctly less promising than those that a boy in the same situation faced a generation ago. And it should be added that the opportunities for the poor boy in America have always been fewer than the history books have implied.[1]

Viewing our mobility situation as a whole, several pressures are working for more fluidity, more openness. Working against these, however, are a number of pressures pushing us insistently toward more rigidness in our social structure. In this pushball contest, as I see it, the ball is slowly moving toward the end of the field labeled "rigid society." I shall devote more attention to the forces for rigidity not only because they seem to be more dominant at present, but because they represent a challenge to our traditional ideology.

First, briefly, what are the pressures toward a more open class system? Here are six forces that have been encouraging a large upward current of strivers from the lower ranks of our society. The first three are definitely diminishing in effectiveness.

1. *The opportunities present in the opening up and settling of new communities.* A frontier town was the ideal place for any person of talent, whatever his origins, to prove his worth. Today, we are still building new communities, but they are mostly mass-produced, mass-merchandised ones at the fringes of our cities. Many builders operating on a modest scale ten or fifteen years ago have become multi-million-dollar operators, thanks in large part to the easy availability of United States government credit for home builders. Many of the nation's most spectacular modern success stories are in the building field.

2. *The differential birth rate.* For years the upper-class families weren't producing enough babies to fill their own ranks. The fecund mothers were in the blue-collar classes. Since World War II, however, the top three classes have been making considerable progress toward reproducing themselves.

3. *The surge of immigrants constantly coming in at the bottom of our society.* For many decades each new contingent helped press upward on the status scale those immigrants who had come a generation earlier. Today, most of the immigration is highly selective: skilled technicians,

---

[1] Richard Centers, "Occupational Mobility of Urban Occupational Strata," *American Sociological Review*, Vol. 13 (April 1948), pp. 197–203; Bernard Barber, *Social Stratification* (New York: Harcourt, Brace & Co., 1957), p. 431; C. Wright Mills, *The Power Elite*, p. 105; W. Lloyd Warner and James C. Abegglen, *Big Business Leaders in America*.

professionals, etc. The raw, unskilled immigrants coming in at the bottom in the old sense are mostly Puerto Rican—and they, of course, are not immigrants at all, but rather fellow citizens.

4. *The billions of dollars being spent by advertisers to persuade Americans to "upgrade" themselves through consumption.* Advertisers are our most ardent crusaders for more upward striving at the material level. I shall survey in more detail the mixed blessings of their dedication to upwardness in the next chapter.

5. *The growing availability of a college education to all classes.* There has been a great increase in all levels of educational accomplishment. In the thirties, most American adults had not attended high school. Today, 6 out of 10 have either a high-school or college education, and 1 in 14 now over the age of twenty has a college degree.

This factor, however, to some degree is illusory. College boys from well-to-do homes have a big edge in the business corporation over poor boys who had to work their way through school. And, as I've indicated, the well-to-do boy has an edge over the poor boy in the more lucrative professions.[2]

6. *Technological progress.* This is perhaps the most massive factor favoring upward mobility. As noted in earlier chapters, this has opened up many new opportunities at the white-collar and technical level. The demand for technicians to manage complex machines and aid the professionals has risen more sensationally than that for any other type of personnel. There has also been a tremendous expansion in the industries that service products, such as TV repair and auto repair.

Some of the gains in the number of white-collar people, it should be added, also are illusory, since a very large proportion of the new white-collar jobs has been for women clerical workers; and there is further a question how much real progress is involved when a man quits a blue-collared factory job to become a white-collared store clerk. At any rate, the growing man-hour productivity in America has produced a rising living standard that has convinced millions of families that they are better off and getting somewhere.

Now let us turn to the pressures toward a more rigid society. I will cite nine such pressures. The first six are on-the-job factors: they affect millions of Americans at their everyday work.

1. *The elimination of steppingstone jobs in office and factory.* Automation is wiping out a broad band of jobs that used to be steppingstones. These jobs call for progressively more skill and talent. The old-fashioned kind of

---

[2] Stuart Adams, "Trends in Occupational Origins of Physicians," *American Sociological Review* (August 1953).

company was organized in such a way that a worker at the bottom could become a skilled worker, then a foreman, and then a manager by gradual steps. Today, most factory jobs lead nowhere.

2. *The trend to require specialized pre-job schooling.* Today, the trend is to recruit from the colleges, technical and business schools rather than from the working personnel. At the Mill in Jonesville, Warner found that every person in a managerial job, with one exception, had been brought in, specially trained, from "outside." In short, managers and technicians are drawn from quite a different population, just as are officers in the military services. Today, you don't move up from enlisted to officer ranks either in military or corporate life just by being a good soldier. You go away to school. And the kind of school you go to pretty well fixes the ceiling on your future potentialities.

The American Management Association made a study of the lives of 325 company presidents. A report on its study advised anyone hoping to become a president first of all to go to college. It suggested Princeton, "if you can make it," but added that in any case you should go somewhere.

Even at the lower laboring level, the requirement of pre-job training is becoming a serious ceiling. To become a skilled worker in the automobile industry, for example, you must graduate from high school, and then go into apprentice training. It is almost impossible for an assembly-line man of several years' experience to become a skilled workman. To qualify for apprentice training, you usually have to be no older than twenty-one. This trend to the pre-schooled specialist is not unique to America.

3. *The fragmentation of skills.* The efficiency engineers, with their time and motion studies, have gone wild in breaking down jobs scientifically to their simplest motion components. By such narrowing of jobs, they enable management to hire lower-skilled—and, of course, lower-paid—people, and to spend less money training them. The mechanical engineers have likewise gone wild designing machines that can be operated by a simpleton. In the offices, many white-collar jobs are being depressed as more and more jobs require primarily finger dexterity. A federal manpower commission has observed that some large-office managers look for the unambitious, not-too-bright girls. Girls are often preferred who have perhaps ten years' total schooling, and who will be content to remain fluttering their fingers over their machines until marriage and/or pregnancy takes them away.

The Yankee City investigators found that in that city's shoe factories the introduction of mechanization had smashed the skill hierarchy by which youngsters gradually learned to become journeymen, and then proud and respected master craftsmen. The investigators couldn't find a single job now requiring more than medium skill. The vast majority of jobs could only be classified as low-skilled.

Throughout American offices and factories, the semi-skilled operatives are coming more and more to dominate the scene numerically. In prefabricated housing factories, jobs once done by skilled craftsmen are now done by semi-skilled machine operators, who may feed a machine that makes twenty-two simultaneous cuts.

Sociologist Ely Chinoy, who worked at a plant among 6,000 automobile workers, reported that only 1 in 20 was rated as a skilled craftsman. And, in other automobile plants, even the skilled men are angry about what is happening to their skill. Toolmakers have complained that many of the automobile companies keep a skilled man on just one machine, and this, in a sense, makes a second-class mechanic of him. They point out that machinists who work in the independent job shops receive broad experience in handling a number of machines.[3]

4. *The growth in bureaucracy.* We have already commented on the relentless growth to bigness in our institutions. (And I am not speaking of just our industrial corporations.) Such big institutions appear to require a well-recognized hierarchy of authority in order to operate efficiently. Sociologist Peter M. Blau, who has specialized in studying bureaucracies, finds that they have four basic traits in common: impersonality, a system of rules, a hierarchy of authority, and specialization.

All add up to a threat to democracy when the bureaucracies are multiplied across the landscape. The impersonality—imposed by necessity--leaves people in the lower ranks feeling isolated and unattached. The system of rules often breeds contempt or resentment toward the organization. The hierarchy of authority, which, as we have seen, seems to require its visible symbols of status, leaves those of low status and power feeling intensely unequal, and inclined to have little interest, initiative, and loyalty. And specialization tends to set up a tight pattern of stratification.

5. *The growing isolation of rank-and-file employees from management.* In older days, when our institutions were smaller, workers often developed warm friendships (or at least intense personal relationships) with their immediate superiors, and often chatted helpfully with the owner-manager. Today, the top management, at most, is likely to show up for the day-before-Christmas handshake. Otherwise, in many offices, shops, and factories, the "higher ups" are never seen. Often they are in other parts of the city, or in other cities. Workers in shipyards, one investigator found, have direct contact with people from the front office so

[3]James C. Worthy, "Organizational Structure and Employee Morale," *American Sociological Review,* Vol. 15, No. 2 (April 1950).

rarely that the occasion is notable. In such rare situations, it was noted, the worker may drop his eyes or remove his hat, but after the front-office officials have passed, the worker is likely to thumb his nose or make other gestures of contempt. (Even off the job, the only contact working-class people have with white-collar types is with their merchants.)

Management, for its part, appears, in many instances, to be developing an attitude of condescending lordliness toward its labor force. In 1958, the *Harvard Business Review* carried a most provocative discussion entitled "Is Management Creating a Class Society?" Its author, Benjamin Selekman, noted that corporate executives are fond of talking about their concern for human relations, and about the social and moral responsibilities that business statesmen (such as themselves) bear. Then he added: "But their statements and actions, on the basis of economic and political views, sharply contradict the moral philosophy they profess in speeches and articles." Selekman noted that businessmen give labor little or no credit for increasing the nation's productivity, and regard labor as a cost to be reduced as far and rapidly as possible. He concludes: "What should concern us is . . . a division in industry creating an elite which looks down on those who do the daily work."

6. *The role of big unions in freezing men and women to their jobs, and discouraging initiative.* Perhaps what we have here is another form of bureaucratization that is an inevitable response to the growth of big corporations. At any rate, the unions are growing in importance as a fixing factor. Whether intended or not, unions are creating for workers a static social order of their own. They are developing a system of fixed "estates" in life reminiscent of medieval guilds. In return for offering the workers security, recognition, and dignity, the workers surrender freedom to arrange their own affairs except as they can influence a union's decisions. Initiative beyond the call of duty becomes pointless because, at least in the automobile industry, whatever promotions to any slightly better-paying jobs are available are decided on the basis of impersonal seniority rules. Chinoy found, in his automobile-industry study, that before union rules came into force an enterprising worker could find ways, informally, to learn enough as a helper to get himself classified as a skilled worker. That possibility was virtually eliminated when the union began insisting that men work only within their job classification.

The result of all these pressures toward rigidity in the work lives of most people in the three supporting classes in America is a diminishing upward mobility, and a slackening of ambition. And these three classes, it should be added, constitute the great bulk of the United States population.

Look, for a moment, at what is happening to the working class, which consists mostly of solid, conscientious people who would like to believe in the American Dream. While these people's material position has improved, their social position has deteriorated. A hard-working semi-skilled operative learns, after twenty-five years on the job, that the seventeen-year-old kid next to him, who just quit high school to go to work, is making, within a few pennies, the same hourly wage he is. The thousands of men around him, in fact, are all making very close to the same money he is.

And the repetitious arm movement he makes hour after hour is excruciatingly boring. His father, he recalls, was poor, but a craftsman who was proud of the barrels he made. Here the machine has all the brains, all the reasons for pride. Perhaps the rules also forbid him to talk to workers nearby, or to get a drink of water except at the break period.

Even if the plant is a marvel of engineering and the bosses are as nice as they can be, the operative is still bored. A study at a meat-packing plant, celebrated in management circles for its solicitude for the worker, showed that the workers, while grateful for the effort, were just as bored and uninspired as assembly-line automobile workers have been found to be.

This average worker also typically has little aspiration. And it is not because he is lazy. He is just realistic. Chinoy found that only 5 of the 62 automobile workers he interviewed at length had any real hope of ever becoming foremen, and these five were all relatively young. In Jonesville, a leading minister asked this challenging question of a member of the Warner investigating group: "Where in this town can a man start to work, and be able to work himself up to a really good job? There isn't any future for anyone who is working at the Mill . . . they never advance into top positions. . . . It is this kind of thing, I think, which is turning us into a class society."[4]

The foremen, too—who are the top sergeants of industry—are typically without aspiration. They realize they have gone as far as they can. C. Wright Mills reports that only 1 foreman in 5 believes he will ever get above the foreman level. The technicians, engineering aides, etc.—although considered by workers to be an elite—know there is a ceiling of realistic aspiration for them. Joseph A. Kahl points out that the modern corporation is very much like government civil service. In both, he says, a person chooses the basic level within which he will work by the type and extent of his education. After that, progress tends to be routinized and is dictated by what is possible within bureaucratic competition.

[4] W. Lloyd Warner, *Democracy in Jonesville*. See "Mobility in the Factory for Managers and Workers."

There are three main levels, or areas, of competition in the corporation, and the overwhelming majority of the personnel begin and end their careers at the same level. Those levels are:

The managers and planners.
The technical aides and functionaries.
The workers.[5]

The pressures toward rigidity apparently are having their effects on the aspirations of our young people. Survey after survey shows a sharp trend away from aspirations to be an adventurous entrepreneur or intellectual pioneer or a social non-conformist. William Zabel, while president of the Princeton debating society in 1958, observed, "Anything you do out of the ordinary brings ridicule." The aggressive ambition, long assumed to be peculiarly American, just doesn't show up on any substantial scale in the surveys any more. Scholastic Magazines, in a study of high-school youths, found that 50 percent more wanted to work for a "large company" than wanted to have their own company. A study made by psychologists at Harvard University and Colby College of attitudes of youths around the world (ten nations) found that Mexicans and Egyptians, for example, showed a great deal more drive and enthusiasm to make themselves and their nations great than Americans. In fact, the main preoccupation of American youths—presumed leaders of tomorrow—was to qualify for a "rich, full life." They typically spelled it out in material terms such as hi-fi sets, outdoor barbecues, and furnishings for their homes. The old saying that "Every boy can grow up to be President" would strike many of the young Americans in the survey as pretty corny.

In addition to the six economic pressures toward rigidity just cited, there are three other principal pressures toward a more rigid society. Since I have already mentioned them in previous chapters, I will just touch on them lightly here.

First is the growing tendency for people to confine their socializing to their own socioeconomic layer. Second is the growing tendency of politicians to treat ethnic and economic groups as blocs, and to base their campaigns on assembling a winning combination of blocs.

And finally we have the rather frightening, headlong trend toward social stratification by residential area. The proliferation of homogeneous developments has accentuated this trend. A developer outside Philadelphia has 1,200 split-level houses. The price of the houses runs between $18,000 and $20,000. He told me he had some executives, attorneys, and

5 W. Lloyd Warner and James C. Abegglen, *Big Business Leaders in America*, p. 230.

doctors, but that most of his buyers were "engineers of the same educational level" from nearby Radio Corporation of America plants. His buyers, he said, have a salary range of $7,500 to $10,000. And he added: "Most have two children."

All in all, we are in the process of becoming a many-layered society. Status is crystallizing. The boundaries between the various layers are becoming more rigid.

For those frozen into the lower layers, frustration is a commonly felt emotion. They still have their vote. If the frustration mounts, and we simultaneously go through an economic setback, we may well get a movement for the nationalization of industry. Such nationalization had frequently developed in countries where the dominant groups refused to work to soften rigid class differentiations that existed.

The opportunities for any notable upward mobility for people in our three supporting classes boil down, in the vast majority of cases, to these three:

1. You can marry off an attractive daughter to a higher-status male. That's still being done occasionally.

2. You can try to see that your children get a college education. That doesn't guarantee anything, but does at least qualify them for consideration for semi-upper-type jobs and friends (see Chapter 24).

3. You can create the feeling that you are getting somewhere by stepping up your consumption of material goods. This is made possible, for most people, by the general rise in buying power. We will see what is being done to encourage people to take this route success, status, and fulfillment through self-indulgence—in the following chapter.

CHAPTER 21

Exploiting the "Upgrading Urge"

The role of advertising men in the emerging class picture is both curious and portentous. For solid business reasons, they are ardent champions of an open-class society.

Advertisers have approximately eleven billion dollars at their disposal to spend each year on persuasive messages that, they hope, will influence our consuming behavior. In the past few years, they have been busily trying to discover the facts of class and status, and to apply their findings in shaping their sales appeals.

Some of their effort and study is directed toward making sales appeals more realistic in terms of the tastes and habits of the members of the particular socioeconomic class they are trying to woo as their most likely customers (i.e., if it is beer you're selling, don't use a drawing-room setting. If it is swimming pools, don't use loud colors). Such realism would seem wholly commendable. If the average American family *must* be subjected to 1,518 sales messages a day—that's the estimate—let them be reasonable, realistic messages.

A great many advertisers, however, are not content with merely being realistic about class. They want to put some sizzle into their messages by stirring up our status consciousness. In fact, they sometimes playfully call themselves "merchants of discontent." They talk profoundly of the "upgrading urge" of people, and search for appeals that will tap that urge.

Many of the products they are trying to sell have, in the past, been confined to a "quality market." The products have been the luxuries of the upper classes. The game is to make them the necessities of all classes. This is done by dangling the products before non-upper-class people as status symbols of a higher class. By striving to buy the product—say, wall-to-wall carpeting on installment—the consumer is made to feel he is upgrading himself socially. Or the limited-success-class housewife can achieve that feeling by paying a few cents more each day for the brand of cigarette that is puffed so elegantly by the genuine Park Avenue matron in the cigarette advertisement.

Much of this exploiting of the "upgrading urge" is aimed at the working-man. As we have noted in the last chapter, the modern factory operative has very little opportunity to upgrade himself in his productive role in life. The advertisers, however, are continuously inviting him to upgrade himself, or herself, at least in his own mind, by adopting the consuming patterns of people in the higher classes.

Ely Chinoy, after studying the automobile workers, makes the point that these people have "anonymous jobs and standardized wage rates." The only visible way left for them to advance in the world, he says, is by acquiring material possessions. And he adds: "With their wants constantly stimulated by high-powered advertising, they measure their success by what they are able to buy." A new car standing in front of one's home is seen as a symbol of advancement. New living-room furniture, a washing machine, and television are seen as further confirmation that one is "getting ahead."

The blue-collar people are adored by the mass merchandisers because, first of all, there are so many of them. And second, they are by nature free spenders and now have more money—and more installment credit—than they are accustomed to handling. In the past their needs have been quite simple, in keeping with low incomes. White-collar workers, in contrast, have less loose money, because of the requirements of their way of life. They are trying to live like the semi-upper-class people, often on working-class incomes.

Selling a higher-class level of living to blue-collar workers, however, is not as easy as it might seem. The snag, of course, is that our way of life simply doesn't offer the workingman a fighting chance to move up to a higher-prestige class. Most of them are resigned to being working folks all their lives, and are not inclined to emulate the upper classes. They know what is what. As the Social Research, Inc., study of Wage Town wives put it: "They have no burning desire to get above their class." They'll buy television because it is a gadget geared to their taste, but they need prodding and "educating" to desire many of the traditionally higher-class products the mass merchandisers desire to move in such vast numbers, such as the electric rotating spits or gourmet foods. Advertisers are being admonished by the marketing experts that these people need to have their desires steered into new directions. At the least they can be induced to want to upgrade themselves by learning to want more wondrous, more expensive, or more sophisticated products.

Advertisers also are being advised of the exciting possibilities offered by the children of blue-collar families who have managed to take up white-collar roles in life. The Institute for Motivational Research suggests to advertisers that they should "welcome" such people into their new status positions, by seeing that they get well launched with the proper status symbols. It has found, from its researchers, that the changes required to take up the new role are far from "painless." There is often considerable uncertainty and self-doubt. The Institute suggests this is the "fertile moment" to develop new brand loyalties by helping the newcomer feel comfortable with his new collar. This can be done, it says, by helping him know the ins and outs of the proper trappings. "The typical 'white-collar' products," it says, "such as fashionable clothing, fashionable home interior products of all kinds, golfing equipment, more sophisticated foods must make this type of person feel that he belongs."

Not only are advertisers ardent champions of upward mobility (or the illusion of it), but they are ardently in favor of more education for everybody, and are in favor of more motherhood. Again, they have some sound, solid reasons for their idealism. A study of consumer expenditures by Alfred Politz Research, Inc., revealed that a household whose breadwinner has had *some* college education spends two-thirds more than the family whose head never went beyond grade school. (Higher income presumably is the primary explanation.) The same study revealed the fact—exciting to marketers—that families with children spend $300 to $500 more a year than families without children.

Advertisers also are enthusiastic champions of the Negro's right to consume the good things of American life. Negroes—as they have acquired skills and buying power—have become a $15,000,000,000 market. (The average Negro family reportedly buys twice as much liquor as the average white family). Also, Negroes are particularly responsive to advertising appeals stressing status because we have forced them to be so preoccupied with status. Their publications take pride in reporting Negro millionaires who ride in Cadillacs; and the publications make the point that "no self-respecting Negro would smoke a cheap cigarette."[1] Another factor that makes Negroes excellent prospects for such products as television is that they are often barred from many places where other Americans enjoy pleasurable pursuits (such as restaurants and country clubs). They must take their pleasures where they can. And they have been repulsed so much that they often seem to need a specific "invitation" from marketers and merchandisers to buy a product, or go to a store, before they feel at ease in doing so.

The prize darlings of the advertisers, however, are the families who move about a great deal. The Interurbia study—conducted by the J. Walter Thompson advertising agency, Yale social scientists, and *Fortune* magazine—found that people who move frequently undergo a tremendous "upgrading urge." With each move a family makes, it tries to get a better house and more of the "extras." These families often leave rented city apartments with only a modest assortment of worldly goods and become people of property with a hunger for hard goods (such as cars, appliances, etc.). If they move into an area where quite a number of the neighbors have clothes driers, they feel they must have one, too, and quickly.

Other studies of new suburbias have disclosed that the residents are ripe for any goods sold to them as keys to social acceptance. And studies of people who have achieved a toehold in the white-collar group reveal that these people like to be told that they now "deserve" the finer, more solid material things in life, and that for them buying the "right" thing has become a "birthright." When people borrow money to achieve all this birthright, they should be assured that by going into debt they are "on their way up."

[1] Max Lerner, *America as a Civilization*, p. 524.

Sales strategies for harnessing the "upgrading urge" have probably been most exhaustively studied—and assiduously employed—in the marketing of automobiles. The automobile makers have spent small fortunes exploring the status meaning of their product. They have noticed that people who live in developments tend to leave their long, bright cars parked out on the street in front of the house, instead of putting them in the garage. It was concluded that such people seek, through the car, a status enhancement which they may not be able to get from a home that looks too much like every other house in the block.

That these advertising campaigns, which promised higher status and exquisite delirium, had achieved no little success is seen in the fact that Americans in the late fifties were spending more of their total income on the family chariot than they were in financing the homestead, which housed the family and its car or cars. Home builders, at their 1958 convention, cited this as a deplorable situation demanding correction.

Over the years, the automobile makers succeeded in building up a status hierarchy for automobiles that was well understood by the public. And it was well understood—motivational studies showed—that one could enhance his own status if he was able in his car buying to move up the hierarchical ladder: from Ford, Chevrolet, or Plymouth; up to Pontiac, Dodge, Mercury, Studebaker, etc.; perhaps to Buick, Oldsmobile, Chrysler, etc.; then up to Imperial, Lincoln, or Cadillac.

Cadillac was at the top of the ladder, or to switch metaphors in mid-sentence, the end of the rainbow. At novelist John P. Marquand's "Happy Knoll" country club, a committeeman seeking to recruit a new member boasted that "Happy Knoll" had eight members who owned Cadillacs, while the rival club only had two members with Cadillacs, "the newest three years old."

The makers of lower-priced lines, under pressure to find new buyers, introduced longer, fatter, more expensive, more powerful, and more luxuriously designed models that competed directly with their traditional superiors in status such as the Pontiac, Dodge, and Mercury. As *Time* magazine has pointed out, the Chevrolet grew two feet in two decades, to become bigger than the Oldsmobile of ten years earlier and more powerful than the Cadillac of five years earlier. Meanwhile, Buick, not content with being the chic, sleek car for doctors and upward-mobile semi-upper-class people, began competing downward for new recruits. It stressed how low priced some of its models were, and underscored this broadening of its image by sponsoring boxing matches on television.

As a result of all this recruiting, both upward and downward, the status gap between different makes of motorcars shrank, and the Detroit-made motorcars in their various multi-hued, elongated forms began seeming less significantly different than they used to. Consequently, some of the makes began losing a little of their effectiveness as status symbols. The way was open for many of the nation's taste makers to show their distaste for the trend toward homogenization in Detroit by becoming enthusiasts of the small—and often expensive—foreign car. In Hollywood, the higher-level status strivers began trying to buy Dual-Ghia convertibles, after Frank Sinatra and Eddie Fisher led the way. Price: about $8,000. One big appeal was that only one hundred a year were supposed to be made.

The typical buyer of foreign cars (even the low-cost, economy ones), it should be noted, was not the workingman but rather the high-status executives, architects, or television directors. As these taste leaders turned in increasing numbers to more compact cars—in their search for visibly distinctive status symbols—the rank and file of automobile buyers, long accustomed to striving for even-bigger cars as symbols of higher status, were confused as to which way to turn.

The automobile makers of Detroit began hedging in their bets by casting dies for additional, more compact lines (which would at least restore readily visual distinctiveness), but they were still convinced from their surveying that the average American wants a big, bright car.[2]

Marketers, then, are striving to promote upward mobility—at least at the consuming level—for solid, business reasons. Should this be considered a healthy or unhealthy factor? One hesitates to draw any decisive conclusions; but in either case the conclusions are depressing.

On the positive side, there is the fact that the marketers, by promoting status striving through the purchase of goods, are giving people the sense that they are getting ahead. This, at the lower levels, is largely a consumption gain. But should we deprive people who are stuck in their jobs of even this psychological satisfaction? If we can't give them a fair chance at making their livelihood in a creative way that offers them the opportunities to advance, should we take away from them—to return to the Roman parallel—their circuses?

On the other hand, what do we do to people when we constantly hold up to them success symbols of a higher class and invite them to strive for the symbols? Does this increase class consciousness in a way that could become dangerous in an economic turndown? And, in this constant conversion of luxuries into necessities, are we pushing people to the point where their expectations are so high—and they live so close to the brink of insolvency—that even a mild prolonged belt-tightening would leave them in an ugly mood? Further, by encouraging people constantly to pursue the emblems of success, and causing them to equate possessions with status, what are we doing to their emotions and their sense of values? Economist Robert Lekachman has observed: "We can only guess at the tensions and anxieties generated."

Finally, aren't the advertisements giving Americans a dangerously distorted picture of how the average American lives?

Clare Barnes, Jr., consultant art director and author of the humorous best-seller *White Collar Zoo*, has taken his fellow directors in the advertising business to task. In *Art in Advertising* (Summer, 1956), he issued a memorable blast. Advertising, he said, "has done more to cause the social unrest of the Twentieth Century than any other single factor." He granted that advertising has done wonders in raising the standard of living, but said that advertisers, in the way they had gone about creating a demand for their products, had concocted "a false and erroneous impression of the social scene today." At this point he invited his colleagues to skim through a few of their advertisements aimed at the masses to see how they picture the "average family." If the scene is outdoors, he said, "we see a house that cost eighty thousand dollars if it cost a nickel. The backyard, where the two beautiful ladies are talking over the fence about a new detergent, is filled with great old trees, beautifully landscaped gardens that extend back to what looks like a golf course for dad. Around in front of the house are several cars this average family owns, the station wagon, the new Cadillac, and a sports car for the kids. When the ads show the interior of the house it is obvious that another eighty thousand bucks has gone into the furnishings of this average American home. Wall-to-wall carpeting, flawlessly decorated, beautiful antiques or even more expensive contemporary furniture, air conditioning, every imaginable facility in the kitchen to give Mrs. Average more time for her many worthwhile activities."

And then he went on to describe the advertisements to sell toilet soap. These advertisements show a gorgeous model with a Hattie Carnegie gown in a setting of marble and mirrors. He said she plays the part of the "average dame." Barnes observed that the average man (or woman) seeing these glowingly distorted depictions of himself then looks at his own setup. Perhaps he is sitting in his union suit with egg on his face, and a 1932 refrigerator behind him. "He becomes understandably restless, to say the least," says Barnes. (There is no suggestion that the average man has to earn all these things.) Mr. Average Man, Barnes continued, "figures he is underprivileged, ill-housed, ill-clothed, ill-fed. He is ripe for any demagogue who comes along and says that air conditioning for every home is a necessity of life, an inalienable right of every citizen. A vote for this demagogue is a vote for free air conditioning for every citizen, regardless of race, creed, or place of national origin. Eventually a law is passed, sure enough, and the Government provides air conditioning for the have-nots at the expense of the haves."

Mr. Barnes expresses apprehension that the whole thing is going to explode, and advertising is going to be blamed.

V. Implications for the Future

CHAPTER 22

Should Status Lines Be Maintained?

In the course of this book I have proceeded on the assumption that a more open society is preferable to a more rigidly stratified one. That assumption, perhaps I should point out, is not unassailable. There is much to be said for a clear-cut hierarchy of status. Here, briefly, are some of the principal arguments for a clearly stratified society.

1. *Stratification is necessary in order to get difficult tasks performed.* A man who undergoes years of arduous training necessary to become an accountant will be motivated to undergo that training only if there is a reward at the end. One reward, of course, is the satisfaction of being an accountant. But most people require additional rewards — even the Soviets are discovering — in the form of pay and prestige.

2. *Many people tend to accept a status hierarchy — and their place in it — naturally.* One of the textile workers in Paterson, New Jersey, who was interviewed by sociologists seemed to recognize the naturalness of differentiation. He asked: "If there were no rich people, who would the poor people work for?"

Many people in the lower classes, further, seem to accept automatically as superior the judgment of their superiors. In the armed services, enlisted men who come up for courts-martial have the right to request that other enlisted men be on their trial panel. This privilege is not typically requested. Most enlisted men prefer to leave their fate up to officers.[1]

3. *Life is said to be more stable and serene in clearly stratified societies.* This viewpoint was most effectively articulated perhaps by anthropologist Ralph Linton after he had studied many of the world's primitive

---

[1] Fred L. Stodtbeck, Rita M. James, and Charles Hawkins, "Social Status in Jury Deliberations," *American Sociological Review*, Vol. 22, No. 6 (December 1957).

societies.[2] In this world, he said, you can have one of two kinds of status. You can have a status that you have "achieved" yourself through your efforts and talents; or you can have a status that society automatically "ascribes" to you. When people are going through a change of adjustment to their environment—as during our own frontier days—there is a great demand for the special gifts that can be provided best by people who achieve their status. Class lines crumble. If, however, your society is well adjusted to its environment, then there is little demand for people of unusual talent, and a society of ascribed status—where little attention is paid to seeking talent outside the born elite—is likely to produce more tranquillity.

4. *A society that encourages status striving produces, in contrast, a good deal of bruising, disappointment, and ugly feelings.* If a society promotes the idea that success is associated with upward mobility, those who can't seem to get anywhere are likely to be afflicted with the feeling that they are personal failures, even though the actual situation may be pretty much beyond their control or capacity to change.

The person standing still in a culture that glorifies upward progress often suffers hurts. The greater menace to society, however, is the person moving downward. Any society that has a good deal of upward circulation is bound to have some downward circulation, too. We can't all stay at the high level our elders or we ourselves achieve. The person being declassed is, as previously indicated, almost invariably in an ugly mood. He is seething with humiliation and apprehension. If society has not developed a mechanism for quickly and gently helping him find a new, more humble niche, then he becomes a bigot, a searcher for scapegoats, and an eager recruit for almost any demagogue who promises to set up a completely new social order.

5. *The culture found in a stratified society, some say, is more satisfying, interesting, and stimulating than that found in a homogenized society.* In such a stratified society you have levels of culture, and you have a long-trained elite dictating what is good and proper for each class. In modern America, where especially at the consuming level the masses have to a large extent become the dictators of taste, we have to endure the horrors of our roadside architecture and billboards; our endless TV gun-slinging; our raw, unkempt, blatantly commercialized cities; our mass merchandising of pornographic magazines; our faceless suburban slums-to-be; our ever-maudlin soap operas. Voices have been crying out for

---

[2] Ralph Linton, *The Study of Man* (New York: D. Appleton-Century Co., 1936), especially Chapter 8, "Status and Role."

the restoration of some kind of elite that can set standards and make them stick.

These, then, are five of the principal arguments that can be offered in favor of stratification. All run counter to the ideals of the prevailing American ideology. A society of ascribed status such as Linton described may offer a Hindu security and happiness in knowing his place, but it is hardly appropriate for mid-twentieth-century America since it shows little interest in the discovery of new talent. We confront in America a historical situation that cries out for a society of achieved status. We are badly maladjusted to our environment and are becoming more maladjusted every month. For example:

— We are in a state of precarious adjustment in our relations with other major societies (notably Russia's).
— We are still desperately trying to adjust to the growth of vast bureaucratic institutions.
— We are still trying to adjust to a way of life that calls for frequent uprooting of our people and moving to new addresses.
— We face the challenge of absorbing 100,000,000 additional persons in our populace within the next twenty to twenty-five years.
— We face the challenge of learning to live with a technological plant more awesome, prodigious, and frightening than anything the world has ever known.

For all these reasons, we need to draw upon all the talent and intelligence we can muster. We need to encourage by every means possible the discovery and advancement of people of unusual potential in our three supporting classes. In a rigidly stratified society, such people are not even considered.

The challenge to us is to recognize the realities of our current class situation. The main reality is our tendency toward greater rigidity in our stratification while pretending that precisely the opposite is occurring. We are consigning tens of millions of our people to fixed roles in life where aspiration is futile, and yet we keep telling them that those who have the stuff will rise to the top. We don't even allow them the satisfaction of feeling secure, dignified, and creative in their low status. And, socially, we look down upon them.

Because of this frustration and isolation imposed upon many members of the supporting classes, we have a frightful shattering of integrity. This shows up in the extraordinarily high psychoses rates we encounter as we approach the bottom of our social scale. And it shows up in the fantastically high delinquency and crime rates among the younger poor of America. In Spain, where class lines are better understood and accepted, you have vastly more poverty but relatively little accompanying juvenile delinquency.

Perhaps it also shows up in something medical investigators have noticed. As you get near the bottom of the social scale, there is an abrupt rise in a disorder called anomie—feeling isolated, loosely attached to the world, and convinced that things are tough all over.

Status distinctions would appear to be inevitable in a society as complicated as our own. The problem is not to try to wipe them out—which would be impossible—but to achieve a reasonably happy society within their framework. If we accept that context, much can be done to promote contentment, mutual respect, and life satisfaction.

There appear to be two principal approaches. One is to promote more understanding between people of the various class groupings in our society. The other is to make class distinctions less burdensome by making certain that people of real talent are discovered and encouraged to fulfill their potential regardless of their station in life. In the two final chapters, we shall explore these two possibilities.

CHAPTER 23

Problems in Understanding

We have seen in earlier chapters that the average American in his friendly associations is becoming more and more limited as far as diversity is concerned. Usually he confines himself to people in his particular niche. He doesn't know much about people on either side of him in the social grid who seem different because they come from outside his world, and may be of different ethnic origin. Furthermore, he doesn't know much about people above or below him on the prestige scale of social classes. His job, his neighborhood, and his church—because of stratifying tendencies— have increased this isolation.

Some would argue that associating only with your own kind makes for a more pleasant life. Otto Butz quotes a Princeton senior of upper-class origin—his father is a successful Midwestern businessman—who articulated this view: "Most people, true enough, I wouldn't invite for a drink to my country club. But this is not a matter of disliking them or feeling superior to them. We are simply different. Intimate social contact would be pointless and probably boring on both sides."[1]

Somehow the lad sounds insufferable. His blinders are on for life. And he likes it. He is oblivious to the other 99½ percent of the people of the United States who live outside his arid little niche. He will never know the exhilaration and fascination of having as friends such colorful and often wonderfully articulate folks as clam diggers, house movers, volunteer fire chiefs, antique salesmen, mental-hospital nurses, bill collectors, farmers, marriage brokers, zoo keepers, divorce lawyers, airline hostesses, rare-bird collectors, and house detectives. The proper young man from Princeton is not like the vice-president I know of a half-billion-dollar corporation who includes among his closest friends a ninth-grade schoolteacher and an amiable, talkative motorboat salesman. He finds them more diverting and relaxing than anyone else he has encountered in recent years.

A lively and friendly curiosity about people around us who lead lives that are quite different from our own can add spice and enrichment to our own. Even if there is no particular desire to develop personal friendships, still an understanding of their way of life and their aspirations can make life for us all a great deal easier in our overcrowded nation of strangers that is developing.

We should begin by taking a hard look at our hundreds of one-layer development communities where the houses are all built to sell to a group with specific socioeconomic and often ethnic characteristics. This new-style segregation conceived by builders is at the root of much of the growing cleavage between status groups. Not only is our neighborhood socializing at Plywood Estates development confined to people all-too-much like ourselves; but our children, in walking to school, see only homes pretty much like their own. And at the school, they learn to know only children pretty much like themselves. At the churches, stores, hospital, and "community" center, we see more of the same. It is all too tidy, too neatly packaged, too sanitary, and too juiceless.

A number of sociological studies have established that genuine acquaintance (rather than simply sight acquaintance) lessens prejudice. This holds true whether the acquaintances are Albanians, Jews, Negroes, or Mohawk Indians. And it holds true with particular force if the people who seemed so different are from a status level in their own group that is equal or superior to our own status.

One comparative study of particular interest (since so many cities are

[1] Otto Butz, *The Unsilent Generation* (New York: Rinehart & Co., 1958).

arguing the issue of interracial public housing) was that made of the attitudes of white housewives living in integrated projects (New York City) and housewives living in segregated (all white) projects (Newark, New Jersey).[2] In one of the comparative tests, only 6 percent of the segregated white wives in Newark indicated they thought of Negroes as being "sociable, friendly, cheerful," whereas 33 percent of the white New York City wives living as neighbors of Negroes checked those traits. On the negative side, fully a third of the segregated white Newark wives (who rarely had any direct acquaintance with Negroes) thought of them as being "low class, noisy, rowdy, impulsive, primitive, drink a lot." Among the New York white wives who knew Negroes as neighbors, only 9 percent checked those traits. A majority of the wives in the integrated New York project reported that their attitudes toward Negroes had become more favorable since living in the project. Only a few said their attitudes had become less favorable.

An Army study among soldiers produced a similar finding. It found that the more personal contact white infantrymen had had with Negro soldiers, the less evidence they showed of harboring any prejudice.

S. I. Hayakawa, the authority on attitude formation, makes the very important point that Negroes now bear a heavy responsibility in helping whites accept them naturally. The battle for equal rights, he says, is now moving from the courts to the field of personal relations. He states: "The Negro, to a degree hitherto impossible, can set the tone of social and business intercourse by the clues he gives in his speech and behavior as to how he expects to be treated." If he acts obsequiously or nervously or self-consciously or over-assertively, the whites will respond accordingly. "If he acts naturally, they will, in 9 cases out of 10, act naturally too and be happy and relieved that meeting a Negro was not the ordeal they thought it was going to be."

Hayakawa went on to explain that "the secret of acting naturally [is to] forget as far as possible that one is Negro." The Negro who is a biochemist or a parent at a P.T.A. meeting should expect to be treated as just another biochemist or parent. "But if you are a biochemist or a parent and expect to be treated as a Negro, people are going to treat you as a Negro, whatever that means to them." Acting naturally, of course, as he points out, is easier said than done.

It is being discovered that people are more willing to accept (with a minimum of protest) a situation that puts them with a previously excluded group if individuals or institutions they respect lead the way. Significantly,

---

[2] Morton Deutsch and Mary Evans Collins, "Interracial Housing," from *American Social Patterns*, pp. 7–42.

on college campuses, it has been the fraternities with the highest prestige that have led the way to integrating minority-group members. (Perhaps the leadership of the socially secure makes it safe for lower-status fraternities to do the same.) The Laurelhurst Beach Club of Seattle, for more than a decade, had accepted virtually no new Jewish members. For ten months every year, Jewish and non-Jewish children of the neighborhood played together; but during the two summer months every year, the non-Jewish children went to the club and the Jewish children could not follow. Several of the most respected citizens of the community, including a law-school dean and a minister, led the way for an anti-discrimination amendment. Later, at a mass meeting, more than five hundred members voiced unanimous support for the change.

In several situations studied, the in-group had vigorously objected when the proposal to eliminate barriers against minorities (on the job, in dormitories, or in housing projects) was first proposed. But when authorities moved firmly and told them they could like it or get out, they accepted the change as something that was beyond their control, and soon were turning their attention to other matters. This firm approach is particularly likely to be successful (and to be secretly welcomed) if the people in the in-group have been a bit conscience-stricken at finding themselves in an anti-democratic stance.

An interesting experiment in promoting understanding between people who seem on the surface different is the Panel of Americans. At twenty-five American colleges and universities, teams or panels consisting typically of five students go about the countryside talking about themselves and inviting searching, blunt questions. Typically, a panel will consist of students of these five group identifications: Catholic, Puerto Rican, Jew, Negro, and white Protestant. They go into high schools and junior high schools, into union halls, churches, P.T.A. meetings, etc. Each member tells what it means to be a member of his or her group. The New York University panel, for example, went to Peekskill, New York, where there had been a great deal of hostility between different groups, and appeared before junior-high-school students in the afternoon. That evening, the panel was to appear before the P.T.A. So many pupils insisted their parents attend that the session drew the largest crowd in the organization's history. Weeks later, reports came back to the P.T.A. that the effects of the meeting were being noted even in supermarkets where more neighborly chatting was observed between housewives of different ethnic and racial groups.

Another place where we should begin taking a hard look is at the tight hierarchical stratification of superiors-subordinates in the large company.

At what point does bureaucratic growth become seriously anti-democratic? What can be safely done in the big company—where Peter M. Blau reported finding "profound feelings of inequality and apathy" in the lower echelons—to restore more democracy and more understanding? A few experiences perhaps will be instructive.

At a large insurance company, a study was made of twenty-four clerical sections to find what kind of leadership produced the best results in output.[3] There has long been an assumption, Blau points out, that the lenient, democratic-type leader in a company is less effective than the disciplinarian who rides herd on subordinates. He is presumed to be a victim of the weakness of indulgence in order to prove what a good fellow he (or she) is.

The insurance study produced clear evidence to the contrary. It was found that the section chiefs who closely supervised the work of their clerks and gave detailed instructions were less successful in meeting production goals than the section chiefs who gave their clerks freedom to do the work in the best way they felt it could be done.

The United States Steel Company stumbled upon an important key to improved employee understanding and efficiency when it sought to find ways to cut financial and man-hour losses due to accidents. In the past, its officials had used the authoritarian approach of posting instructions on the bulletin board. Violators of the instructions were sent home for a day. Still, accidents persisted. There seemed to be a point below which the accident rate could not be cut. The company's leadership decided upon a new "psychological" approach. It began calling in the employees in groups of three or four and asking for their suggestions on how their particular operation could be made safer. These sessions are held in clean conference rooms. Thousands of them have been held. Coffee is served. At a plant near Pittsburgh, I listened as a group of four workmen analyzed step by step their job, in which a team of eight men lift one-thousand-pound rails and take them to a designated spot. It was an exciting experience. These workmen argued about who should give the signal to lift, how they should place their feet, and so on. A gray-haired man named Charlie got up and gave a demonstration of the theories he had developed over the years. For the first time these men were seeing that their job, physical as it is, was important; that their advice was important; and that they could help improve the safety and efficiency of their own operation.

This new approach to safety—called "Operations Attitude"—was first introduced in the Chicago plant that had the highest accident rate of any of the company's main plants: 2.29 accidents per million man-hours. Within

---

two years, that rate had been cut to the sensationally low .66, the best in the company's entire history. More impressive, the company began getting some pleasantly unexpected dividends. Wherever employees were consulted about their job, morale generally rose, and so did production.

Still another area where large improvements can be made in understanding is between our upper-class professional people and the people of the lower classes they are supposed to serve. (We will discuss educators in the next chapter.) As we have noted, there is often a grievous lack of communication or insight that diminishes the professionals' effectiveness.

Consider the matter of sex. The marriage manuals, written by "authorities" from the upper classes, are enormously preoccupied with elaborate pre-union techniques of foreplay. For couples of lower educational levels, such recommended techniques actually diminish the likelihood that the woman will find satisfaction from the experience. Furthermore, such techniques so earnestly pontificated are viewed by these couples as so much intellectual eroticism and dillydallying. The upper-level doctor who brusquely requests the lower-level patient to strip for a physical examination also is revealing his lack of understanding of the mores of people in the lower classes, who typically are deeply embarrassed by such requests.

And psychiatrists, for all their erudition, have a great deal to learn about the public they are supposed to serve, according to the findings of the Yale group of sociologists and psychiatrists (see Chapter 18). These psychiatrists expressed annoyance and revulsion at the behavior of lower classes that they encountered during therapy. They were shocked by the sex mores of the lower classes and they were disgusted at wives from the lower classes who accepted beatings from their husbands as a natural reasonable part of life.[4]

A part of the problem is that the people in the two lower classes tend to be dubious that anything worthwhile can be accomplished by a head doctor. They prefer to think of ailments as having a physical basis. For example, they account for the mental illness of relatives as being due to such things as "bad blood," a "bump on the head," and "too much booze."[5]

August B. Hollingshead and Frederick C. Redlich, speaking for the Yale team, advise psychiatrists to examine their professional biases. They feel much must be done to improve communication between psychiatrist and

---

[4] August B. Hollingshead and Frederick C. Redlich, *Social Class and Mental Illness,* p. 344.

[5] Ibid., p. 341.

lower-class patient. And psychiatrists, they conclude, should undertake to school themselves on the social structure within which they operate, and the life values of people of the various classes.

All of us might lead more effective lives, and quite probably more serene ones, if we sought to understand our whole society and not just our particular niche in it.

CHAPTER 24

Widening the Gates to Opportunity

While relaxing at a coffee house in Buffalo near the campus of a local college (State University of New York) in late 1958, I heard an all-too-typical story of the changing opportunity picture in mid-century America. My informant was a waiter (named Joe) who was a tall, thoughtful, personable, husky, articulate young man with a crew cut. Joe was working to keep himself in college and he explained to me, under questioning, why he was still only a freshman at the age of twenty-two. He had believed in the American Dream, and lost four years as a result.

Joe has six brothers and sisters; and his father is a financially strapped Civil Service clerk. When Joe graduated from a local high school with good grades, he decided it would be too much of a burden on his family to try to go to college. Besides, he had a girl and he wanted a car and spending money. So he went to work for a large manufacturing corporation in the area. He began on the assembly line. Soon convinced that there was no possibility of progress there, he switched to being a crane operator, and later became a stock-room clerk. He worked hard, and everyone seemed satisfied with his work. But he felt he wasn't getting any place. Joe related: "I had just taken it for granted that I could qualify for better jobs, but I was bumping my head against a very low ceiling. Even in the cafeteria there was a wall between where I could eat and where the office force ate. I was labeled 'plant.' "

Every few months Joe went to the personnel office to ask about getting on the "office" force. The people there at first seemed surprised by his appearance before them. They took out his file card, which showed he had a high-school education, and said they couldn't think of anything he might qualify for at the moment. Later they seemed to treat him as a nuisance. Joe continued: "It took me a long time to realize just what the situation was. In twenty years I would still be in the stock room or operating a machine. So," said Joe with a sigh, "I'm trying college. It is hard to get the hang of studying after four years, but I'm doing all right." He is studying abnormal psychology. A university professor who knows Joe's background spoke of him in admiring terms.

Not all corporations require a diploma to "enter the race"—to use Arnold Green's phrase—but the trend is strongly in that direction. A number of studies agree that more than three-quarters of the higher executives of our larger companies now have had some college education. And one study found that, during the quarter century from 1928 to 1952, there was a 78 percent rise in the number of top executives who were college graduates.

Joseph A. Kahl quotes an executive who states that, while only half of the executives of his own age group are college men, about 90 percent of the men "starting out now" are "college."

The large corporations looking for management trainees appear to be more insistent on confining their search to college men than the smaller companies, which often are more old-fashioned and have to scratch harder to find qualified men willing to take a chance on a smaller company.[1]

Each year, more than six hundred large companies send recruiters to college campuses in search of possible management material. What has convinced many large companies that they should confine their management-training programs to college men? There is little question, of course, why this is happening when they are looking for men with skills in law, chemistry, engineering, etc. Many eventually become executive material. But what about the non-professional college men who go into the large companies in such large numbers?

One explanation, of course, is the growing complexity of management and production problems. College-trained experts in business methods are said to be needed. But if that is so, why do so many college-trained executives preside in fields far removed from their course of study? Sociologist Melville Dalton found that 62 percent of the college-educated executives he studied "were engaged in duties not related to their formal training."[2]

Another explanation offered is that in these complex times corporations

---

[1] Otto Butz, *The Unsilent Generation.*
[2] Melville Dalton, "Informal Factors in Career Achievement," *American Journal of Sociology*, Vol. 56 (March 1951), pp. 407–15.

need "brains." That, too, has a large element of truth. But what kind of brains? Patricia Salter West reported, after studying 10,000 college graduates, that "academic ability, or whatever ability is measured by college marks, makes very little difference to success in business."[3]

Certainly, college adds *something* in the way of know-how or viewpoint or social poise that enhances a businessman's chance of progressing in the corporation. At the same time, however, we should not overlook two technical, informal factors that undoubtedly have a great deal to do with the trend toward making the executive suite a college club.

One is the growing use of the blueprint approach to the selection of personnel, with the growth of thousands of vast business institutions. In any bureaucracy, we noted earlier, impersonality is a pervading feature. It is easier for a personnel department to draw up its job specifications and then "go by the book." Its officials impersonally build their organization tables and, for each level, assign minimum qualifications. Typically, the minimums become higher in terms of schooling with each step up the hierarchy. It's neater that way.

The other informal factor is the growing "professionalization" of business executives. The growth of business schools and management-consulting firms has perhaps helped this trend along. At any rate, we are seeing an effort by the executives themselves to protect their in-group by limiting the number of possible challengers and at the same time enhance its prestige by confining it pretty much to a diploma elite.

In many areas, the kind of education we have largely determines the status we will have throughout our adult life. Although this has its oppressive implications, at least it should be noted that education is a more humane and enlightened measure for stratifying society than ancestry or family wealth. The educational have-nots in our adult world at least have the hope that their children can succeed through education, where they did not.

If education is to be the main key to a higher-status way of life, then the availability of education to all of high native abiltiy becomes crucial. If the channels of access to higher education become clogged at the lower levels, then we will indeed have a rigid society, and a potentially inflammatory situation.[4]

As I see it, the situation, then, is this. If the American Dream is to have reality—and if we are to have available the talent of our most capable

[3] Patricia Salter West, "Social Mobility among College Graduates," from *Class, Status, and Power,* p. 474.
[4] Richard Centers, *The Psychology of Social Classes,* p. 148.

young people for the challenging years ahead—it seems imperative that we clear and broaden the channels of access to higher education for those qualified.

As things stand today—despite the clamor for more scientists—a vast amount of brain power is going to waste. And most of the wastage is in the three supporting classes.

All estimates appear to agree that the number of bright high-school seniors who do not go on to college each year runs into the hundreds of thousands.

Furthermore, class position seems to have a good deal to do with the failure to go to college. A study of 1,000 Milwaukee high-school graduates who were all rated as "college material" showed that, while nearly 100 percent of those from upper-income families had gone on to college, the percentage dropped to around 25 percent for lower-income families.

One reason for this unquestionably is the cost of going to college. Higher education, the key to higher status, must be bought with money. And as social psychologist Herbert H. Hyman points out, money is "the very commodity which the lower classes lack."

The cost of going to college has doubled since 1940 and is expected to double again by 1970. America's colleges typically are desperately short of funds. They can't pay faculty members anywhere near the salaries their skills command in private industry. And college enrollments are expected to double in the coming decade. As a result of these pressures, Columbia University's Eli Ginzberg points out, a trend is under way in which "more and more of the costs of a college education are assessed against the student."[5] The social danger here, he agrees, is that "if tuition is raised to cover cost, without a simultaneous increase in the number of scholarships and loans, parental income rather than personal ability will determine who gets an advanced education and who does not."

Currently, the average American student must pay between $1,600 and $1,700 to stay a year in college. The costs vary, of course, according to the type of college. Here, very roughly, is what I have found one may expect in the way of total cost per year at five types of college today:

State university	$1,300
Private coeducational school	$1,800
Institute of technology	$2,050
Private men's college	$2,175
Private women's college	$2,425

[5] Eli Ginzberg, *Human Resources: The Wealth of a Nation* (New York: Simon & Schuster, Inc., 1958), p. 144.

Another serious handicap of the bright youngster from the lower classes is his (or her) lack of motivation. He could often find a way to get to college if he had a burning desire, but he hasn't learned to aspire to a college education or to dream in large terms. This factor of low motivation has been, until recently at least, widely overlooked by educators. The common lack of motivation encountered at the lower levels has developed for several reasons. A youngster from the lower classes, first of all, may be rather sour on the educational process as a result of being snubbed at the dating age by youngsters from the upper classes.[6]

Furthermore, the most tempting goal in life for many in the lower levels, because of the environment of defeatism they live in, is to get by and live it up. Money for the moment becomes the goal. With money they can buy a car and have more fun with the girls and free themselves from dependency on their parents. They haven't been encouraged to think further than that. Quitting school to get a job promises the money they desire.

While Joseph A. Kahl was working with the Harvard Laboratory of Social Relations, he and his colleagues sought to explore this matter of low motivation with youngsters in the Boston area.[7] The investigators found that, in general, the boys who did not plan to go to college, and their parents, too, had an attitude toward life different from that of the college-oriented boys and their parents. Sons reflected parents, Kahl relates, to a remarkable degree in their values about life. Families that were not college-oriented lived by a philosophy of "getting by." They were resigned to life and felt that college—when they thought about it at all—was beyond their grasp. Families that were college-minded were geared to "getting ahead," and the fathers typically felt they had been frustrated in life by lack of education. Of the twelve boys who had no plans to go to college, eleven came from families where the "getting by" philosophy was dominant. They had been conditioned by their families not to expect much from life. They were bored with school, and felt that running around with their gang of friends was the most important thing they could do. And they tended to look upon the boys taking the college-preparatory course as stupid and sissified, as "fruits" who carried books home at night. On the other hand, the boys who yearned to go to college viewed the non-strivers as being "irresponsible" and not knowing "what was good for them."

Those two factors then—the high cost of college and the low motivation toward college caused by an environment of resignation, ostracism, and hedonism—help account for the "wastage" of a very large percentage

---

[6] August B. Hollingshead, *Elmtown's Youth*, p. 346.
[7] Joseph A. Kahl, *The American Class Structure*, p. 286.

of our brighter young people. Some of the youngsters, those who feel they have been priced out of the college picture, feel badly frustrated. For the others, the resigned hedonists, the frustration typically comes later. If the American Dream is to have meaning to the majority of our young people, they must be encouraged to do their best. And they must be convinced that, if they do their best, they will be considered on their merits.

How can they be encouraged to do their best, and be assured that if they do they will be considered? These are questions that deserve the most earnest attention of our business leaders, our government leaders, and our educational leaders. Each of these groups has a heavy responsibility if we are to achieve the goal of a genuine circulation of talent. Consider first the implied responsibility of the nation's business leaders.

Every large business institution would seem to have a responsibility to recruit at least some of its management personnel from its own family of employees. A number of companies are meeting this responsibility and have been recruiting some of their management trainees from the ranks of foremen and clerical workers.

Those corporate executives who feel their upper ranks should consist primarily of college men would seem to have a responsibility to offer college scholarships to talented youngsters in communities where they have plants. And with every scholarship, their company should offer a supplemental grant to the college accepting the youngster. Our hard-pressed colleges typically lose money on every youngster they educate. The loss must be made up by gifts or government grants. A substantial number of companies now offer scholarships, but only a very few offer with them supplemental grants to the colleges.

Finally, if our business enterprises are going to demand that their management men and women have college degrees, they would seem to have a responsibility to help ambitious, capable people already with the company to get that degree. A number of companies now are starting to accept this responsibility and opportunity. Many have been instituting job-training programs—sometimes confined to younger employees—to increase their supply of needed technical skills. And a growing number have been instituting programs to assist the ambitious employee to acquire either a two-year or four-year college degree.[8]

To conclude the thought, the leaders of America's major enterprises seem to have a responsibility—if they persist in confining their management to college-trained men—to make certain that the colleges are

[8] *Popular Science*, September 1957, p. 115.

available to any ambitious youngster of talent whatever his background. This would mean they must help the private colleges maintain high standards of scholarship while simultaneously maintaining reasonably low charges for promising applicants. And it would mean the companies must set aside far more money for scholarships and tuition payments than most of them have considered doing thus far.

Government leaders, state and national, also need to start thinking in larger terms about education. With the growing depletion of our natural resources, people are becoming our main resource. And here quantity is not enough. Adding another hundred million people to our population is going to create far more problems than it will solve.

Thought might well be given to exempting from taxation money spent for higher education. The state governments should consider undertaking periodic state-wide testing programs to uncover their potential future leaders, so that the youngsters and their parents can be encouraged to harness the talent. Oklahoma, which has been anxious to attract new industries involving advanced technology, has done this with gratifying results (with tests provided by Science Research Associates). Furthermore, the state and federal governments, if the wasted talent of the supporting classes is to be utilized, must vastly expand their programs of aid to public institutions of higher learning and of individual subsidies or scholarships.

In America, government assistance seems especially urgent in aiding students in graduate school seeking to qualify as professionals. It is in the scientific professions requiring long and intensive training, particularly medicine, that the poor youngsters of talent are finding themselves most clearly frozen out.

One of the more hopeful developments, in terms of the government's role, is the growing interest the military services are showing in encouraging men of promise to study toward craft skills, technical proficiency, and college degrees while in the service.

Our nation's educators, particularly at the public-school level, have perhaps the greatest responsibility in developing a greater circulation of talent. They are the arbiters of whether it is ever recognized and ignited in the first place.

Teachers, it would seem, should first of all examine their own subconscious biases. Bevode McCall reports that most teachers are unskilled in the nuances of social-class differences. And Hollingshead found in Elmtown that in both guidance and grading teachers showed a preference for the upper-level students. On the I.Q. tests, 30 percent of the brightest students were in the working class. That was not accurately reflected in the grades given. One reason the lower-level students don't produce up to their capacity, Hollingshead speculates, is that they come from a home environment of frustration, worry, or failure and haven't been trained to respond positively to competitive situations such as tests (as the upper-level youngsters have). They need guidance. Yet they are least likely to get it from the schools. The lower a child's social status, the fewer the chances were that the teacher would take an interest in him or her. This, perhaps, is because those youngsters in the lower classes do not invite help. If teachers had a better understanding of the psychology of the various classes, they would be more likely to identify, inspire, and guide the youngsters of talent in the two lower classes.[9]

A combination of aptitude testing and sympathetic attention to each youngster from the start should go a long way toward promoting the discovery of talent in our lower classes. This discovery and encouragement of talent among those of modest status seems to offer our best opportunity for keeping our social arteries open and forestalling the further development of sclerosis.

This book began as an exploration of the class behavior in the United States in this era of unparalleled material abundance. One of the most insistent themes that developed was that status seekers are altering our society by their preoccupation, in the midst of plenty, with acquiring evidences of status. The people of this country have become increasingly preoccupied with status primarily because of the impact on their lives of big housing developments, big advertisers, big trade-unions, and big corporate hierarchies. As a result, democracy is still more of an ideal than a reality.

The forces of the times seem to be conspiring to squeeze individuality and spontaneity from us. We compete for the same symbols of bigness and success. We are careful to conform to the kinds of behavior approved by our peers. We are wary of others who don't look like our kind of people. We tend to judge people by their labels. And all too often we judge people on the basis of the status symbols they display.

All this is hardly a credit to us as a people. We profess to be guided in our attitudes by the body of ideals set forth by our Founding Fathers. The Founding Fathers would wish us to be individualists, free thinkers, independents in mind and spirit. They would admire, I believe, a delightful elderly Negro woman I know who is widely beloved despite her strong preferences and dislikes in people. She runs a private enterprise that

---

[9] C. C. North, *Social Differentiation* (Chapel Hill, North Carolina: University of North Carolina Press, 1927), p. 247.

possibly nets her $2,000 a year and is, despite more-than-ordinary adversity, a supremely serene woman. A few weeks ago, she and I were discussing a family we both know. The family is probably worth $250,000. It has two fashionable homes, three cars, and full-time help. This elderly lady, however, has no use for them. She dismissed them scornfully as "common." She had judged them strictly on their personal qualities. And in her view they were found wanting. She found them shallow, crude, pleasure-minded people and felt they had botched the job of giving their children decent standards to live by.

I think we should all be happier, and live more stimulating lives, if, like her, we judged people not by the symbols they display and the labels they wear but rather by their individual worth.

And while becoming practicing individualists we should work to make opportunity a reality in our land of the free. Our people should be able to believe in this reality from personal and observable experience rather than by reading about it on billboards.

In this time of transcendent challenge and danger to our way of life, it seems clear that we can endure and prevail only if the vast majority of our people really believe in our system. They must be genuinely convinced that our system offers fairer rewards and opportunities for the fulfillment of human aspiration than any other.

Right: In a Ned Hilton cartoon, a woman looks up from reading *The Status Seekers* and asks her husband about their social position.

Below left: Cartoonist William F. Brown warns social climbers not to let people know they rely on *The Status Seekers* for how-to information.

Below right: Brown dramatizes how aspiring consumers carefully calibrated the social meaning of automobiles in their quest to keep up with the Joneses.

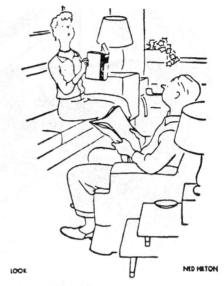

LOOK   NED HILTON

"Are we in the uppermost upper part of the lower middle class, or the mid-lower part of the upper middle class?"

"The Junior League is coming over this afternoon, Fred. Don't leave our copy of The Status Seekers *lying around."*

"Well, if we can't afford a Cadillac, how about a low license number for the Chrysler? That'll show the Wilsons and their new Mercedes."

*"Maybe at future parties you'll leave
it to Vance Packard to tell people what strata they belong to."*

"If there's one thing I can't abide, it's an out-and-out status seeker."

Top: Stevenson dramatizes the danger of using *The Status Seekers* to identify the social position of people at a cocktail party.
Bottom: Another Stevenson drawing depicts the one-upmanship of a status-seeking commuter arriving at a suburban railroad station.

*"Is stopping coming in and kicking tires like you
were official big shot with money to buy car,
comrade 'status seeker' peasant . . . !"*

Above: Playing on a cold war theme, in a "Grin and Bear It" cartoon dated March
26, 1961, George Lichty depicts Soviet "comrades" seeking status just like
Americans.
Below left: Frank Owen captures how the quest for status symbols was transforming American lives.
Below right: This drawing by Gardner Rea demonstrates the spread of Packard's
ideas into the corners of American society.

*"It took our life savings, but Agatha had her
heart set on a status symbol!"*

"Status seeker!"

Above: Like other corporations, a liquor company in 1962 turns the critique in *The Status Seekers* to its own advantage, linking its brand with foreign cars, French restaurants, and custom-made clothes as an item that is "something special for status seekers."

Right: This cartoon by Ed Dahlin highlights the possibilities of downward mobility.

Below: Almost five years after the publication of *The Status Seekers,* when the space race was on the minds of Americans, a cartoon by Eric illustrates the struggle middle-class families faced as they piled up installment debts.

"Here we are—Downward Mobility!"

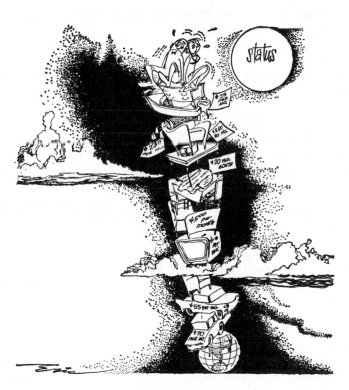

MOON PROBE

The United States and Vance Packard from the 1940s to the 1960s
A Chronology of Political Events, Consumer Culture, and Social Criticism

1941

December 7: The Japanese attack Pearl Harbor and, several days later, the United States enters World War II.

1942

Summer: Packard leaves the Associated Press and joins the staff of *American Magazine*.

1945

April 12: With the death of President Franklin D. Roosevelt, Vice President Harry S. Truman becomes president.

Spring: The Packards purchase first home, in Connecticut suburb of Darien.

August 6: The United States drops an atomic bomb on Hiroshima, and Japan surrenders on August 14, ending World War II.

1946

March 5: On a visit to the United States, former British Prime Minister Winston Churchill declares that "an iron curtain has descended across the Continent."

1947

March 12: To prevent Communist takeover of Greece and Turkey, the Truman Doctrine is proclaimed, committing the United States, in the battle against the spread of communism, to "support free peoples who are resisting attempted subjugation by armed minorities."

March 21: By executive order, Truman creates the Loyalty Program for federal employees, giving the government the power to dismiss "subversives" without due process.

June 5: Secretary of State George C. Marshall proposes the Marshall Plan to aid the postwar recovery of Europe and stop the spread of communism.

June 23: Congress overrides Truman's veto of the Taft Hartley Labor-Management Act, which reverses some of the gains labor unions had made during Roosevelt's New Deal in the 1930s.

1948

Spring: Vance, Virginia, and the three Packard children move to a house in New Canaan, Connecticut.

November 2: Truman is reelected president.

1949

September: Communist forces, under the leadership of Mao Zedong, establish control of mainland China. Arthur M. Schlesinger, Jr., publishes *The Vital Center,* a statement of cold war liberalism.

September 17: North Atlantic Treaty Organization (NATO) is established. NATO was a military pact that, in response to the possibility of Soviet aggression, committed its member nations to defend one another.

1950

Americans have eight million television sets in use; the Diners Club, the first general-use credit card, is introduced.

January 21: Alger Hiss, once a State Department official, is convicted of perjury following his denial of espionage.

February 9: In Wheeling, West Virginia, Senator Joseph McCarthy alleges the existence of Communists in the State Department.

June 25: The Korean War begins.

July 3: On its cover *Time* uses a picture of William J. Levitt, the developer of mass-produced suburban homes in a town that bore his name; 1.4 million new houses are under construction this year.

September: David Riesman publishes *The Lonely Crowd,* an influential book on the problem of achieving autonomy in affluent America.

1951

Gerber Products introduces MSG into its baby foods so that mothers will find the taste more appealing.

February 11: "Dennis the Menace" is first published as a cartoon strip.

May: Editors of *Fortune* publish *U.S.A.: The Permanent Revolution,* a celebration of America's achievement of freedom and prosperity.

September: C. Wright Mills publishes *White Collar.*

1952

April: Ralph Ellison publishes *Invisible Man,* arguably the best American novel written by an African American and a powerful exploration of the struggle of the individual against the system.

May—October: *Partisan Review* devotes three issues to a symposium, "Our Country and Our Culture," in which leading intellectuals celebrate postwar America.

November 4:   Dwight D. Eisenhower is elected president.

1953

April 3:   *TV Guide* first appears.

June 19:   Alleged Communist spies Ethel and Julius Rosenberg are executed.

July 17:   Disneyland opens in Anaheim, California.

July 27:   Armistice agreement ends the war in Korea.

Fall: Packards purchase a summer residence on Chappaquiddick Island, Martha's Vineyard, Massachusetts.

December: *Playboy* begins publication, with a photo of a nude Marilyn Monroe. C. A. Swanson and Sons introduces ninety-eight varieties of frozen TV dinners.

1954

Elvis Presley makes his first commercial record.

The franchising of McDonald's fast food restaurants begins.

January 12:   Secretary of State John Foster Dulles announces a policy of "massive retaliation" against Soviet aggression.

March: Northland, America's first enclosed shopping mall, opens in the Detroit area.

Spring: First issue of *Dissent* is published, a magazine whose editors were committed to democratic socialism and whose founding underscored the persistence of opposition to the celebration of American life.

April 22:   The U.S. Senate begins the Army-McCarthy hearings, which lead to Senator Joseph McCarthy's censure by the Senate on December 2.

May 7:   The Viet Minh defeat the French at Dien Bien Phu signaling the end of French colonial rule in Vietnam and the triumph of Ho Chi Minh.

May 17: The Supreme Court declares that separate but equal schools are unconstitutional in *Brown v. Board of Education of Topeka.*

June: The phrase "under God" is added to the Pledge of Allegiance.

August 2: Eisenhower signs the Housing Act of 1954, which provides funds for urban renewal, public housing, and mortgages.

August 24: Eisenhower signs the Communist Control Act, effectively outlawing the Communist party.

1955

January 1: U.S. aid to South Vietnam begins.

January 5: Marian Anderson becomes the first African American to sing at the Metropolitan Opera in New York.

July: Sloan Wilson publishes *The Man in the Gray Flannel Suit,* a novel that dramatized the dilemmas members of the suburban white middle class faced in the 1950s.

October: The movie *Rebel without a Cause,* starring James Dean, is released. *The Mickey Mouse Club* begins broadcasting on ABC television.

October 7: Poet Allen Ginsberg reads "Howl" in San Francisco, California, marking the emergence of the Beat generation.

November: Herbert Marcuse publishes *Eros and Civilization,* a philosophical critique of modern society that influenced 1960s radicals.

November 19: William F. Buckley launches the conservative journal *National Review.*

December 1: In Montgomery, Alabama, Rosa Parks refuses to relinquish her seat on a bus to a white man; Martin Luther King, Jr., leads a bus boycott in Montgomery.

1956

Suggesting that not only "fallen" women color their hair, "Miss Clairol" begins an advertising campaign based on the question "Does she or doesn't she?"

Americans buy 20,000 television sets per day; they spend more time watching television than working for pay.

February 14: Soviet Premier Nikita S. Khrushchev attacks Stalin's cult of personality and acknowledges the terror Stalin had inflicted in the 1930s and 1940s.

April: C. Wright Mills publishes *The Power Elite,* a sociological exploration of the concentration of power in the United States that would influence 1960s radicals.

August: The last issue of *American Magazine* is published. Packard transfers to *Collier's.*

September: Grace Metalious publishes the novel *Peyton Place*, which portrays an American community that contradicts the widely held picture of quiet and respectability.

November: John Keats publishes *The Crack in the Picture Window*, an exposé of some of the problems of suburban life.

November 4: The Soviet army crushes a revolt in Hungary.

November 6: President Eisenhower is reelected.

December: William H. Whyte, Jr., publishes *The Organization Man*, a best-selling nonfiction book that explored the tensions between individualism and conformity among managers in the nation's large corporations.

December 24: *Collier's* announces cessation of publication; Packard becomes unemployed.

1957

February 14: The Southern Christian Leadership Conference (SCLC), a civil rights organization led by Martin Luther King, Jr., is founded.

April: Vance Packard publishes *The Hidden Persuaders;* soon after, Packard settles on the topic for his next book, an examination of status consciousness and social divisions in America.

May 6: *I Love Lucy*, first shown on television in October 1951, ends its first run.

May 11: Eisenhower and President Ngo Dinh Diem of South Vietnam announce an agreement to cooperate against the spread of communism in Vietnam.

August 29: Civil Rights Act of 1957 is passed; it is a weak law but the first civil rights legislation since Reconstruction.

September: Jack Kerouac publishes his classic Beat novel *On the Road.*

September 2–4: Arkansas Governor Orval Faubus uses the National Guard to prevent integration of Central High School in Little Rock.

September 25: Eisenhower orders federal troops to escort nine African American students to Central High School in Little Rock.

October 4: The Soviet Union launches *Sputnik I*, the first Earth satellite.

November: The National Committee for a Sane Nuclear Policy is founded.

1958

January 31: The United States launches the first successful space satellite.

April: Vice President Richard M. Nixon encounters protests while on a goodwill trip to Latin America.

June: John Kenneth Galbraith publishes *The Affluent Society,* a critique that decried the imbalance in American society between private wealth and the poor state of public facilities.

September: Responding to fears over *Sputnik,* the U.S. Congress passes the National Defense Education Act, authorizing the expenditure of billions of dollars for education to enable the United States to catch up with the Soviet Union in the technology race.

1959

The Barbie doll is introduced.

Glen Raven Mills introduces panty hose, thus eliminating the necessity of garters and corsets.

Although they are only 11 percent of food stores, supermarkets account for 60 percent of food sales in the United States.

April: Vance Packard publishes *The Status Seekers.*

November 2:   Scandal erupts over rigged TV quiz shows.

1960

February 1:   African Americans protest segregation in Greensboro, North Carolina, by staging lunch counter sit-ins.

April 15:   The first conference of the Student Nonviolent Coordinating Committee (SNCC), a civil rights group that would eventually challenge Martin Luther King, Jr.'s leadership and approach.

May 6:   The Civil Rights Act of 1960 is signed, strengthening federal control over voting rights in the South.

May 9:   The Food and Drug Administration approves the sale of the birth control pill.

October: Paul Goodman publishes *Growing Up Absurd,* which helped shape the counterculture of the 1960s and blamed large organizations for causing the disaffection of the young. Vance Packard publishes *The Waste Makers,* a study of planned obsolescence in the United States.

November 8:   John F. Kennedy is elected president.

1961

March 1:   The Peace Corps is established, a testament to President Kennedy's commitment to activism; the program would send thousands of Americans to aid people in remote parts of the world.

May: Freedom Rides in southern states protest segregation of public facilities, prompting violent retaliation by southern whites and drawing national media attention.

October: Kennedy agrees to send additional military advisers to Vietnam. Joseph Heller publishes *Catch-22*, which explored the problems of alienation and absurdity in a modern, organized world.

1962

February 20: John H. Glenn, Jr., becomes the first American to orbit the earth.

March: Michael Harrington publishes *The Other America: Poverty in the United States*, revealing the extent of poverty in the nation and preparing the ground for Lyndon B. Johnson's War on Poverty.

June 11–15: A meeting of Students for a Democratic Society (SDS) adopts the Port Huron Statement, an influential analysis of American society by the New Left. SDS was the principal organization of the New Left, the movement among white college students who worked to achieve civil rights for African Americans and who opposed the war in Vietnam.

September: Rachel Carson publishes *Silent Spring*, a pioneering work that calls attention to threats to the natural environment.

October: Vance Packard publishes *The Pyramid Climbers*, a study of the problems faced by aspiring executives in large corporations.

1963

February: Betty Friedan publishes *The Feminine Mystique*.

August 28: Martin Luther King, Jr., gives his "I Have a Dream" speech before hundreds of thousands of participants in the March on Washington.

November 22: President Kennedy is assassinated; Vice President Lyndon B. Johnson assumes the presidency.

Questions for Consideration

1. What does Packard's *The Status Seekers* tell us about the United States in the 1950s? What does it omit?
2. What evidence is there in *The Status Seekers* that the atmosphere of the cold war, especially the American struggle with communism, shaped Packard's approach?
3. Where does Packard articulate a challenge to those who believed that prosperity had helped Americans fulfill the American Dream? How effective is his challenge?
4. What kinds of evidence does Packard draw on for his analysis? What other types of evidence might he have used? How would an academic sociologist approach the questions Packard addressed?
5. How accurate and deep is Packard's analysis? To what extent does it capture root causes? If it misses them, why?
6. What is Packard's view of the relationship of social class, ethnicity, gender, and race?
7. How effective were the solutions Packard offered in Part V to the problems his analysis highlighted?
8. How convincing do you find the assertions of some critics: that Packard offered a nostalgic picture; that the book was more useful as self-help than as social criticism; that the presentation was popularized and superficial; that Packard's politics were ambivalent and shallow?
9. Are Packard's findings, concerns, and suggestions still relevant today?
10. Analyze and critique university or local communities in the terms provided by Packard.
11. How much has changed since Packard wrote *The Status Seekers* and how much has remained constant in U.S. society?

Selected Bibliography

The text of this edition of *The Status Seekers* is a condensed version of Vance Packard, *The Status Seekers* (New York: David McKay, 1959). For a full treatment of Packard's life and career, see Daniel Horowitz, *Vance Packard and American Social Criticism* (Chapel Hill: University of North Carolina Press, 1994).

Many books explore the history of the entire postwar period but a good starting point is William H. Chafe, *The Unfinished Journey: America since World War II*, 2nd ed. (New York: Oxford University Press, 1991). For general books on the late 1940s and 1950s, see John P. Diggins, *The Proud Decades: America in War and Peace, 1941–1960* (New York: W. W. Norton and Co., 1988); Godfrey Hodgson, *America in Our Time* (New York: Random House, 1976); David Halberstam, *The Fifties* (New York: Villard Books, 1993); Marty Jezer, *The Dark Ages: Life in the United States, 1945–1960* (Boston: South End Press, 1982); Douglas T. Miller and Marion Nowak, *The Fifties: The Way We Really Were* (Garden City, N.Y.: Doubleday and Co., 1977); J. Ronald Oakley, *God's Country: America in the Fifties* (New York: Dembner Books, 1986); William L. O'Neill, *American High: The Years of Confidence, 1945–1960* (New York: Free Press, 1986); Geoffrey Perrett, *A Dream of Greatness: The American People, 1945–1963* (New York: Coward, McCann and Geoghegan, 1979); Stephen J. Whitfield, *The Culture of the Cold War* (Baltimore: Johns Hopkins University Press, 1991).

Several books deal with American intellectual life in the postwar period, including Alexander Bloom, *Prodigal Sons: The New York Intellectuals and Their World* (New York: Oxford University Press, 1986); Howard Brick, *Daniel Bell and the Decline of Intellectual Radicalism: Social Theory and Political Reconciliation in the 1940s* (Madison: University of Wisconsin Press, 1986); Richard H. Pells, *The Liberal Mind in a Conservative Age: American Intellectuals in the 1940s and 1950s* (New York: Harper and Row, 1985); and Alan M. Wald, *The New York Intellectuals: The Rise and Decline of the Anti-Stalinist Left from the 1930s to the 1980s* (Chapel Hill: University of North Carolina Press, 1987).

Among the discussions of the 1950s that focus on significant social and cultural changes are Erik Barnouw, *Tube of Plenty: The Evolution of American*

Television (New York: Oxford University Press, 1975); Taylor Branch, *Parting the Waters: America in the King Years, 1954–1963* (New York: Simon and Schuster, 1988); Wini Breines, *Young, White, and Miserable: Growing Up Female in the Fifties* (Boston: Beacon Press, 1992); W. T. Lhamon, Jr., *Deliberate Speed: The Origins of a Cultural Style in the American 1950s* (Washington, D.C.: Smithsonian Institution Press, 1990); Manning Marable, *Race, Reform, and Rebellion: The Second Reconstruction in Black America, 1945–1982* (Jackson: University Press of Mississippi, 1984); Roland Marchand, "Visions of Classlessness, Quests for Dominion: American Popular Culture, 1945–1960," in *Reshaping America: Society and Institutions 1945–1960*, edited by Robert H. Bremner and Gary W. Reichard (Columbus: Ohio State University Press, 1982), pp. 165–90; Elaine T. May, *Homeward Bound: American Families in the Cold War Era* (New York: Basic Books, 1988); Lary May, ed., *Recasting America: Culture and Politics in the Age of Cold War* (Chicago: University of Chicago Press, 1989); Richard Polenberg, *One Nation Divisible: Class, Race, and Ethnicity in the United States since 1938* (New York: Viking Press, 1980); Ellen W. Schrecker, *No Ivory Tower: McCarthyism and the Universities* (New York: Oxford University Press, 1986); Harvard Sitkoff, *The Struggle for Black Equality, 1954–1980* (New York: Hill and Wang, 1981).

Many books have been published on suburban life in the 1950s and 1960s, among them Bennett Berger, *Working-Class Suburb: A Study of Auto Workers in Suburbia* (Berkeley: University of California Press, 1960); Scott Donaldson, *The Suburban Myth* (New York: Columbia University Press, 1969); Herbert J. Gans, *The Levittowners: Ways of Life and Politics in a New Suburban Community* (New York: Pantheon Books, 1967); Kenneth Jackson, *Crabgrass Frontier: The Suburbanization of the United States* (New York: Oxford University Press, 1985); John Keats, *The Crack in the Picture Window* (Boston: Houghton Mifflin Co., 1956); John Seeley et al., *Crestwood Heights: A Study of the Culture of Suburban Life* (New York: Basic Books, 1956); Sloan Wilson, *The Man in the Gray Flannel Suit* (New York: Simon and Schuster, 1955). The footnotes to *Status Seekers* call attention to many of the contemporary community studies.

Those wishing to read other influential or popular works of social commentary published between the end of World War II and the early 1960s should begin with Daniel Bell, *The End of Ideology: On the Exhaustion of Political Ideas in the Fifties* (Glencoe, Ill.: Free Press, 1960); Betty Friedan, *The Feminine Mystique* (New York: W. W. Norton, 1963); John Kenneth Galbraith, *The Affluent Society* (Boston: Houghton Mifflin Co., 1958); Paul Goodman, *Growing Up Absurd: Problems of Youth in the Organized System* (New York: Random House, 1960); Max Lerner, *America as a Civilization: Life and Thought in the United States Today* (New York: Simon and Schuster, 1957); Herbert Marcuse, *Eros and Civilization: A Philosophical Inquiry into Freud* (Boston: Beacon Press, 1955); C. Wright Mills, *Power Elite* (New York: Oxford University Press, 1956) and *White Collar: The American Middle*

Classes (New York: Oxford University Press, 1951); David Potter, *People of Plenty: Economic Abundance and the American Character* (Chicago: University of Chicago Press, 1954); David Riesman, *The Lonely Crowd: A Study of the Changing American Character* (New Haven: Yale University Press, 1950); A. C. Spectorsky, *The Exurbanites* (Philadelphia: J. B. Lippincott Co., 1955); and William H. Whyte, Jr., *The Organization Man* (New York: Simon and Schuster, 1956).

Index

Contents

Animal Planet

Mini Mice

1 package (about 18 ounces) chocolate cake mix, plus ingredients
to prepare mix
1 container (16 ounces) chocolate frosting
1 container (16 ounces) white frosting
Small black and pink hard candies or decors
Small fruit-flavored pastel candy wafers
Black string licorice

1. Preheat oven to 350°F. Line 60 mini (1¾-inch) muffin cups with paper baking cups.

2. Prepare cake mix according to package directions. Spoon batter into prepared muffin cups, filling almost full.

3. Bake 12 minutes or until toothpick inserted into centers comes out clean. Cool in pans 10 minutes. Remove to wire racks; cool completely.

4. For brown mice, frost cupcakes with chocolate frosting; use knife or small spatula to pull up frosting and create fuzzy appearance. For speckled mice, frost cupcakes with white frosting; use toothpick to add streaks of chocolate frosting.

5. Arrange candies on one side of each cupcake for eyes, nose and ears. Cut licorice into 3-inch lengths; press into opposite end of each cupcake for tail.

Makes 60 mini cupcakes